KU-113-556

# THE E.C. DIRECTIVE ON
# RENTAL AND LENDING RIGHTS
# AND ON PIRACY

AUSTRALIA
The Law Book Company
Brisbane ● Sydney ● Melbourne ● Perth

CANADA
Carswell
Ottawa ● Toronto ● Calgary ● Montreal ● Vancouver

AGENTS:
Steimatzky's Agency Ltd., Tel Aviv;
N.M. Tripathi (Private) Ltd., Bombay;
Eastern Law House (Private) Ltd., Calcutta;
M.P.P. House, Bangalore;
Universal Book Traders, Delhi;
Aditya Books, Delhi;
MacMillan Shuppan KK, Tokyo;
Pakistan Law House, Karachi, Lahore

# THE E.C. DIRECTIVE ON RENTAL AND LENDING RIGHTS AND ON PIRACY

*By*

JÖRG REINBOTHE, M.C.L., DOCTOR AT LAW
*E.C. Commission (Directorate-General, Internal Market and Financial Services)*

and

SILKE VON LEWINSKI, DOCTOR AT LAW
*Max-Planck Institute for Foreign and International Patent, Copyright and Competition Law, Munich*
*Consultant to E.C. Commission on Rental Directive*
*Adjunct Professor, Franklin Pierce Law Centre, Concord, N.H., U.S.A.*

LONDON ● SWEET & MAXWELL ● 1993

KJE 230

Published in 1993 by
Sweet & Maxwell Limited
of South Quay Plaza
183 Marsh Wall, London E14 9FT
Phototypeset by MFK Typesetting Ltd.,
Hitchin, Herts.
Printed and bound in Great Britain
by Hartnolls Ltd., Bodmin

A CIP catalogue record for this book
is available from The British Library

ISBN 0421 493909

*All rights reserved. No part of this publication may be
reproduced or transmitted in any form or by any means,
electronic, mechanical, photocopying, recording or otherwise,
or stored in any retrieval system of any nature, without the
written permission of the copyright holders and the publisher,
application for which shall be made to the publisher.*

No natural forests were destroyed
to make this product only farmed
timber was used and re-planted.

The index was prepared by Robert Spicer

*The Authors' Right to be Identified has been asserted in accordance with
the Copyright, Designs and Patents Act 1988*

©
Jörg Reinbothe and
Silke von Lewinski
1993

# Preface

On November 19, 1992, the Council of Ministers of the European Community adopted Council Directive 92/100/EEC "on rental and lending rights and on certain rights related to copyright in the field of intellectual property." It was the second Directive in the area of copyright (after the Directive 91/250/EEC on the legal protection of computer programs), but the first one to present a broad and comprehensive harmonisation of copyright and neighbouring rights for several groups of rightholders, with "horizontal" impact on the whole legal field.

The rental Directive contains many different elements, all of which have a particular importance of their own. First, it harmonises Community-wide a rental and lending right for all works and subject matter, such as performances, phonograms and videograms. It does so by granting an exclusive right to authors, performers, phonogram producers and film producers to authorise or prohibit rental and lending of their respective works, performances, phonograms or films. As a consequence, commercial rental is recognised in the whole Community as an activity which should be controlled by the rightholders of intellectual property.

At the same time, the rental Directive harmonises a broad range of neighbouring rights: performers, broadcasting organisations, phonogram producers and film producers are to be vested with important basic rights, such as rights of reproduction, fixation, broadcasting and communication to the public, and distribution. This particular part of the Directive aims at improving the fight against piracy.

With the adoption of the rental Directive, a rather ambitious project was successfully concluded: in one go, modern forms of exploiting intellectual property were made subject to exclusive rights throughout the Community, and a clear signal was given in favour of a high level of protection for copyright and neighbouring rights.

To achieve this goal was by no means easy. The initiative started with the Green Paper on Copyright and the Challenge of Technology of 1988, which mentioned the issues of piracy and rental in its Chapters 2 and 4 respectively. A two-day hearing organised by the Commission in 1989 marked the direction to be followed for the proposal: comprehensive and ambitious harmonisation was called for, harmonisation which would both help to build the Internal Market and to reinforce the position of those who are actively involved in the creation of intellectual property. Consequently, the Commission proposal for the rental Directive went beyond what had been announced or set down for discussion in the Green Paper of 1988.

The proposal was made in December 1990. What followed were more than 18 months of most intensive lobbying from all affected interested parties. As

v

never before, such lobbying focused on copyright questions of a fundamental, and at times even dogmatic nature, such as: should rightholders have a right to control commercial rental and/or lending, or would a right to remuneration suffice? Should film producers enjoy protection based on copyright or based on neighbouring rights? Should the rights of authors and performers be subject to a presumption of transfer?

In the end, all these questions and problems were mastered by the European Parliament and by the Council. Both institutions successfully resisted the temptation to engage in "religious wars" about dogmatic concepts and copyright traditions; while approving of the substance and of the main thrust of the Commission proposal, they presented pragmatic modifications which never lost sight of the common goal to be achieved, namely the Internal Market for important copyrights and neighbouring rights.

Against this background, it is only natural that the text of the Directive makes complicated reading. The Directive is clearly a compromise, but certainly one of great value. In order to fully understand all the nuances and details of this Directive, and the subtle structure of the compromise contained therein, one is bound to look at its legislative history. This legislative history and the discussions in the various institutions quite often hold the key not only to understanding the text of the rental Directive, but equally to the transposition of its elements into the national laws of the Member States.

It is for this purpose, that this Commentary seeks to explain the Directive on the basis of its historical background and development in the legislative process, as described in Section I. Every Article of the Directive, together with the relevant recitals, is commented on in Section II in some detail and with reference to the discussions held in the various legislative bodies. With a view to the implementation of the Directive into national law, Section III of this Commentary is dedicated to the present legal situation, and the position under the Directive, in all 12 Member States. Section IV does the same with respect to the Member States of EFTA, most of which are following very closely the legislation in the Community whether they have already applied for membership of the Community or not. While the rental Directive by its nature is designed to harmonise Member States' laws with a view to establishing the Internal Market, it may have some impact on the international obligations which the Member States of the Community have under the international conventions in this field. Moreover, the rental Directive may have its own influence on developments in international copyright and neighbouring rights protection. These international questions are dealt with in Section V of this Commentary.

The concept of this Commentary is to offer background information, interpretative guidance and assistance to the legal profession practising in the field of copyright and neighbouring rights, and to legislators faced with the transposition of the rental Directive into national law. Both authors have been closely involved in the preparation and drafting of the original proposal, and in the whole legislative process up to the final adoption of the Directive. However, this Commentary only reflects their personal opinion and should not be interpreted as an official expression of the view of the E.C. Commission.

Every attempt has been made to take account of all recent developments until September 1, 1993.

We wish to express our thanks to all those whose efforts have contributed to the adoption of the rental Directive, and we would like to thank especially all those who have assisted us in our work on this Commentary with their patience and constructive advice.

*October 1993*                                               *Jörg Reinbothe*
                                                             *Silke von Lewinski*

# Foreword

Ever since its coming into play, copyright has been a rather delicate and complicated area, as it is at the interface between creativity, cultural identity, social policy, economic aspects, cultural traditions and technological developments. All these aspects are usually wrapped together into a complex national legal framework.

The driving engine behind developments in copyright has for centuries been new technology; the invention of the printing-press was an important starting point in this respect. In our modern times, where videograms, digital recording techniques and all sorts of new forms of interactive electronic communication are the media our children grow up with, this is even more true. New technology has become a real "challenge" for all those who are creative or otherwise active in the cultural field: authors, performers, broadcasters, phonogram and film producers.

If this is the challenge we are faced with in the area of copyright, then the Internal Market of the European Community is our chance. The Internal Market offers the unique opportunity to provide those rightholders with a wide market, without frontiers, for what they have created or produced — in fact it is at present the biggest common market for cultural goods in the world. For the rightholders concerned, this market gains its true value only if we provide for a high level of protection for copyright and neighbouring rights, and ensure at the same time that the cultural identity of any creative person and the cultural diversity within the Community remains untouched. I am convinced that this creativity, based on the cultural diversity in the Community, is our strength and our most forceful weapon against tendencies to "commercialise" culture.

To apply this underlying philosophy to the harmonisation of copyright when building the Internal Market, may indeed appear to be an attempt to square the circle. But the E.C. Directive on rental right and lending right and on certain rights related to copyright in the field of intellectual property proves that we are able to achieve this goal. This Directive is an important step towards a broad copyright and neighbouring rights harmonisation, and takes the most comprehensive approach so far; it may well be called a milestone in this field.

Thanks to the joint efforts and the constructive spirit of all the institutions and persons involved, this important Directive was initiated, successfully discussed and adopted during my term of responsibility for the Internal Market as Member of the E.C. Commission. I am particularly thankful to the co-authors of this Commentary; their contribution to this part of building the Internal Market was essential. Furthermore, this Commentary not only provides legal advisers, practitioners and legislators with an exemplary insight into the structure and the details of the Directive; it also shows how important the harmonisation of intellectual property laws is for the Internal Market, and how much work and effort has been put into its achievement.

*October 1993*                                        *Martin Bangemann*
                                                     *Vice-president of the*
                                                     *E.C. Commission*

# Contents

## SECTION II: COMMENTARY ON THE ARTICLES OF THE DIRECTIVE

CONTENTS

## SECTION III: THE POSITION IN THE MEMBER STATES

## SECTION IV: THE POSITION IN THE EFTA COUNTRIES

## SECTION V: THE POSITION AT INTERNATIONAL LEVEL

## APPENDICES

# E.C. Treaties

# E.C. Legislation

# RESOLUTIONS

# COMMISSION PROPOSALS AND OTHER DOCUMENTS

# National Legislation

# International Treaties, Conventions and Agreements

# The Evolution of the Directive

# 1. Background to the Proposal for a Council Directive

## 1. Initiatives by the Commission

According to the EEC Treaty, it is up to the E.C. Commission to take the initiatives for Community legislation, in particular for, although not limited to, the harmonisation of the legal provisions of Member States. Copyright and related rights were already mentioned as a subject of future harmonisation of the laws of the Member States of the European Community in a resolution of the European Parliament of 1974,[1] as well as in several communications from the Commission, the initial one being published in 1977. More concrete measures were announced by the Commission's Green Paper on "Television Without Frontiers,"[2] and in the Commission's White Paper of 1985, entitled "Completing the Internal Market."[3] However, these two documents were rather selective, addressing only certain specific issues in this field.

## 2. The Green Paper of 1988

The first Commission document to present an (at that time) comprehensive choice of priority items for harmonisation in the area of copyright and neighbouring rights was the "Green Paper on Copyright and the Challenge of Technology – Copyright Issues Requiring Immediate Action."[4] In its seven chapters, this Green Paper of 1988 described and analysed the areas in which the Commission saw a need for action, or at least for observance. Chapter 4 was dedicated to "Distribution Right, Exhaustion and Rental Right," and Chapter 2 was given the rather simplistic name "Piracy."

It is these two Chapters (2 and 4) of the 1988 Green Paper ("the Green Paper") which are the source of the Community Directive described in this book.

---

[1] [1974] O.J. C62/5.
[2] Document COM (84) 300 final.
[3] Document COM (85) 310 final.
[4] Document COM (88) 172 final.

## (a) Copyright piracy

Copyright piracy was a subject to which the Commission obviously attached particular importance in its Green Paper. The largest part of it, approaching one third, was dedicated in Chapter 2 to improving the means to fight such piracy inside the Community. The Commission defined piracy for the purposes of the Green Paper as "the unauthorised reproduction of works protected by copyright or allied rights for commercial purposes as well as all subsequent commercial dealing in such reproductions." In a detailed sectorial analysis the Green Paper demonstrated that this piracy had emerged as a serious problem for industries and persons active in the creative field. It highlighted in this context certain specific sectors: books, sound recordings, films and video recordings, computer programs, broadcasts and cable transmissions.

The Commission arrived at the conclusion that on the domestic, *i.e.* Community level, fighting piracy more effectively required in particular the harmonisation of

- the rights of performers to authorise the reproduction for commercial purposes of their fixed performances and their commercial distribution;
- the rights of producers of films and of phonogram producers to authorise the reproduction for commercial purposes and the commercial distribution of their products; and
- the rights of broadcasting organisations to authorise the fixation and reproduction for commercial purposes of their broadcasts, as well as the commercial distribution of such fixed broadcasts.

Besides these measures of substantive harmonisation, the Commission in the Green Paper suggested several initiatives on the enforcement of rights which would complement the harmonisation steps. It has to be noted that the Commission in Chapter 2 of the Green Paper focused on the trade aspect of piracy; it followed from this that the proposed initiatives were limited to the holders of rights related to copyright (the neighbouring rightholders), and not extended to authors of literary and artistic works.

## (b) Rental Rights

These conclusions of the Commission on piracy were, at least at first sight, not related to its statements on rental rights in Chapter 4 of the Green Paper. In fact, rental rights were described in legal terms as being an element in the framework of distribution rights and exhaustion. In economic terms, they were considered to be a rather novel way of exploiting certain categories of protected material, in particular sound recordings and films, where potential damage to the rightholders was involved. The most obvious example which the Commission had in mind was of course the commercial rental of compact discs or of videograms in videoshops; and with respect to this commercial activity, the legal situation in Member States varied considerably.

In conclusion, the Commission in Chapter 4 of its Green Paper saw a need to harmonise in the Community a rental right for certain areas of copyright and for certain recording media. It suggested the introduction and harmonisation of

- a right for authors, performers and phonogram producers to authorise or prohibit the commercial rental of sound recordings; and
- a right for the producers of cinematographic works to authorise or prohibit the commercial rental of videograms.

Clearly, just as in Chapter 2, the initiatives proposed by the Commission in Chapter 4 concentrated on the rightholders of neighbouring rights; however, as far as sound recordings were concerned, it was suggested that authors should also be entitled to their own rental right.

It was the Commission's view that these rental rights should be structured as strong, and therefore exclusive rights (to authorise or prohibit rental), as opposed to a right to remuneration only, in order to provide rightholders with the choice as to the time, place and sector of the market for the exploitation of their products. While the Commission in this respect took a rather firm view in the Green Paper, it interestingly saw no obvious need for the harmonisation or introduction of a general right for authors to control the commercial distribution of their works, or for the harmonisation of the various schemes of exhaustion of rights. Moreover, the Commission did not deem it necessary also to include non-commercial lending in its harmonisation efforts.

## 3. FOLLOW-UP AND HEARING

The Commission asked for comments on these suggestions in Chapter 2 and Chapter 4 of the Green Paper by December 1, 1988. The number of submissions received by the Commission during this period, and also for many months thereafter, was beyond expectation.

On the whole, the comments made were quite positive with regard to the Commission's conclusions on piracy and rental; at least such comments were less critical by far than the reactions to the other chapters of the Green Paper, in which the Commission was accused of taking too narrow-minded an approach in favour of the "cultural industry," proposing "authors' rights without authors."

However, while the conclusions of the Commission on piracy were practically accepted by interested circles, those on rental rights met with two main objections: some asked for the rental right for videograms to be extended also to rightholders other than film producers, and others held that a right for non-commercial lending should be introduced and harmonised as well.

Under these circumstances, the Commission was certainly well advised to organise a hearing of interested circles on these issues. It was the third hearing that the Commission had organised in the context of the follow-up to the Green Paper of 1988, and took place on September 18 and 19, 1989.

It was at this hearing that the two issues of piracy and rental, which – as has been stated above – are at first sight barely related, were combined for the first time. There were rather pragmatic reasons for this combination: on both issues, the rightholders concerned, as well as the rights to be harmonised, were to some extent overlapping. As the Commission in the context of Chapter 4 of the Green Paper intended to submit a proposal on the harmonisation of a rental right, as quite a specific right for holders of rights related to copyright such as performing artists and phonogram producers, it had to make sure that the introduction of more fundamental rights for the same groups of right-holders, such as the right of reproduction envisaged in Chapter 2 of the Green Paper, was discussed at the same time. Moreover, rental in some legal systems is considered to be a form of distribution; since both Chapter 2 and Chapter 4 of the Green Paper dealt with the harmonisation of the legal protection of various forms of distribution, their joint discussion was only logical.

As a result of the hearing, this interaction between rental and piracy was accepted. In substance, the approach the Commission had taken in the Green Paper was supported, and participants agreed to the need for harmonisation in these fields.

The concept of an exclusive right (to authorise or prohibit) for rental as suggested by the Commission, was firmly supported. The so-called "Japanese" model, according to which the rental right would be of an exclusive character for a limited period of time only, followed by a right to remuneration, was put to discussion as an alternative, but gained no support.

An overwhelming majority, however, held that the Commission's proposal should go beyond the suggestions made in the Green Paper. In the view of this majority, a Directive on the harmonisation of rental right would be incomplete if it did not cover non-commercial lending as well, preferably in the form of a lending right to remuneration, to be exercised by collecting societies or similar bodies. In addition, there was unanimity that not only sound recordings and videograms should be covered by such a rental/lending right, but equally all the other categories of rental/lending objects.

Finally, in the view of most participants not only producers should be entitled to the rental/lending right in respect of videograms, but all main right-holders, namely authors, performers and producers.

## 4. The Proposal

On the basis of the Green Paper, the results of the hearing and the numerous written and oral comments submitted to the Commission, the proposal for a Council Directive was prepared. The original "Proposal for a Council Directive on rental right, lending right, and on certain rights related to copyright" was adopted by the Commission on December 5, 1990.[5]

In its substance, the proposal was clearly based on the Green Paper of 1988. As already envisaged in the hearing of 1989, it combined the issues of Chapter 2 and Chapter 4 of the Green Paper and, just like the Green Paper, limited itself to proposing harmonisation in these sectors and only to the extent which was considered to be absolutely necessary, rather than submitting a Community-wide concept for copyright and related rights. Thus, for instance, the proposal did not attempt to harmonise more horizontal aspects of copyright

---

[5] Document COM (90) 586 final.

law, such as questions of ownership of rights, the definitions of authors and performing artists, or the test of originality. It was also as part of this "self-restraint" that the proposal, at least in general terms, sought not to affect adversely the copyright concepts existing in the national laws of the Member States: it tried to offer pragmatic solutions for problems with actual import-ance, without touching upon dogmatic discussions of principle.

On the other hand, the proposal deliberately went several steps further than the Green Paper of 1988. It did so against the background of the quite critical public reactions to the Green Paper, and as a result of the Commission's reflec-tions in the light of the hearing of interested parties. Besides, this proposal for the rental Directive was published nearly at the same time as the document on the working program in the field of copyright and related rights[6]: just as this working program tried to offer a comprehensive and somewhat revised view of the intentions of the Commission in this field for the sake of transparency and oriented at the highest possible level of protection for authors and other rightholders, so the rental proposal pointed in the same direction. In contrast to the Green Paper, the proposal suggested the harmonisation of a lending right in addition to the rental right, and extended the proposed exclusive rental right to authors and performing artists in respect of films.

Right from the time of its submission, it was the generally declared inten-tion of the proposal to present comprehensive solutions and a carefully struck balance of interests, with a view to setting the right signals for a Community-wide protection of copyright and related rights. It was therefore also the credi-bility of the Commission which was at stake, and which made the proposal a cornerstone of, and a proof of, the modified and more author-oriented approach of the Commission.

---

[6] "Follow-up to the Green Paper – Working Programme of the Commission in the field of Copy-right and Neighbouring Rights," Document COM (90) 584 final.

# 2. Main Elements of the Proposal for a Council Directive

## 1. THE LEGAL BASIS

The E.C. Commission based the proposal for a Council Directive on Articles 100A, 57(2) and 66 of the EEC Treaty.

According to the declared intention of the Commission, the proposal formed part of the Commission's program for the completion of the internal market before December 31, 1992. Article 8A of the EEC Treaty defines the internal market as "an area without internal frontiers in which the free movement of goods, persons, services and capital is ensured in accordance with the provisions of this Treaty." This provision makes explicit reference to a choice of Articles which may serve as a legal basis for harmonisation measures, including Article 100A and Article 57(2).

The Commission explained the choice of Article 100A as a legal basis for the Directive in its explanatory memorandum to the proposal. In the view of the Commission, the differences in legal protection between Member States, as regards rental rights as well as neighbouring rights, had a negative impact on intra-Community trade and on the functioning of the internal market; furthermore, they created considerable distortions of competition.[7] In concluding that the harmonisation of the laws of Member States on rental rights was necessary for the functioning of the internal market, in particular in relation to the free movement of goods and services, the Commission referred to the decision of the European Court of Justice of May 17, 1988 in the case *Warner Bros. Inc. et al.* v. *Christiansen.*[8] In this decision, the ECJ had held that the differing legislation in the Member States with respect to rental rights was likely to affect indirectly intra-Community trade in products such as videocassettes.

Articles 57(2) of the EEC Treaty was applied as a legal basis in addition to Article 100A, because it provides for the harmonisation of Member States' legislation "concerning the taking up and the pursuit of activities as self-employed persons." Article 66 was added, as it renders Article 57(2) applicable to services. In the view of the Commission, creative authors as well as performing artists normally act as self-employed persons, and their activities are often in the nature of services. In the field of copyright and related rights, just as in areas such as insurance and banking, the laws of Member States regarding the activities which self-employed persons pursue in their own

---

[7] Proposal for a Council Directive, COM (90) 586 final, p. 25.
[8] Case 158/86, *Warner Bros. Inc.* v. *Christiansen*: [1988] E.C.R. 2605, [1988] 3 C.M.L.R. 684.

8

interest or in the interest of others had to be harmonised in accordance with the purpose of Articles 57(2) and 66 in order to achieve the internal market.

Although the Commission developed these considerations about the legal basis of the proposal primarily in respect of rental rights, it applied the same legal basis also to lending rights. In the view of the Commission, rental rights could not be dealt with in a comprehensive way without also dealing with lending rights, as the lending of media in public libraries is closely connected to rental by commercial rental shops: the lending of protected material is by its very nature an exploitation of rights which from a copyright point of view is comparable to rental.

Likewise, the Commission also based the chapter of the proposal on piracy (Chapter II) on Articles 100A, 57(2) and 66 of the EEC Treaty. The lack of Community-wide protection for neighbouring rights, which Chapter II sought to overcome, clearly affected the functioning of the internal market and created considerable distortions of competition, furthering piracy and causing prejudice to European industry.[9]

## 2. THE TITLE OF THE PROPOSAL

It is worth having a brief look at the title of the proposed Directive, and not only because this title was changed at a later stage due to a proposal from the European Parliament, as will be explained in Chapter 3 below.

The original title did not adopt the somewhat vague headings of Chapters 2 and 4 of the Green Paper of 1988. Instead, it reflected accurately the contents of the proposed Directive. The rental right and lending right were dealt with in Chapter I of the proposal. Chapter II itself was entitled "Protection in the field of Rights Related to Copyright." The neutral expression "rights related to copyright" used in the title was synonymous with the terms "related rights" or "neighbouring rights" used elsewhere in the explanatory memorandum to the proposal. It signified the rights of performers, phonogram producers, film producers and broadcasting organisations.

The Commission chose a neutral term for this category of rights in order to avoid any interference with grown legal traditions of Member States. The Commission did not intend to enter into, or attempt to decide, the dogmatic discussions about the concepts of copyright, "droit d'auteur" or neighbouring rights. With respect to the above-mentioned category of rights, the proposal therefore did not prejudice the ability of Member States to choose to implement the new rights as "copyright" in the narrow sense, or as "neighbouring rights." It was the scope of rights which was intended to be harmonised, not the dogmatic approach of Member States in the field of copyright.

---

[9] Proposal for a Council Directive, COM (90) 586 final, p. 29.

## 3. The Concept of Rental and Lending Rights

### (a) Exclusive Rights

Chapter I of the proposed Directive contained the provisions on rental and lending rights. In accordance with the Green Paper and the outcome of the hearing, the Commission proposed in Article 1 an exclusive right, rather than only a right to remuneration: this exclusive right would enable the rightholder to prohibit or to authorise rental and/or lending with or without payment.

The exclusive nature of the rights proposed in fact corresponded to the traditional and classical concept of exploitation rights in the field of copyright, as only this exclusive nature would provide the rightholder with the possibility of controlling the exploitation of his works. As far as rental is concerned, it may in some sectors be essential for the protection of the rightholders for them to exercise the right to prohibit rather than allow rental activities; this may be the case in particular for the rental of newly released compact discs, with its potentially damaging effect on sales.

Moreover, only an exclusive right would provide its rightholder with the strong bargaining position which is necessary to negotiate adequate royalties for licensing. A mere statutory right to remuneration, in contrast, would not provide such a strong position, as the use would be allowed and the rightholder would not be able to enforce higher royalties in return for his authorisation.

It should be noted that the proposal did not limit this exclusive right to the rental/lending of sound recordings and videograms, as had been the concept of the Green Paper. Instead, a broader approach was chosen which no longer discriminated between different categories of protected works or subject matter. According to Article 1(1), the exclusive rental and lending right applied to all "originals and copies of copyright works and other subject matter," namely performances, phonograms and films.

### (b) Definitions of Rental and Lending

The definitions of rental and lending in Article 1(2) and (3) were the only definitions included in the proposal.

First, rental and lending were distinguished from sale by defining them as making available "for a limited period of time"; it followed from the nature of rental or lending that the respective object had to be returned to the outlet after use.

Secondly, in order to distinguish rental from lending, the proposal used the term "profit making purposes": to qualify as rental, the act would have to be done for direct profit making purposes, whereas the act of lending was described as done "not for direct profit making purposes." The main criterion was therefore whether the act in question served the economic interests of rental/lending businesses. Other possible criteria, like the payment of rental/lending fees, or reference to the commercial nature of rental, were explicity rejected by the Commission as being too blurred.[10] In addition, for an act to

---

[10] Proposal for a Council Directive, COM (90) 586 final, p. 34.

qualify as lending was made dependent upon it being done by institutions which were accessible to the public; a non-exhaustive list of such institutions (public libraries, school libraries, etc.) was added in Article 1(3) of the proposal.

These definitions did not include any specific reference to what some might consider to be borderline cases, such as the "rental" of a film copy by a distributor to a cinema. However, no further clarification was felt to be necessary for such cases, since the definitions, by using the expression "making available for use" already limited rental/lending to the use by final consumers only; acts of exploitation rather than of use by the consumer were therefore not intended to be covered by the Directive in any case.

## (c) The Rightholders

As stated above, the proposal went beyond the approach taken in the Green Paper by granting exclusive rental/lending rights for all protected works and subject matter. In Article 2 of the proposal, the Commission also chose a broader approach than in the Green Paper in respect of the relevant rightholders.

Thus, the exclusive rental and lending rights were to be given to authors in respect of all categories of protected works, to performers in respect of their fixed performances (be it a sound recording or a visual recording), to phonogram producers in respect of their phonograms, and to film producers in respect of their films.

It should be noted that the Commission did not attempt to define the terms author, performing artist or phonogram producer. It could rely in this context on the respective provisions, or even on the definitions, in the relevant international conventions, and actually did so explicitly in the Explanatory Memorandum for the proposal.[11]

As far as the fourth category of rightholders listed in Article 2(1) of the proposal – film producers – is concerned, there is no specific mention in the relevant conventions. Some Member States give film producers separate neighbouring rights, others consider them to be the "authors" of those films which qualify as protected works. The Commission offered a rather pragmatic solution to this problem: the producer of a film (be it a film work in the strict sense, or just moving images, such as documentary recordings without "work" character) was explicitly declared to have his own exclusive rental and lending rights, provided that he was the producer of the first fixation of that film. Producers of further fixations, in particular the producer of the videogram version of a film, were not among these genuine rightholders. The question whether film producers could be the authors of their film works, or whether they should be put into the category of neighbouring rightholders, was left to Member States to decide.

---

[11] Proposal for a Council Directive, COM (90) 586 final, p. 37.

### (d) Sharing of Payments

When the Commission decided to propose in Article 2 that four groups of rightholders should enjoy their own exclusive rental and lending rights, it was of course aware of the necessity for the rights to be assignable. A product which was subject to rental, for instance a videocassette, could only be marketed on the rental market if all rightholders involved agreed, and if the decisions on the marketing were concentrated in one place; this situation would not be much different from the management of reproduction rights, so that assignment would be the common practice for exclusive rental and lending rights, too.

In Article 3, entitled "Authorisation of Rental and Lending," the Commission intended to take account of this practice of assignment of the exclusive rights. It tried to ensure at the same time that the assigning rightholders would participate in the financial revenues obtained from the new rights. Therefore, this provision was shaped as a safeguard clause in the interest of those rightholders who assigned their exclusive rental and lending rights to others for exploitation. The application of Article 3 was limited to phonograms and videocassettes, as in these areas the assignment was expected to be of most relevance in practice.

It seems important to stress these underlying ideas, as the wording of the proposed Article 3 gave rise to a number of misunderstandings, and was to be changed accordingly in the course of the legislative process. But the real meaning of this provision, as reflected in the Commission's Explanatory Memorandum, was that those rightholders (normally: authors and performers) who had assigned their exclusive rental and/or lending right to others (normally: the producers of phonograms or films) for exploitation, should be entitled to obtain an adequate part of the payment which was received from rental outlets for the exploitation of the rights.

This right to participate in the revenues was declared to be unwaivable in Article 3. Whether it was to be administered by the individual rightholders themselves, by their collecting societies or by the assignees (the producers), was left for the Member States to decide.

### (e) Derogation from the Exclusive Lending Right

As already stated, the harmonisation of a lending right had not been envisaged in the Green Paper of 1988. When the Commission nevertheless, due to the comments received from interested circles and the outcome of the hearing, proposed that a lending right be made part of the Directive, it was aware of the potential opposition from some Member States' governments. It was foreseeable that some Member States would consider a lending right to be an inappropriate interference with the availability and accessibility of books and other cultural goods in public libraries.

It was against this background that Article 4 of the proposal gave Member States the ability to derogate, for cultural or other reasons and for one or several categories of objects, from the exclusive lending right as established under Article 1(1). If Member States were to make use of this option, however, they were to be obliged under Article 4 to provide (at least for authors) a right to equitable remuneration instead.

This provision clearly aimed to leave Member States with the utmost flexibility with respect to any legislation on the lending right. On the other hand, such flexibility would always be limited by the provisions of the EEC Treaty. The Commission deemed it useful to put explicit stress on Article 7 EEC Treaty: Article 4 of the proposal stated that, when introducing or maintaining a remuneration scheme for public lending, Member States would have to comply with Article 7 EEC and not discriminate between Community rightholders on the basis of their nationality.

## 4. Chapter II on Related Rights

The issues dealt with in Chapter 2 of the Green Paper of 1988 concerning copyright piracy were taken up in Chapter II of the proposed Directive, entitled "Protection in the Field of Rights Related to Copyright."

The provisions in Chapter II, Articles 5 to 8, were based on and structured closely according to the Rome Convention.[12] However, they included several "plus" elements as compared with the Rome Convention, namely further-reaching protection in terms of rights granted and rightholders concerned. The main improvements in this respect were the exclusive nature of performers' rights (rights to authorise or prohibit), the granting of their own reproduction right to film producers and the distribution right for performing artists, phonogram producers, film producers, and broadcasting organisations. None of these features were to be found in the Rome Convention, but the Commission, in accordance with the arguments of interested parties, felt that they were essential in order to establish effective Community-wide tools for the fight against piracy.

Article 5 of the proposal (fixation right for performing artists and broadcasting organisations) was based upon the respective provisions of the Rome Convention (Article 7, para. 1(b) and Article 13(b)), but gave performers an exclusive right (to authorise or prohibit fixation), instead of the mere "possibility of preventing" referred to in the Convention. No definitions had to be offered for such terms – as "performing artists" or "broadcasting," as the Rome Convention already did so in its Article 3.

Article 6 of the proposal set out an exclusive reproduction right for performers in respect of their fixed performances, for phonogram producers in respect of their phonograms, for film producers in respect of the first fixations of their films,[13] and for broadcasting organisations in respect of fixations of their broadcasts. With the exception of the right for film producers and the different nature and scope of performers' rights, these rights have their mirror image in Articles 7(1)(c), 10, and 13(c) respectively of the Rome Convention.

---

[12] International Convention for the Protection of Performers, Producers of Phonograms and Broadcasting Organisations of October 26, 1961.
[13] For the term "first fixation" see above, 3. c).

13

Article 7(1) proposed a new right, as compared with the Rome Convention. Under this provision, the exclusive right of distribution was to be granted to the same groups of rightholders and for the same subject matter as the reproduction right. Distribution was defined as making available to the public for an unlimited period of time by sale or otherwise. With this definition, a clear line was drawn between distribution within the meaning of Article 7, and rental which by itself also is an act of distribution in the wide sense, but was treated as a separate right under the Directive with respect to acts of making available for a limited period of time. Article 7(2) limited itself to restating the established rule on Community exhaustion: once a phonogram or videocassette, etc., has been put into circulation within the Community with the consent of the rightholder, the distribution right cannot be invoked to prevent the free circulation of these goods inside the Community. The proposal remained silent on the rules of exhaustion that Member States could choose to apply to imports from outside the Community.

Article 8 on the limitations to the rights granted in Chapter II of the proposed Directive was almost identical with Article 15 of the Rome Convention, as it restated the limitations which are allowed for under that provision. Article 8(3) however, was new: this paragraph was intended to deprive Member States of the potential excuse that the permitted exception for private use under Article 8(1)(a) of this proposed Directive would prevent future Community legislation in the field, in particular the harmonisation levy schemes for private copying already envisaged, and mentioned in the Commission's working programme.[14]

## 5. CHAPTER III ON DURATION

Under the proposed Directive, several rights were to be introduced which were not yet included in the international conventions, particularly the rental right, the lending right and the distribution right for neighbouring rightholders. Moreover, some Member States had not yet made any provision for the protection of neighbouring rights. Therefore, some rules on the duration of these rights were necessary, in order to obtain harmonisation also with respect to the terms of protection.

The Commission chose not to harmonise the duration of these rights in an isolated manner within the framework of the rental Directive. First, a separate proposal for a Directive on the harmonisation of the duration of copyright and neighbouring rights, with a broad and horizontal coverage, had already been announced.[15] Secondly, the discussions on the duration of the rental right and the other new rights would have to be co-ordinated in any event with those regarding the duration of copyright and neighbouring rights in general.

As a consequence, Chapter III of the proposed Directive, while being entitled "Duration," only provided for a minimum duration of the authors'

---

[14] "Follow-up to the Green Paper – Working Programme of the Commission in the field of Copyright and Neighbouring Rights," Document COM (90) 584 final.
[15] In the Working Program, see n. 14 above.

rights included in the proposal in accordance with the Berne Convention,[16] *i.e.* in general until at least 50 years after the death of the author (Article 9). On the other hand, pursuant to Article 10, it was proposed that the rights of performing artists, phonogram producers, film producers and broadcasting organisations included in the proposal should last at least as long as provided for in Article 14 of the Rome Convention (*i.e.* until 20 years after the fixation, performance or broadcast respectively).

## 6. COMMON PROVISIONS: APPLICATION IN TIME

Among the "Common Provisions" in Chapter IV (Articles 11 and 12) of the proposal, the Article on the "application in time" of the Directive is worth mentioning.

The question as to which works and subject matter (phonogram or film productions) the Directive was to apply to was of great importance. If the Commission had proposed that the Directive should apply to new works or productions only, legal certainty would have been provided for, and acquired rights or interests would have been left untouched; however, as a consequence, the effect of harmonisation would have been delayed far into the future. Instead, in Article 11 a faster path of harmonisation was chosen: the Commission proposed that the provisions of the Directive should apply also to all the already exisiting works, performances and productions still enjoying protection under national legislation, *i.e.* those which had not yet fallen into the public domain because of the expiry of the term of protection.

This approach was certainly ambitious, and necessarily so. As will be shown, it has survived into the final version of the Directive, albeit with several modifications.

---

[16] Berne Convention for the Protection of Literary and Artistic Works, of September 9, 1886, as revised at Paris on July 24, 1971.

# 3. Reactions and Legislative Process

## 1. THE REACTIONS IN INTERESTED CIRCLES

### (a) General Reactions

When the proposal for a Directive was published and available in January 1991, reactions from interested circles came promptly, and as to their substance they were in general no surprise to the Commission. On the whole, these reactions were quite positive. The proposal was welcomed and appreciated as offering a more balanced approach than the Green Paper of 1988 which had been the starting point for harmonisation in this field.

In particular, interested parties were struck by the complexity of the proposal. It was widely recognised that the text, while pursuing some new avenues in the search for sound and balanced copyright solutions, tried to accommodate different legal systems and traditions in a pragmatic manner. Moreover, the extensive Explanatory Memorandum was taken as a proof of the expertise and the solid legal background reflected in the proposal. The responses received were therefore of a rather different tone when compared with the criticisms that the Green Paper of 1988 had been faced with.

### (b) Reactions from Authors

Authors naturally appreciated the proposal, as it clearly offered them more than the Green Paper had done. They welcomed the proposed new entitlement to a genuine exclusive rental right in the video sector. Other points of particular importance for authors were the inclusion of the lending right, and the right to obtain an unwaivable share in the revenues received from the rental and lending rights under Article 3.

### (c) Reactions from Performers

Performers were pleased that the Commission proposed to "correct" the, in this respect, somewhat weaker provisions of the Rome Convention[17] by granting performing artists clear-cut exclusive rights. Performers understood that the exclusive rental right, lending right, fixation right, reproduction right and distribution right established for them under the Directive would provide them with a comprehensive range of strong rights which could be exercised in a meaningful way against users, as well as against potential licensees.

---

[17] International Convention for the Protection of Performers, Producers of Phonograms and Broadcasting Organisations of October 26, 1961.

Performing artists felt particularly satisfied about the right to share the rental/lending revenues under Article 3. They expected that this right would play an important role to their advantage, especially in the film sector where their rights had so far often been subject to a "buying-out."

At the same time, performers regretted that Chapter II of the proposal remained silent on the rights of broadcasting and communication to the public, and did not include provisions on the secondary use of phonograms similar to Article 12 of the Rome Convention. With respect to these rights, however, they accepted the idea that some harmonisation would be provided for after all, once the Commission's proposal for a Council Decision[18] concerning the accession of Member States to the Rome Convention was adopted.

As far as the lending right was concerned, performers would have preferred to have been included in Article 4 on a mandatory basis, side by side with authors as holders of a right to remuneration for public lending.

### (d) Reactions from Phonogram Producers

In view of the increasing digitalisation in the music market, in particular with respect to consumer recording equipment, phonogram producers had always insisted on the exclusive nature of the rental and lending rights. Accordingly, they welcomed the relevant provision in Article 1 of the proposal. But it was equally consequent that they considered the concept for the lending right as proposed by the Commission – an exclusive lending right combined with the possibility to derogate by providing a right to remuneration only – to be too weak. They argued that rightholders would also have to have the right to prohibit lending, if the sales of phonograms were not to be negatively affected by widespread lending in public libraries.

Phonogram producers also had reservations about the provision for the sharing of rental and lending revenues under Article 3. While they accepted the underlying idea of letting other rightholders, like performers, participate in the revenues received under the new rights, they were worried that Article 3 might preclude payments on a lump sum basis, and might even by its nature require management by collecting societies.

On the other hand, phonogram producers reacted very positively to the provisions included in Chapter II on related rights, even if the secondary use of phonograms was not dealt with there.

### (e) Reactions from Broadcasting Organisations

Broadcasters were widely satisfied with the harmonisation of the rights of fixation, reproduction and distribution as envisaged in Chapter II of the proposal. Similarly to performing artists, they regretted the absence of any rights

---

[18] "Proposal for a Council Decision concerning the accession of the Member States to the Berne Convention for the Protection of Literary and Artistic Works, as revised by the Paris Act of July 24, 1971, and the International Convention for the Protection of Performers, Producers of Phonograms and Broadcasting Organisations (Rome Convention) of October 26, 1961," Document COM (90) 582 final; Amended Proposal for a Council Decision, Document COM (92) 10 final.

of communication to the public or (re-)broadcasting in the proposal. They accepted, however, that the necessary harmonisation in this field was intended to be covered by the proposal for a Council Decision[19] concerning the accession of Member States to the Rome Convention.

### (f) Reactions from Film Producers

Film producers reacted positively to the harmonisation as such of rental and lending rights, and of the other rights included in Chapter II; this corresponded to the position they had held in the hearing in 1989. On the whole, however, they were the group least satisfied with the proposal.

They were opposed to the structure of the rights proposed, and particularly to film producers being treated as holders of "related rights." Even though the proposal remained neutral on the question of authorship of films, it clearly treated film producers as a separate category of rightholders: in the chapter on rental/lending rights they were listed just like phonogram producers, as rightholders besides (and not necessarily identical with) authors; and again, in the chapter on related rights, they figured side by side with the other neighbouring rightholders. Film producers understood this to be a step in the "wrong" direction, *i.e.* in the direction of the continental legal systems, where film producers are not considered to be among the authors of a film, but rather neighbouring rightholders instead.

Moreover, film producers did not want to be faced with genuine exclusive rights of those who contribute to a film, particularly performing artists. In the view of film producers, such exclusive rights would not take due account of the investment situation in respect of films, and might even be detrimental to their efficient marketing.

For similar reasons, film producers disapproved of the unwaivable right to share the revenues from rental and lending under Article 3. This right, in their view, would render the current practice of lump sum payment of artists impossible. Furthermore, it would put the economic essence of the rental and lending rights into the hands of collecting societies; film producers, it was argued, would in consequence have to bear the losses of a production alone, but would be obliged to share any gains.

Indeed, this opposition from the side of film producers, whether justified in substance or not, turned out to be the main cause of controversy in the context of the legislative process, as will be seen below.

### (g) Reactions from the Users' Side

Of course, the proposal would have direct consequences for users, in particular consumers, but also for those involved in the exploitation of rental and lending, such as libraries, video outlets and CD rental shops. Some of these groups put forward criticisms, though rather late in the day.

Libraries were worried about the exclusive nature of the lending right in Article 1, and about the possible effects on their budgets of remuneration for

---

[19] See n. 18, above.

public lending under Article 4. CD rental shops saw the danger of rightholders prohibiting CD rental altogether on the basis of the new exclusive right, and thus putting their very existence into question. Both these concerns were discussed and taken account of in the legislative process.

## 2. THE LEGISLATIVE PROCESS

### (a) The Economic and Social Committee

The Economic and Social Commitee is an institution established under Article 193 of the EEC Treaty. It has to be consulted in the context of the procedure envisaged under Article 100A for the harmonisation of the laws of Member States for the completion of the internal market. This ECOSOC, as it is called in short, consists of "representatives of the various categories of economic and social activity," such as producers, consumers and unions. Its members are appointed by the Council (Article 194 EEC Treaty).

During the Spring of 1991, the ECOSOC's Section for Industry, Commerce, Crafts and Services, which was responsible for preparing ECOSOC's Opinion on the subject, discussed the proposal several times. The Opinion of ECOSOC was adopted in plenary on July 3, 1991.[20] In substance, this Opinion essentially included the following comments on the proposal.

First of all, ECOSOC agreed to the need for harmonisation in this field, and explicitly welcomed the choice of an exclusive right (to authorise or prohibit) for rental. It also approved of widening the scope of the rental right to all protected works and subject matter, beyond what had been suggested in the Green Paper of 1988.

As to the ability of Member States, included in Article 4 of the proposal, to derogate from the public lending right, ECOSOC seems to have had somewhat mixed feelings. On the one hand, it held that this derogation was too wide and too flexible with respect to rightholders and categories of works: in its view, the lending of videograms and phonograms may decrease sales and should therefore always be subject to an exclusive right without the possibility of derogation. On the other hand, ECOSOC felt that the remuneration to be paid, at least to authors, in the context of that derogation for public lending might be too high a burden for the budgets of public libraries and thus for public funds to bear.

The provision on the sharing of the rental/lending right revenues under Article 3 of the proposal was recognised by ECOSOC to be inventive and difficult to construe. It recommended re-examination of the text, with a view to making it more understandable, more easily applicable by Member States, and in order to keep interference with contractual relations in the field to a minimum.

As far as the provisions on related rights in Chapter II of the proposal were concerned, ECOSOC approved of their substance and drafting, but regretted the absence of harmonisation of the rights of broadcasting and communication to the public, and of the secondary use of phonograms. According to

---

[20] [1991] O.J. C269/54.

ECOSOC, the Commission should "lose no time in submitting proposals for harmonisation" in these areas too.

## (b) The European Parliament

The European Parliament[21] has a decisive role to play in the legislative process in relation to initiatives for harmonisation under Article 100A of the EEC Treaty. While it is the Council which finally adopts Directives under that provision, it is obliged to co-operate closely with the European Parliament in the process, the procedural details being laid down in Article 149 of the EEC Treaty. According to that Article, the European Parliament is twice given the opportunity to comment on a proposal: once, in first reading, the Parliament gives its opinion before the Council in a so-called "Common Position" agrees upon the substance of the proposal; then, in second reading, the Parliament may comment on, or suggest modifications to, this Common Position.

With respect to the proposed Directive on rental right, lending right and related rights, the European Parliament certainly did not have an easy task, as this was the first pure or "classic" copyright initiative taken by the Commission, and a very complex one at that. However, the Parliament clearly met this challenge, and took the task very seriously. From the very beginning, it was aware of the horizontal impact of the proposal on the whole field of copyright and neighbouring rights in the Community. As a consequence, it was faced with a degree of intensive lobbying almost unheard of before.

The Commission communicated its proposal for a Directive to the European Parliament on February 6, 1991. It was submitted to, and discussed by, three Committees of the Parliament, with the Committee on Legal Affairs and Citizens' Rights having the main responsibility for the proposal.

The Committee on Youth, Culture, Education, the Media and Sport adopted its Opinion on September 26, 1991. The Committee on Economic and Monetary Affairs and Industrial Policy adopted its Opinion on October 18, 1991. The Legal Affairs Committee, however, due to the degree of lobbying already mentioned and the various interests involved, organised a hearing of interested parties on the proposal on September 26, 1991. The fact that this hearing was not held in public in view of the strong lobbying constitutes an exception and a rather remarkable detail in this context. The Legal Affairs Committee adopted its Opinion on January 21, 1992.

The proposal was discussed in the plenary of the European Parliament on February 10, 1992. All interventions in the debate, including that of the rapporteur of the Legal Affairs Committee, Mr. Anastassopoulos, recognised and stressed the importance of the proposal as a first cornerstone of general harmonisation in the field of copyright and neighbouring rights. Moreover, its importance for the completion of the internal market was stressed, and the Commissioner in charge of the dossier, Vicepresident Bangemann, called the proposal an indispensable measure for the recognition of authors' and performers' rights in the Community.

---

[21] EEC Treaty, Arts. 137 *et seq.*

Two days later, on February 12, 1992, the Parliament almost unanimously adopted its Opinion in first reading on the draft Directive. The main thrust of the proposed Directive as well as most of its substance were endorsed. About half of the 41 amendments to the text of the proposal originally put to vote in plenary were adopted and therefore formed part of the Parliament's Opinion. In more detail, the following points were subject to proposed amendments:

- The Parliament suggested that a reference to "intellectual property" should be added to the title of the Directive, in order to give a clearer indication of the type of rights dealt with. Two other amendments concerned recitals: one proposed the addition of a phrase according to which the exercise of the rights dealt with in the proposed Directive would entail a liability to pay a compensatory levy for home copying; the other proposed an additional recital concerning the necessity for negotiations on national treatment for third countries.
- As far as the definitions in Article 1 were concerned, the Parliament suggested that both rental and lending should be explicitly stated not to include "making available for the purpose of public presentation and performance"; this clause was intended to ensure that rental or lending was not covered by the Directive unless it served the "use" by the consumer. Another amendment on this Article proposed to add to the definition for rental, as being done "for profit-making purposes," the formulation "and for direct or indirect economic advantage."
- Some important amendments concerned Article 2. It was suggested that a new separate paragraph should be added to this Article, stating that for the purpose of the rental and lending right, "at least the main director of an audiovisual work shall be deemed to have the status of author." This amendment clearly addressed those countries – including the United Kingdom – where the film producer is for the time being considered to be the (only) "author" of a film work; thus, a limited rule on authorship was introduced into the Directive. The second amendment proposed the addition of a presumption of transfer of rights: subject to contractual provisions to the contrary, a performer would be presumed to have transferred his rental and lending rights in a contract with a film producer. This amendment was intended to outweigh to some extent the strong new exclusive rental right of performers, redressing the balance in favour of film producers.
- The unwaivable right under Article 3 to obtain an adequate part of the revenues received for rental or lending was subject to several proposed amendments. The Parliament suggested modification of the reference to the rightholders concerned, and replacement of the supposedly somewhat strong phrase "the right to obtain" with the expression "the right to enjoy." In an attempt to offer more precise criteria for the determination of the "adequate part of the payment," it was suggested that the text should state that "the adequate part shall be duly proportional to the contribution to the work and its exploitation." Furthermore, in order to facilitate the administration of this right, a provision was proposed to be added to the effect that the administration of the right "may be entrusted

21

in particular to collective administrative associations representing the professional categories concerned."

- The Parliament suggested the insertion of a new Article 4A into the text, stating that the protection of neighbouring rights in the Directive "shall not prejudice protection of the copyright as such." The underlying idea for this amendment was to take up a non-prejudice clause of the same kind as included in Article 1 of the Rome Convention.[22]
- Another new Article which the Opinion of the Parliament proposed to add to the Directive concerned a prohibition of alterations: this new Article 4B was supposed to state that "no changes, cuts or additions may be made to a work by the letter, the hirer, the lender or borrower."
- With respect to the right of reproduction in Article 6, the Parliament suggested that the Directive should include a similar rebuttable presumption of transfer of the right of the performing artist in a contract with the film producer, as already proposed for the rental and lending right.
- The Parliament proposed a new Article 6A. This provision was intended to add a comprehensive list of broadcasting rights and rights of communication to the public. These rights had not been mentioned in the original proposal for a Directive, because its Chapter II had been closely following the Green Paper of 1988, which had defined piracy in a more limited way as relating to unauthorised reproductions only. On the other hand, the reason that the rights in question were not dealt with in the original proposal was that the adoption of the proposal for a Council Decision concerning the adherence of all Member States to the Rome Convention[23] would already have had a harmonising effect in this respect. In the view of the Parliament this situation had changed: by the time of the adoption of its Opinion on the rental proposal, it had become clear that prospects for adoption of that Council Decision were not good.

Consequently, the new Article 6A introduced into the Directive those Rome Convention rights which had not yet been covered. Article 6A(1) set out an exclusive right for performers to control the broadcasting and communication to the public of their unfixed and unbroadcasted performances, based on Article 7(1)(a) of the Rome Convention. Article 6A(2) followed closely Article 12 of the Rome Convention in providing for "fair payment" for performers and phonogram producers with respect to the use of phonograms for broadcasting or communication to the public. Finally, Article 6A(3) established an exclusive right of broadcasting for broadcasting organisations, similar to Article 13(d) of the Rome Convention.

- With respect to the right of distribution, the Parliament proposed a rebuttable presumption of transfer of the rights of performers in contracts with film producers along the lines of the rebuttable presumption of transfer of the rental and lending right.
- As regards Article 11 (Application in Time), the European Parliament suggested the addition of a new paragraph safeguarding acquired rights:

---

[22] See n. 1, above.
[23] See n. 2, above.

rights and obligations deriving from legislation enacted prior to the Directive were not to be affected by its provisions. However, contracting parties were put under an obligation to "review the terms of their contracts within three years" from the entry into force of the Directive.

It is worth noting that the European Parliament did not vote any amendments at all on the concept of the lending right as contained in the proposal. Even where the Parliament proposed amendments to the Directive, they followed its main thrust, although a number of important modifications were made.

### (c) The Commission's Amended Proposal

As long as the Council has not acted on a Commission proposal, the Commission has the right under Article 149(3) of the EEC Treaty to submit an amended proposal. Actually, it can do so at any time during the legislative procedure, as long as the discussions of a proposal in the framework of the proceedings envisaged in Article 149(1) and (2) of the EEC Treaty for harmonisation initiatives are not concluded.

Clearly, the presentation by the European Parliament of its Opinion in first reading constitutes the most significant input in substance on a proposal, before the Council itself takes a position. The conclusion of this first reading in Parliament is therefore the right moment for the Commission to reconsider its initiative, and to come up with a modified proposal, if appropriate. It gives the Commission the opportunity to adjust its proposal in response to the Parliament's deliberations, without losing time in the proceedings: while the modified proposal virtually replaces the original one, the Parliament does not engage in another "first reading" on it and the ongoing proceedings are continued.

For all these reasons, the Commission took the opportunity to work out an amended proposal for the rental Directive, based on the findings of the European Parliament. This amended proposal was adopted by the Commission on April 29, 1992, and was presented one day later.[24] Its declared intention was to take account of the Opinion of the European Parliament.

Only two of the amendments proposed by the European Parliament were not adopted in the amended proposal. The one concerned a phrase on the payment of a compensatory levy on home copying, which the Parliament wanted to be added to a recital; the Commission did not accept it, because it had no relation to the contents of the Directive. The other proposed amendment that was rejected was of a mere technical nature. All the other amendments suggested by the Parliament were incorporated into the amended proposal, though some of them underwent quite significant drafting changes.

First of all, the Directive changed its title: in accordance with the Parliament's proposal, a reference to "the field of intellectual property" was added. Besides other less important additional recitals, one new recital concerned the relations of Member States with third countries. With respect to this recital,

---

[24] "Amended Proposal for a Council Directive on Rental Right and Lending Right and on Certain Rights Related to Copyright in the Field of Intellectual Property," Document COM (92) 159 final; [1992] O.J. C128/8.

the Commission accepted the Parliament's underlying concerns, but – not being entirely convinced – came up with a largely modified wording. It was this recital which was to be the only real point of contention in the context of the second reading.[25]

As regards the definitions, the Commission accepted that clarification should be inserted to the effect that rental and lending for the purpose of public performance were not covered, and that therefore such acts, in particular the rental of film copies to cinemas or to broadcasting organisations, and the rental of sheet music for the purpose of public performance, remained outside the scope of the Directive. In addition, the element of "economic advantage" was adopted as part of the definition of rental.

The amended proposal adopted all of the Parliament's proposals on Article 2, those on the authorship of film works and on the rebuttable presumption of assignment of rights of performing artists being the most important ones. Both provisions were "streamlined," however, in order to facilitate their application in practice. The same is basically true for the modifications to Article 3 (the right to obtain an adequate part of the revenues received for rental).

As the European Parliament had proposed no amendments on the derogation from the exclusive lending right under Article 4, this provision remained unchanged. Pursuant to the Opinion of the Parliament, the Commission included a separate Article on the non-prejudicial relationship between neighbouring rights and copyright, as is already to be found in Article 1 of the Rome Convention. Since this provision is of a general character and would apply to the Directive as a whole, the Commission did not place it in the first chapter as proposed by the Parliament, but as Article 11 bis in Chapter IV of the text under the "Common Provisions." The other additional provision, proposed by the Parliament as an Article 4A was also accepted and given the title "Moral Rights."

In Chapter II of the amended proposal, the Commission again incorporated the substance of what the European Parliament had suggested. Of particular importance was certainly Article 6 bis on "Broadcasting and Communication to the Public."

In Chapter IV on Common Provisions, the Commission included the Parliament's proposal for a new Article 11(2). Furthermore, the Commission took the opportunity to clarify in paragraph 1 of this provision that not only works and subject matter still protected were to be covered by the Directive, but also those still "protectable." This formulation was intended to ensure that the Directive would not be ineffective in respect of already existing works and productions in those Member States which as of yet had no protection whatsoever for whole categories of rights; without such a clause, the Member States in question would have been allowed to apply the new rights under the Directive only to new works or productions. In addition, and for the first time in this context, the Commission introduced into Article 11(2) a safeguard provision for the protection of those who had engaged in rental or lending before the entry into force of the respective exclusive right under the Directive, with

---

[25] See (d), below.

respect to rental/lending objects already acquired. This provision was intended, in particular, to safeguard the ability of videoshops or compact disc rental outlets to continue to rent from their already existing stock.

### (d) The Council of Ministers

It is the Council of Ministers[26] which finally decides upon the adoption (or otherwise) of all Directives. However, a proposal based on Article 100A of the EEC Treaty may be adopted in the Council by qualified majority; no unanimity is required.[27] The size of the majority obtained has to be calculated on the basis of the number of votes each Member State holds in the Council according to Article 148(2) of the EEC Treaty. Particularly with respect to complex proposals, the chances for adoption obviously depend upon which Member States are opposed to which elements of the proposal, and how many votes they hold.

Of course, the Council does not take decisions in isolation. It is obliged to co-operate with the European Parliament under Article 149(2) of the EEC Treaty and to consult the Economic and Social Committee, as was described in more detail above. Moreover, as far as its internal decision-making process is concerned, the Council employs the established procedure of discussion in Working Groups. These Working Groups discuss the proposals in detail, in parallel with the European Parliament and ECOSOC, and prepare them for the decision of the Council. Only when the Working Group considers the proposal ripe for a political decision is it submitted via the Committee of the Permanent Representatives ("Coreper") to the Council of Ministers.

The Working Group consists of expert representatives from each Member State and from the Commission. In the area of copyright, it is usually the expert from the national ministry of culture, justice, trade or the like, depending on the internal distribution of dossiers in the respective Member State, who represents his or her government in the discussions about a proposal. The chairman of the Working Group is usually a representative of the Member State which holds the Presidency in the Council.

In the case of the proposed Directive on rental and lending right, the usual procedure was followed. The Working Group started its discussion on the proposal as early as in January 1991, immediately after it was published, under the Presidency of Luxembourg. Some preliminary conclusions on points of substance were reached in the Working Group under the Dutch Presidency during the second half of 1991; for instance, consensus had already largely been attained on Chapter II of the proposal on piracy.

However, real progress could not be made by the Working Group until the European Parliament had concluded its first reading of the proposal. As soon as this was the case, as of February 12, 1992, the Presidency of the Working Group (at that time Portuguese) pushed for progress. Working in parallel with the Commission preparing its Amended Proposal,[28] it prepared several "consolidated texts" and internal memoranda which followed closely the line of

---

[26] EEC Treaty, Art. 145 *et seq.*
[27] EEC Treaty, Art. 149(2)(a) and (e).
[28] See (c), above.

the original proposal, but were at the same time intended to take account of the findings of the European Parliament in first reading, and of the Commission's reactions thereto.

This enabled the Working Group to finalise its text in only six meeting days after the adoption of the Opinion in first reading by the European Parliament, and to make it ready for political decision-making in the Council itself. Immediately after the publication of the Amended Proposal by the Commission, the proposed Directive was thus submitted to the Internal Market Council meeting of May 14, 1992, with a view to adopting a Common Position.

Three points of substance had been most controversial: the rule on authorship for film works, the provisions on the presumption of assignment of exclusive rights, and the structure of the public lending right. It was these controversial points which prevented the immediate adoption of a Common Position on May 14, 1992: it was finally adopted, after these points had been settled, on June 18, 1992. Adoption was unanimous, with only the United Kingdom abstaining. In substance, it was certainly facilitated thanks to several statements which either the Commission on its own, or the Council jointly with the Commission made in the Council meeting for the records. These statements do not form part of the text of the proposal, nor are they public; they nevertheless clarify to some extent the interpretation which should be given to certain provisions of the Directive. The statements are taken account of and explained in detail, in the article by article commentary on the Directive contained in Section II below.

Amongst the solutions which the Common Position found for outstanding or controversial items, the following deserve particular mention:

- The definitions for rental and lending in Article 1 were co-ordinated; they both now applied the test of "direct or indirect economic or commercial advantage."
- It was now explicitly stated in Article 2(4) that the exclusive rental or lending rights were assignable. Member States had to provide for a rebuttable presumption of assignment of the exclusive rental right by the performer in individual or collective contracts with film producers concerning film production (Article 2(5)). Member States could provide for similar presumptions with respect to authors (Article 2(6)). Furthermore, they could provide that written contracts between performers and film producers concerning the production of a film which provide for an equitable participation in the revenues from exploitation would have the effect of authorising rental, or the other acts, that performers were entitled to prohibit under Chapter II of the Directive, (Article 2(7)).
- The right for authors and performers to participate in the revenues from rental was declared under Article 4 to be an "unwaivable right to equitable remuneration." Member States were free to impose collective administration of this right by collective societies, and to decide from whom this remuneration could be claimed or collected. What was to be understood by "equitable" could only be accurately decided *ex post*, but lump sum advances or payments were possible.

- Member States could now widely derogate from the exclusive lending right, Article 5, provided that at least authors obtained a remuneration for such lending. Other than with respect to the lending of phonograms, films and computer programs, Member States were free to determine the amount of the remuneration according to their cultural objectives. They could even exempt certain categories of establishments completely from paying remuneration. Before July 1, 1997, the Commission had to draw up a report "on public lending in the Community."
- By Article 13(1), Member States had to extend the rights granted under the Directive to already existing works and subject matter which were "still protected" by their "legislation in the field of copyright and related rights or meet the criteria for protection under the provisions of this Directive" on July 1, 1994. Member States were given the option of not applying the provision on authorship for films (Article 2(2)) before July 1, 1997, or of not applying it at all to film works created before July 1, 1994. Likewise, Member States would not have to apply the unwaivable right to equitable remuneration (Article 4) before July 1, 1997 (Article 13(8)). In addition, there were several new safeguard clauses concerning old contracts (Article 13(6)) and acquired rights or expectations of assignees (Article 13(7) and (9)) and of rental or lending outlets (Article 13(3)).

The proceedings which apply to a Common Position are laid down in detail in Article 149 of the EEC Treaty. In line with these provisions, the Common Position, together with an explanatory note from the Secretariat of the Council and comments from the Commission,[29] was submitted to the European Parliament, where it was officially received on July 9, 1992.

According to Article 149(2)(b) and (c) of the EEC Treaty, the European Parliament has to conclude its second reading of the proposal within a period of 3 months, calculated from that date of reception. Due to the summer break, this period was extended by one month (Article 149(2)(g)), so that the actual deadline for the conclusion of the second reading was November 9, 1992.

In the course of the plenary debate in the European Parliament, the rapporteur, Mr. Anastassopoulos, pointed out that the Commission had adopted in its amended proposal a remarkable number of amendments from the Parliament's Opinion in first reading. He stressed that this, in his view, had provided the Parliament with a maximum impact on the substance of the proposal. After this debate, the Parliament adopted its Opinion in second reading on October 28, 1992. It endorsed the Common Position with one exception: the Parliament insisted on the reintroduction of a recital concerning the relations of Member States with third countries.

This recital suggested that the Directive "may create a new situation in regard to Member States' relations with certain third countries," and that therefore, it would be "necessary to step up negotiations and consultations with such third countries, in particular with the relevant international organisations, with a view to securing at least reciprocal legal protection." It was

---

[29] "Communication from the Commission to the European Parliament," Document SEC (92) 1323 final.

thus exactly the same recital as the European Parliament had come up with in first reading,[30] and which the Commission had then – obviously only half convinced – adopted in its amended proposal.[31] The Council had dropped it from the Directive, as it saw no need for such a recital, and held that it would create confusion rather than constitute a useful statement. The Commission in its comments[32] on the Common Position had agreed to the deletion of this recital as, in its view, "the statements included therein are of no particular importance for the understanding of the operational provisions, nor are they necessarily connected with the scope of this Directive."

The Council was thus faced with only one amendment to its unanimously adopted Common Position. In order to encourage the Council to adopt the Directive in the unamended form of the Common Position, the Commission issued an Opinion[33] stating that it rejected the Parliament's proposed amendment and accepted the Common Position as it was and "without any amendments." In such a situation, the Council could, if necessary, have adopted the Directive in the form of the unamended Common Position by qualified majority.[34]

In fact, the unamended text was adopted unanimously, and without further discussion, on November 19, 1992 as Council Directive 92/100/EEC on rental right and lending right and on certain rights related to copyright in the field of intellectual property.[35]

## Table of Events

| July 7, 1988 | Presentation of Green Paper on Copyright and Challenge of Technology, COM (88) 172 final. |
| --- | --- |
| Sept. 18/19, 1989 | Hearing of interested parties on the issues of Chapter 2 and Chapter 4 of the Green Paper, organised by the Commission. |
| Dec. 5, 1990 | Adoption of the Proposal for Council Directive on rental right, lending right, and on certain rights related to copyright by the Commission. |
| Jan. 24, 1991 | Publication of the Proposal as document COM (90) 586 final; [1991] O.J. C53/35. |
| July 3, 1991 | The Economic and Social Committee adopts its Opinion on the Proposal; [1991] O.J. C269/54. |
| Feb. 12, 1992 | The European Parliament adopts its Opinion on the Proposal in first reading; [1992] O.J. C67/92. |
| April 29, 1992 | The Commission adopts its Amended Proposal on the Directive as document COM (92) 159 final; [1992] O.J. C128/8. |

---

[30] See (b), above.

[31] See (c), above.

[32] See n. 29, above.

[33] "Opinion of the Commission," Document SEC (92) 2091 final.

[34] EEC Treaty, Art. 149(2).

[35] [1992] O.J. L346/61. The United Kingdom abstained, as it had on the adoption of the Common Position.

| | |
|---|---|
| June 18, 1992 | The Council adopts a Common Position on the Proposal. |
| July 3, 1992 | Communication from the Commission to the European Parliament on the Common Position, document SEC (92) 1323 final. |
| Oct. 28, 1992 | The European Parliament adopts its Opinion on the Proposal in second reading; [1992] O.J. C305/73. |
| Nov. 9, 1992 | Opinion of the Commission on the amendment proposed by the European Parliament, document SEC (92) 2091 final. |
| Nov. 19, 1992 | The Council adopts Council Directive 92/100/EEC on rental right and lending right and on certain rights related to copyright in the field of intellectual property; [1992] O.J. L346/61. |

## SECTION II

# COMMENTARY ON THE ARTICLES OF THE DIRECTIVE

# Article 1. Object of Harmonization

Article 1 lays down the principle that the rental and lending rights shall be granted in the Member States, and that they shall be exclusive rights to authorise and prohibit. It contains definitions of "rental" and "lending."

## 1. ARTICLE 1(1)

*Article 1*

**Object of harmonization**

1.   In accordance with the provisions of this Chapter, Member States shall provide, subject to Article 5, a right to authorize or prohibit the rental and lending of originals and copies of copyright works, and other subject matter as set out in Article 2(1).

...

COMMENTARY

### (a) Exclusive Nature of the Rental Right

The Commission, in its original proposal, had already decided in favour of the exclusive nature of the rental right, since this not only reflected the classical nature of the exploitation rights in the field of copyright, but it also constituted the most efficient form of protection in the particular case of rental. Rental without the possibility of prohibition would, particularly in the field of phonograms, have resulted in continued extensive copying and in a corresponding decrease of sales.

The European Parliament did not propose any amendment with respect to the exclusive nature of the rental right.

Within the Council Working Group, two Member States were strongly opposed to the exclusive nature of the rental right. They held a reservation on this point until the day on which the Internal Market Council adopted its Common Position. These Member States would have preferred, in accordance with their respective national legislation and legislative intentions, a remuneration right.

The expressions "(the right) to authorize or prohibit (rental)" and "exclusive" are synonymous. The combined use of these terms in Articles 2(1), 6(1) and (2), 7(1) and 8(1) and (3) does not reflect any difference in the meaning.

The fact that the word "exclusive" has been added to the original wording "a right to authorize or prohibit" in these Articles is due to one Member State's wish to use the word "exclusive right" throughout the whole Directive, and not just in Article 7 (distribution right), as the original proposal did for mere reasons of syntax.

The reference to "other subject matter as set out in Article 2(1)" is a reference to fixations of performers' performances, phonograms, and originals and copies of films as defined by Article 2(1), 4th indent, of the Directive.[1]

It is to be expected that the exclusive rental right will be exercised by selective prohibition in the music sector. The right-owners might, for example, forbid rental of compact discs for several months after release, in order to encourage sales instead of rental and copying activities. They might also authorise a particular outlet to rent only a limited number of copies of a certain recording. In the video sector, the rental right will not primarily be necessary to avoid the problem of copying, at least as long as CD-videos have not appeared on the market in large numbers. It will probably be used to allow a parallel exploitation on both the sales and rental markets.

### (b) Exclusive Nature of the Lending Right

The Commission, having considered proposing a public lending right in the form of a remuneration right only,[2] finally proposed an exclusive right as a basic principle but, at the same time, offered Member States the opportunity to choose a remuneration right as set out in Article 4 of the original proposal instead of the exclusive right. This double structure was chosen, *inter alia*, in order to emphasise that lending in principle is, at least from a rightholder's point of view, a form of copyright exploitation which is similar to rental and must accordingly be covered by an exclusive right. The possibility of derogation provided by Article 4 was intended to allow for the Member States' cultural policies, in particular the need to guarantee access for consumers to public libraries. In addition, it was intended to facilitate a compromise between the Member States, which have strongly differing provisions, if any, on lending rights.

In order to underline the need for a lending right, in whatever form, the Commission pointed out the economic connections between rental and lending and the fact that the increase in lending activities in the music and film sectors might end up considerably affecting the rental business and thereby depriving the rental right of its importance.

The appropriateness of covering the lending right in the Directive was highly controversial. The Legal Affairs Committee of the European Parliament voted against several proposed amendments to delete the lending right from the Directive; finally, the plenary of the European Parliament did not

---

[1] For further analysis of the "subject matter", see comments on Art. 2(1) of the Directive, pp. 50–51, below.

[2] In the Green Paper (COM (88) 172 final), it did not see any need for harmonisation of the lending right: see paras. 4.4.4. to 4.4.10. of the Green Paper.

adopt any amendment with respect to the lending right as set out in Article 1(1).

In the Council Working Group, the lending right as such, as well as its exclusive nature, were two of the most disputed issues of the Directive. About one half of the Member States were not keen on introducing a lending right at all, whether because of the financial implications or because of (unjustified) doubts as to how a public lending right would be administered in practice. Some Member States which seemed less reluctant to have a lending right only recognised its importance in respect of certain categories of media. Other Member States were in principle favourable, while some insisted on the lending right being covered by the Directive. Another Member State wanted even the exclusive lending right to apply mandatorily to certain categories of media. Finally, a compromise was found within the framework of Article 5 (Common Position/Directive).[3]

Most of the Member States will probably not provide for an exclusive lending right but will make use of the right of derogation set out in Article 5. However, it may be expected that some Member States will provide an exclusive right for certain media, such as sound recordings, videograms and computer programs, in order to provide more efficient means to cope with the problem of copying related to those categories of media.

The words "subject to Article 5" which did not appear in the original proposal were introduced at a Member State's request, in order to clarify the relationship to Article 5. This supplement does not change the meaning of the original Commission proposal.

The above comments on the expressions "right to authorize or prohibit," "exclusive right" and "other subject matter"[4] apply also to the lending right.

## 2. RECITALS (12) TO (14) AND ARTICLE 1(2) AND (3)

### Recitals

(12) Whereas it is necessary to define the concepts of rental and lending for the purposes of this Directive;

(13) Whereas it is desirable, with a view to clarity, to exclude from rental and lending within the meaning of this Directive certain forms of making available, as for instance making available phonograms or films (cinematographic or audiovisual works or moving images, whether or not accompanied by sound) for the purpose of public performance or broadcasting, making available for the purpose of exhibition, or making available for on-the-spot reference use; whereas lending within the meaning of this Directive does not include making available between establishments which are accessible to the public;

(14) Whereas, where lending by an establishment accessible to the public gives rise to a payment the amount of which does not go beyond what is necessary to

---

[3] Discussed at pp. 80–81, below.
[4] See p. 33.

cover the operating costs of the establishment, there is no direct or indirect economic or commercial advantage within the meaning of this Directive;

*Article 1*

. . .

2.   For the purposes of this Directive, "rental" means making available for use, for a limited period of time and for direct or indirect economic or commercial advantage.

3.   For the purposes of this Directive, "lending" means making available for use, for a limited period of time and not for direct or indirect economic or commercial advantage, when it is made through establishments which are accessible to the public.

. . .

## COMMENTARY

### (a) Making Available for Use for a Limited Period of Time

The Commission, in its original proposal, considered it to be necessary to include in the definitions of "rental" and "lending" the words "*for a limited period of time,*" in order to exclude forms of making available for use for an unlimited period of time, such as sale or gift. This part of the definition did not meet any objections, either from the Parliament or from the Council.

The definition comprises all cases where the rental or lending object has to be or may be returned after a certain time. Hence, even sale with an option to repurchase at a price which is lower than the selling price is covered by the definition. Generally speaking, the definition also covers acts which have a different legal structure from rental or lending within the meaning of civil law but which are intended to have the same result as acts of rental or lending (and which may in fact amount to acts of attempted circumvention). Otherwise, the rental and lending right provisions of the Directive could easily be avoided by users such as rental outlets and thereby lose their importance or become obsolete.

In connection with the expression "*making available for use,*" the question arose whether this use should cover only private use by an end user, for example listening at home to a compact disc, or also use for public purposes, for example showing a rented film to a cinema audience (films which are shown in cinemas are regularly rented by the cinema owner from the film distributor). The original Commission proposal did not contain any explicit comment on this question; it was however not intended to cover use for public purposes. In order to deal with this question the European Parliament adopted amendments according to which the making available "for public presentation and performance" should be excluded from the definitions of rental and lending. The Commission endorsed in a clearer version of this amendment in its own amended proposal, *i.e.* "for the purpose of public performance." According to the Commission, this addition did not change the original content, since the word "use" had to be distinguished from "exploitation" and was never intended to include acts of exploitation such as the public performance of a film.

In the course of the discussions in the Council Working Group, for similar reasons several Member States wanted to exclude explicitly certain forms of making available, in particular the case already mentioned, namely the making available of a film to a film theatre which then publicly performs the film. Other cases mentioned were the making available of works of art by one museum to another for the purpose of exhibition, intra-library lending, and the rental of sheet music for the purpose of broadcasting or public performance.

It proved difficult, however, to find an appropriate wording for the exclusion of these and similar cases. A possible definition of rental and lending as "making available for use *by an end user*" was discussed but rejected because it seemed too vague and the notion of an "end user" did not present a proper copyright term. Another possibility, the mere specification of the mentioned cases, did not seem suitable since further comparable cases, which would have to be included, might exist or arise in the future. Despite long discussions no satisfactory definition providing for such an exemption was established and the Member States continued to disagree on certain points, in particular on the question of whether the rental of sheet music for purposes of broadcasting or public performance should be excluded from the definition. Therefore, instead of providing a definition in the text itself, Member States agreed to the introduction of an additional recital, which is, as are recitals in general, not of an operative nature but represents only a means of interpretation.

According to the resulting Recital (13), it is desirable that Member States exclude from the definition of rental and lending certain forms of making available, for example the "rental" or "lending" of a film to a cinema which then shows the film to its audience; the "rental" or "lending" of a film to a broadcasting organisation which will then broadcast the film; the "rental" or "lending" of a work of art by a private person or a museum to a certain museum which then shows the work in a specific exhibition or the "lending" of a certain book by a library to another library which then may lend it to a reader who requests the book (libraries fall under the expression "establishments which are accessible to the public," which has the same meaning as under Article 1(3)). There may be similar cases which do not involve any "use" within the meaning of Article 1(2) and 1(3) and therefore are not covered by the Directive. This is suggested by the fact that the recital only lists examples (the wording reads: "as for instance").

Recital (13), in interpreting Article 1(2) and (3), also mentions acts of making available for on-the-spot reference use. Indeed, it may be concluded from the words "making available" in Articles 1(2) and (3) that mere on-the-spot reference use does not lead to having objects *available* and therefore is not covered by Articles 1(2) and (3). This part of the recital was introduced pursuant to a request by several Member States – in particular, those which were opposed to the inclusion of the lending right at all – which wanted to exclude explicitly lending by reference libraries. In addition, some Member States wanted to exclude explicitly on-the-spot rental which did not appear to be economically important. Accordingly, amongst other examples, lending by libraries which lend books or other material only on their premises but do not allow users to take the material home is excluded from the Directive.

Rental outlets at present do not seem interested in making phonograms or videograms available only in their premises. It is, however, conceivable that rental outlets will do so in future and, at the same time, will offer the use of copying machines, so that a client may rent a compact disc, make a copy within the same premises and return the disc. This hypothesis would represent a case of attempted circumvention of the Directive and would, corresponding to the view of all Member States in the Council, thus be covered by the rental right in any case.

### (b) (Not) for Direct or Indirect Economic or Commercial Advantage

This part of the definitions of rental and lending was one of the most discussed concepts in the Directive. It seems that the Commission, the Member States and the Parliament largely agreed on the substance, but it proved extremely difficult to agree on the concrete wording.

The Commission, in its original proposal, had defined the terms "rental" and "lending" according to whether or not the activity was for profit-making purposes. The most important cases were meant to be rental by video and CD rental shops and lending by public libraries. The wording "not for *direct* profit-making purposes" in the original definition of "lending" was intended to cover a particular kind of lending library which is organised or sponsored by public or private companies and which is accessible to the general public in much the same way as a public library.

The European Parliament proposed, with respect to rental, to replace the words "for profit-making purposes" with the words "for direct or indirect economic advantage." With respect to lending, it proposed to replace the words "not for *direct* profit-making purposes" with the words "not for profit-making purposes." The Commission, in its amended proposal, endorsed these amendments by the Parliament since it held that the new wording did not cause any change of substance – except in the case of lending. The deletion of the word "direct" in the definition of lending would limit the scope of lending, in favour of rental. Accordingly, the above mentioned libraries, which act towards users largely like public libraries but are organised by private companies, would no longer fall under lending (which allows for a mere remuneration right), but under rental.

It was also the view of several Member States that these libraries should be governed by the rental provisions. However, the discussions in the Council Working Group focused upon a different issue, namely the wording which would characterise the rental and lending activities respectively and thus be a means to distinguish rental from lending. Several possibilities were examined, particularly the phrases "(not) for profit-making purposes," "without/ against payment," "(not) for commercial purposes" and "(not) for economic advantage," as well as definitions of rental and lending under national civil laws. During the discussions it became clear that "rental" and "lending" could not properly be defined by the words "against payment" and "without payment." This was so because public libraries which charge users with some kind of library fees would fall, against the Member States' intention, under the rental provisions, which do not permit any derogation from the exclusive right.

Many Member States arrived at the conclusion that the Commission's original proposal ("(not) for profit-making purposes") was to be preferred to all the other versions proposed. However, one Member State was suspicious about the possibility of rental activities being carried out by organisations established in the form of non-profit associations, which could thereby possibly escape the rental provisions. Not least because of the Parliament's proposal to employ the words "economic advantage," the version "(not) for profit-making purposes" was given up.

The phrases "for commercial purposes" and "for economic advantage" gave rise to controversy between two Member States in particular. One of them considered the expression "commercial purposes" to be too narrow because, according to its national commercial law, private organisations undertaking a rental business for economic advantage would not act for commercial purposes, simply because they were private organisations. The other Member State considered the phrase "economic advantage" to be too wide, since even the public libraries, which charge user fees or fees for delayed return of books would, according to this Member State's interpretation, operate for an economic advantage and therefore fall under the rental provisions.

Other Member States, given the background of their national laws, did not perceive any major difference between the two expressions. Finally, by way of compromise, both were included in the definitions. In order to ensure that the very large definition of rental would not cover the case of public libraries charging their users some kind of fee, recital (14) was added. It reflected the reasoning which had already been expressed in the original Commission Explanatory Memorandum.[5]

The expression "making available for economic or commercial advantage" does, in the end, seem to be rather vague. However, one may conclude from the wording that it implies a business-like behaviour – indicated by the words "economic" and "commercial," for the purposes of profit – indicated by the words "advantage" and "economic or commercial." As a guide-line for interpretation, it is worth repeating that the main examples for rental and lending are the activities carried out by video and CD rental shops and public libraries respectively. Under the definition there are four situations in which rental or lending respectively may occur: making available (not) for (1) direct economic, (2) direct commercial, (3) indirect economic or (4) indirect commercial advantage. In any of these cases, it is irrelevant whether an economic or commercial advantage is obtained in fact; it is sufficient that the purpose of the rental activity is to obtain such an advantage.

---

[5] See the original Commission proposal: document COM (90) 586 final, para. 1.2, p. 34.

"Making available for use for *direct* economic or commercial advantage" means rental carried out with a view to obtaining such an advantage. "Making available for use for *indirect* economic or commercial advantage" means rental producing such an advantage as a side-effect only.

One example of such making available for use for indirect economic or commercial advantage is the type of library organised or sponsored by business companies. Typically, access to such libraries is free of charge to the general public, which means that no direct economic or commercial advantage is sought. However, this service to the public might have an advertising effect and thereby aim at an indirect economic advantage.

The making available of video cassettes to guests of a hotel for use in a hotel room will, if there is no direct charge, be made for indirect economic or commercial advantage, since such a service might attract further clients. Likewise, the service offered for example by hairdressers' shops and doctors' and lawyers' offices, of making available journals for use in the waiting rooms, is for indirect economic or commercial advantage. The two last-mentioned examples however do not constitute rental activities under the Directive, because making available for on-the-spot reference use is excluded.[6] Other examples of an indirect economic or commercial advantage being sought are the rental of a hotel room, in which a painting is displayed, and the rental of a car which includes an audiocassette player and some recorded tapes. Although these cases may be covered by the wording of the Directive, they are certainly not covered by its purpose, since the rental of the painting and the tapes occurs incidentally to the rental of the room and the car.

The Directive does not allow avoidance of the definitions of rental and lending. All Member States in the Council Working Group were agreed that it must not be possible to avoid the application of the Directive by deliberate circumvention. However, because of the difficulties of finding appropriate wording, no explicit provision was introduced; in any case, the Member States agreed that it was not necessary to introduce any explicit provision, since it went without saying that deliberate circumvention of the provisions of the Directive was not allowed. Therefore, such acts which are intended to have the same result as acts of rental or lending, will be covered. In particular, it is irrelevant whether rental is exercised by non-profit associations, private video clubs or public enterprises; solely the kind of activity matters, and not the legal structure of the renting organisation.

Libraries and other establishments accessible to the public perform lending (and not rental) activities when they do not act for economic or commercial advantage, *i.e.* when they charge their users either no fees at all or fees which do not go beyond what is necessary to cover their operating costs (Recital (14)). The kind of fees involved do not matter; they may consist of annual fees per user, fees per lent book or other material, or something else. The imposition of surcharges on library users who return books after the agreed return date will not transform lending into rental activities. In the normal course of things they will not go beyond what is necessary to cover the operating costs. Moreover, in this case books or other materials are not given to readers "*for*

---

[6] See Recital (13) and the comments on it, above.

economic or commercial advantage," namely *in order to* collect a surcharge; rather, the surcharge applies only in cases of delayed return and is intended to induce library users to return the lent items on time.

### (c) "Electronic Rental or Lending"

In the future, it will probably be possible to "rent" or "lend" (for example a film) by way of electronic data transmission (downloading), *i.e.* to get a film transmitted electronically for reproduction on the television screen of a private household. This form of exploitation may be called "video on demand"; the user may determine what film he wants to see at what time. "Video on demand" must be distinguished from "pay-per-view," which is clearly a form of transmitting cable programmes. Unlike regular cable programmes, the subscriber to the "pay-per-view" programme pays only an amount relating to the time during which he actually watched the programme. In contrast to "video on demand," he is dependent on the programme transmitted simultaneously to all subscribers and can neither choose any film to be transmitted to him independently of this programme, nor the time of transmission. Accordingly, since "pay-per-view" is clearly a form of transmission of cable programmes and does not resemble rental or lending, "electronic rental and lending" as used in this section refers only to "video on demand."

The Commission, in its original proposal, did not consider that this electronic form of "rental" or "lending" was covered by the proposed Directive. This was, in particular, because this form of exploitation will represent a public performance (or communication to the public) under the laws of most Member States and, hence, will be protected by that right or would at least have to be regulated in the framework of a harmonisation of that right, but not of rental or lending. The Commission wanted to avoid inconsistencies within the national copyright laws of the Member States. Such inconsistencies could have been created if this particular form of immaterial exploitation, "which represents only one aspect of the right of public performance and only one aspect of the range of copyright questions related to electronic data transmission, [had been] singled out in the framework of this Directive."[7]

The Parliament did not express any opinion on the question of electronic "rental" or "lending." The Commission raised the question in the Council Working Group. The Member States did not discuss the subject exhaustively, but simply stated that they did not want to deal with it in the framework of the rental Directive because this would be premature.

The wording of Articles 1(1) and 2(1) would seem to support the view that electronic "rental" and "lending" are not covered by the Directive. According to these provisions, the making available for use always refers to material copies, for example to "originals and copies" of a work, or "fixations" of a performance. Such material objects, and not just the work or performance, must be made available to the user.

The purpose of the Directive, however, suggests that electronic "rental" and "lending" should be covered, because they will have, in practice, the same

---

[7] Explanatory Memorandum, para. 1.2, p. 35.

effects as the traditional rental and lending of material objects. By harmonising rental and lending rights, the Member States envisaged the situation in which, for example, a film or video cassette is made available to a person who may watch the film and/or make a copy and who has to return the cassette after a certain time. The situation does not seem to be substantially different if the person, instead of going to a videoshop or library, simply orders a particular film by telephone which is electronically transmitted to and appears on his television screen at the time he indicates. The person can watch the film and copy it just as before. It may be presumed that the Member States wanted to regulate this situation, whatever the technical form of making a film available, be it by handing over a video cassette, or electronically transmitting the film to a television screen. They would certainly not want the Directive to lose its effects or even become obsolete simply because the technical means of "rental" and "lending" have changed. Accordingly, the Directive should be interpreted as covering the electronic "rental" and "lending," but leaving to the Member States the concrete means of incorporation into the national law, so that they can incorporate it into the scope of the right of public performance or communication.

### (d) Establishments which are Accessible to the Public

The Commission's original proposal included a long list of establishments which were considered to be examples of "institutions which are accessible to the public." The Commission wanted to cover all kinds of lending institutions. The Parliament did not object to that. However, several Member States – mainly those which were opposed to the inclusion of lending rights in the Directive at all – preferred to reduce the list to one example, namely "public libraries." Later on, even this example was deleted because it was considered to be superfluous. Some Member States pointed out that university and school libraries are not considered to be accessible to the public under their national laws and that the notion of "public" should continue to be interpreted according to national law.

Certainly, the Directive does not provide for a definition of "public," and the Member States did not agree on a specific meaning for the term. However, the Directive will not allow it to be declared, for example, that a local library which is accessible to the general public or to all inhabitants of the municipality is not accessible to the "public." On the contrary, one may conclude from Article 5(3) of the Directive that Article 1(3) has to be given a wide interpretation. Since Article 5(3) allows Member States to exempt certain categories of lending establishments, Article 1(3) has to cover a number of different categories of such establisments, not only "public libraries." Accordingly, besides libraries which are open to the general public, libraries open to a specified public such as students or pupils, hence university, school or church libraries or other establishments may be taken to be covered by Article 1(3). Member States which want to exclude such libraries may do so under Article 5(3). Beyond these principles of interpretation derived from the Directive, national law will continue to apply to provide a more detailed definition of "accessible to the public."

The term "institution" in the original Commission proposal was replaced with "establishment" because the English version was adapted to the French version, which itself had been amended at the request of France. According to the French delegation, the term "*établissement*" instead of "*institution*" had to be used in the French language in order to refer to libraries and similar establishments. Accordingly, this replacement did not cause any change of meaning. "Establishment" is a very broad term; it is not limited to any specific legal form if any at all. The establishment may hold collections of books only, of compact discs, phonograms, video cassettes or even paintings only, or of several of these items, or of any lending object which incorporates any kind of copyright work or subject matter as set out in Article 2(1).

## 3. ARTICLE 1(4)

*Article 1*

. . .

4.   The rights referred to in paragraph 1 shall not be exhausted by any sale or other act of distribution of originals and copies of copyright works and other subject matter as set out in Article 2(1).

COMMENTARY

The wording of the Commission's original proposal, according to which the rental and lending rights should "*not be affected*" by any act of distribution, was replaced by the wording "*not be exhausted*" in accordance with a proposal by the European Parliament and by some Member States, which held that the new wording would better correspond to the terminology of copyright. However, the term "exhaustion" is used in copyright law with respect to the distribution right (a distribution right is exhausted for example after the first sale), but not with respect to the rental and lending rights themselves. Notwithstanding this question of terminology, the indicated change of wording did not cause any change in substance.

The laws of a number of Member States provide for a distribution right which covers the acts of rental and lending. Such a distribution right is in normal circumstances exhausted with respect to a certain copy of a work by any sale or some other act of distribution of such a copy of a work, when the author or right owner consents to the act. Consequently, he loses his right to authorize or prohibit any kind of distribution of that copy, including rental and lending.

The present paragraph clarifies that the exhaustion of distribution rights will not affect the subsistence of the rental and lending rights as set out in Article 1(1). Accordingly, the author will retain his exclusive rental or lending right even after a copy of the work has been sold or otherwise distributed.

Article 1(4) does not provide that all Member States must incorporate the rental and lending rights in to the scope of a larger distribution right. It remains possible to provide for a narrow distribution right which covers only sale and other forms of distribution made for an unlimited period of time, and to provide for completely separate rental and lending rights. Likewise, Article 1(4) does not have any effect upon the existence of *droit de destination*[8] systems. The exclusive rental and lending rights which are inherent in the *droit de destination* simply have to be confirmed expressly by law and put into practice. Wherever the national law of a Member State provides for the exhaustion of a distribution right which covers rental and lending, Article 1(4) ensures the subsistence of the exclusive rental and lending rights after any act of distribution.

---

[8] The *droit de destination* has been developed by French jurisprudence and is applied in several Member States; it enables the right-owner to control the exploitation of copies of his work even after the first act of distribution, for example by rental or lending.

# Article 2. Rightholders and Subject Matter of Rental and Lending Right

Article 2 specifies who the first rightholders of the rental and lending rights will be and in respect of what kind of works and other protected subject matter these rights are to exist. In addition, it deals with the transferability of these rights and with presumptions of transfer.

## 1. ARTICLE 2(1) TO (3)

*Article 2*

**Rightholders and subject matter of rental and lending right**

1.   The exclusive right to authorize or prohibit rental and lending shall belong:

– to the author in respect of the original and copies of his work,
– to the performer in respect of fixations of his performance,
– to the phonogram producer in respect of his phonograms, and
– to the producer of the first fixation of a film in respect of the original and copies of his film. For the purposes of this Directive, the term "film" shall designate a cinematographic or audiovisual work or moving images, whether or not accompanied by sound.

2.   For the purposes of this Directive the principal director of a cinematographic or audiovisual work shall be considered as its author or one of its authors. Member States may provide for others to be considered as its co-authors.

3.   This Directive does not cover rental and lending rights in relation to buildings and to works of applied art.

…

COMMENTARY

### (a) Rightholders

*The title of the Article*

In the title of Article 2, the words "first owner" in the original proposal were replaced in the Directive by the word "rightholders." This is because Article 2 now includes provisions on the transfer of the rental and lending rights and no longer deals exclusively with the first rightholders. The rightholders mentioned in Article 2(1) and (2), however, are indeed "first rightholders," *i.e.* rightholders in whom the rental and lending rights are originally vested and not persons who gain the rights by way of transfer, presumption of transfer or otherwise.

*Authors*

The term "author" in Article 2(1), first indent, was deliberately left undefined in the original Commission proposal, since it is of relevance not only to the rental and lending rights, but to all author's rights. Defining the "author" only in respect of the rental and lending rights could have created undesirable inconsistencies within the national laws of Member States. Furthermore, the meaning of the term had already been influenced, to a certain extent, by the application of the Berne Convention in all Member States.

The European Parliament did not propose any amendment as to the author in general[9] being one of the first rightholders of the rental and lending rights. In the Council Working Group, only one Member State doubted whether authors should be included as rightholders; this Member State at present provides an exclusive rental right only for producers of films and phonograms and for authors of computer programs.

The term "author" covers authors of the same categories of works as are recognised under the Berne Convention. Accordingly, authors of computer programs, as well as translators, adaptors, writers, composers, architects, painters, sculptors, authors of collections of works and others are "authors" under the Directive. Since works by their nature are personal, intellectual creations, their authors may only be the natural persons who created them. Even employed authors are authors of the works created under their employment contracts, although they may, of course, transfer their rights to the employers and employers may benefit from presumptions of transfer of the rights (Article 2(4) and (6)). Persons or entities who are not genuine creators can not be regarded as "authors" under the Directive. This is evident, as regards phonogram and film producers (and performers), from the context of Article 2(1), which enumerates these three groups of rightholders as distinct, separate groups from "authors". This conclusion is reinforced by the fact that Article 2(6) would make no sense if the term "author" was interpreted otherwise.

These general comments on the author require further analysis with respect to films. Originally, the Commission proposed that national law should continue to govern the question of who is the *author of a film* – be it the film director and other creative persons as in most Member States, or, as in a few Member States, the film producer.[10] Consequently, the original proposal did not include any provision in this respect. Although the Commission considered that the protection of creators of film works, such as film directors, was desirable,[11] it did not regard the harmonisation of the general issue of film

---

[9] This excludes the author of a film.
[10] See the Explanatory Memorandum of the original proposal, para. 2.1.2.1, p. 38–39.
[11] Explanatory Memorandum, para. 2.1.2.1, p. 40.

authorship as appropriate in the context of the Directive, particularly since any comprehensive solution of this highly controversial issue appeared to be misplaced in the original proposal.

The idea of ensuring, within the Directive, that at least the principal film director was recognised as an author of a film originally emerged in the European Parliament's Committee on Culture, which passed an amendment in much those terms. At the same time, it rejected another amendment which proposed that national law should determine who was the author of a work. The amendment concerning the principal film director was, however, then rejected by the Committee in charge, the Legal Affairs Committee, but was finally adopted in plenary session, with 211 votes in favour, 125 against and 4 abstaining. The Commission respected the Parliament's opinion and integrated this amendment, in a slightly modified form but without any change of content, into its amended proposal as Article 2(2). The Commission by way of explanation pointed out that "at least" in the context of this Directive, the principal director of a film would be guaranteed legal protection as an author throughout the Community and would no longer be disadvantaged in those Member States which did not provide protection.

This new Article 2(2) was, indeed, the most disputed issue until the Council adopted the Common Position. The three Member States which did not provide an author's right for film directors were fundamentally opposed to the provision. They were joined by two other Member States which did not see any need for harmonisation of this issue in the context of the Directive. In the end, a compromise was possible because, amongst other things, exemptions with respect to the application in time of this provision were granted in Article 13(4) and (5).[12]

The expression "principal director" derives from the wording of Article 14 bis (3) of the Berne Convention and has to be construed in the light of that provision. The term "cinematographic or audiovisual work" is intended to be very broad and covers cinema films, films made for broadcasting organisations and any other film works, such as films on videograms, and whether or not accompanied by sound.[13]

Article 2(2) allows other contributors to a film, such as the screenplay writer, the cameraman, the editor and others, to be considered its co-authors. Since the Directive does not want to interfere unnecessarily with existing national concepts, it allows Member States to consider the producer of a film as its co-author with the principal director.

In those Member States where film directors do not yet enjoy author's rights, the application in time of Article 2(2) may be limited to works created after July 1, 1994, and to acts of exploitation after July 1, 1997.[14] The controversial nature of the issue of authorship of films gave rise to a joint statement by the Council and the Commission, minuted at the Council meeting on June

---

[12] See p. 123, below.
[13] For further comments on film works see p. 52, below.
[14] See the corresponding exemptions in Art. 13(4) and (5), and the comments thereon, p. 123.

18, 1992, to the effect that the Commission will conduct a report on the matter.[15]

*Performers*

With respect to performers, the Commission in its original proposal[16] decided that they would have to be included amongst the rightholders entitled to rental and lending rights. In the view of the Commission which was shaped by the European Parliament, the omission of performers would have been misplaced, given in particular the importance of performers' contributions to phonograms and films. Doubts as to their inclusion in the Directive were expressed by only two Member States, which did not share the view that performers made notable contributions and which feared that the exercise of parallel rights by several groups of rightholders (authors, performers, phonogram and film producers) would not be feasible. Most of the Member States, however, rejected these arguments by reference to the important role of, for example, musicians and actors in the music and film industries, and to some situations where the parallel rights of several groups of rightholders are already exercised in practice.

As in the case of the "author," the Directive does not provide any definition of a "performer." Thus, it is largely left to the Member States to define the term, which is in any event used in more or less the same way throughout the Community, due to the influence of the Rome Convention. Articles 3(a) and 9 of the Rome Convention may aid interpretation. Accordingly, the Directive does not prevent Member States from using their national laws to protect other kinds of performers in addition to those protected under the Rome Convention, in particular performers such as circus artists and music hall entertainers who do not perform "works."

*Phonogram producers*

As far as phonogram producers are concerned, no problems arose with the concept presented in the Commission's original proposal, either in the Parliament or in the Council.

Again, the Directive leaves the definition of "phonogram producers" to the Member States, but Article 3(c) of the Rome Convention may help interpretation. In particular, only those who "first fix" sounds are eligible for protection; this is supported by the parallel definition of film producers in Article 2(1), fourth indent.

*Film producers*

The Commission's original proposal to grant film producers throughout the Community separate rights which they would own as first rightholders was based, as in the Commission's Green Paper of 1988, on the idea that their achievements are comparable to those of phonogram producers and that the

---

[15] The statement reads: "The Council and the Commission agree that the Commission will draw up before 1 July 1997 a report on the question of authorship of cinematographic or audiovisual works in the Community."

[16] See the Explanatory Memorandum to the original proposal, para. 2.1.3, at p. 41 *et seq.*

existing presumptions of transfer of authors' rights in favour of film producers may not always provide sufficient protection. In addition, the protection for film producers would not be limited to film works, but would include films which were not works, due to lack of originality. The proposal for separate rights for film producers as first rightholders was not called into question by the European Parliament, but was opposed by several Member States which did not consider the protection to be necessary.

As was acknowledged during the discussions in the Council, it is irrelevant whether the film producer is granted his right as first right-owner in the form of a copyright as, for example, in the United Kingdom, or a neighbouring right, as in France. This view is supported by a statement from the Commission made for the records of the Council meeting of June 18, 1992.[17] Member States would, however, not meet the requirements of Articles 2(1), 7(1) and 9(1) simply by providing presumptions of transfer of authors' rights in favour of film producers, because this would lead to derived rights, rather than rights originally vesting in the film producer.

As there are no definitions of the term "film producer" in international conventions which would have influenced the national law of the Member States, the Commission, in its original proposal, thought it necessary to provide at least a partial definition based on the definition of phonogram producers in the Rome Convention. The idea behind this definition, which was adopted by the Council, is that the producer is a person or legal entity which *first fixes* a film; this idea is introduced into the text by the wording "producer of the *first fixation* of a film." This excludes from protection in particular producers of simple copies of films, such as copies made from cinema films and adapted for video distribution.[18] Member States are free to give the term "producer" further definition, for example by requiring that he or she takes economic risk. With respect to the definition of "film" as set out in Article 2(1), fourth indent, reference is made to the comments below.[19]

*Parallel rights*

The fact that the four groups of rightholders set out in Article 2(1) will be granted parallel rights, leading to each of the contributors (for example, the composer of the music, the musician and the phonogram producer) enjoying his own right to prohibit rental and lending, were not likely to create any problems in practice. This situation occurs every day in relation to other rights such as the reproduction right. In the same way as it is reasonable to expect the

---

[17] The statement on Arts. 2(1), 7(1) and 9(1) reads: "The Commission considers that the provisions of Art. 2(1), fourth indent, Art. 7(1), third indent, and Art. 9(1), third indent, do not oblige Member States to create a separate neighbouring right for film producers where they enjoy in their own right, elsewhere in their national law, the same rights as are introduced by the provisions mentioned."

[18] The underlying philosophy according to which such an activity has insufficient merit to warrant protection is reflected, *e.g.* in s.5(2) of the UK Copyright, Designs and Patents Act 1988.

[19] See p. 50, below.

producer to acquire the reproduction right from the author and performer, it is reasonable to expect him to acquire other exclusive rights, such as the rental right, whether directly from the author or performer, or from a collecting society to which they may have assigned their rights. In the film sector, producers will even benefit across the Community from a presumption of transfer of the performer's right (Article 2(5)) and may do so in some Member States in the case of the author's right (Article 2(6)).

If producers want to prohibit rental they may effectively do so merely by exercising their own right; even if the authors or performers authorise the rental, the act of rental is authorised only if all rightholders involved give their consent. If, on the other hand, producers want to authorise rental, they will have to acquire the rights of the authors and performers involved. This should not be a problem because they will usually be in a stronger bargaining position or will be able to benefit from a presumption of transfer. In addition, the author and performer will usually find it in their best interests to assign their rental rights. The more likely scenario for disagreement is where the performer wishes to exploit his performances by rental but the producer withholds his consent.

## Other rightholders

In principle, the list of rightholders set out in Article 2 is exhaustive; otherwise, the wording of Article 1 would have to include expressions such as "at least," "in particular" or "for instance." Accordingly, broadcasting organisations can not be granted a rental or lending right in the Community, except if they also qualify as phonogram or film producers. Film producers may only enjoy a rental and lending right if they fall within the definition of Article 2(1), fourth indent, but not if they produce, for example, copies of cinema films for video distribution, thus not being responsible for the "first fixation." These two examples were mentioned in the discussions of the Council Working Group. Notwithstanding the exhaustive character of the list, it seems to have been the common understanding of the Commission and the Member States that the Directive does not intend, with respect to existing public lending right schemes, to abolish the existing rights of certain groups of rightholders, particularly when the cases in question are of minor economic significance. Accordingly, the existing neighbouring rights of photographers, scientific editors and publishers with respect to lending may continue to exist.

## (b) Subject Matter

### Definitions

Article 2(1) makes reference to four categories of protected subject matter, namely works, performances, phonograms and films. Article 2(3) specifies categories of subject matter not covered by the Directive. Article 2 does not include any definitions of the protected subject matter, except for films. This lack of definition was intentional by the Commission, as in the case of the rightholders.[20] The Parliament did not propose any amendment in this respect; only at the beginning of the discussions in the Council Working Group did a few Member States suggest the inclusion of definitions.

In theory, the subject matter as set out in Article 2(1) and (3) will have to be defined by national law. The Berne and Rome Conventions may provide the basis for definitions and interpretation.

## Works

Works include in particular musical compositions, poems, drawings, translations, adaptations of other works and works of painting and photography.[21] The standard of originality to be attained is determined according to national law. In general, works will have to be personal, intellectual creations.

The context of the provisions of Article 2(1) shows that a "work" within the Directive does not include a performance, a phonogram or moving images. This does not, however, prevent a Member State from designating, for example, phonograms as "works" under national law, provided that the provisions of the Directive which refer to phonograms are in substance properly incorporated into the national law.

The words "original and copies" of the author's work mean the first materialisation of a work and all further copies thereof, as for example the manuscript of a novel (the original) and books (copies thereof). The rental or lending of an "original" of a work is particularly relevant in the case of works of art such as paintings or sculptures. It has to be stressed that the word "original" does not in any way refer to the concept of "originality" of a work.

## Performances

Corresponding to the meaning of "performers," discussed above, performances include, for example, interpretations of musical compositions by musicians and singers and of theatre plays by actors, readings of novels by actors and performances by music hall entertainers.

## Phonograms

Phonograms are any fixations of sounds, including the sounds of a musical performance, of a speech, or even sounds emanating from machines or animals. The material object on which the sounds are fixed may be of any kind; examples are music cassettes, compact discs and digital compact cassettes. No discussion took place on new technologies for the manufacturing of phonograms, which might provoke the need for more specified definitions including, for example, the "fixation of digital presentations of sounds," as has been proposed by WIPO in its memorandum concerning a possible "New Instrument."[22]

---

[20] See the Explanatory Memorandum to the original proposal, para. 2.1.1, p. 37, and pp. 45–50, above.

[21] For the exclusion of certain works see p. 52, below.

[22] WIPO, Committee of Experts on a Possible Instrument for the Protection of the Rights of Performers and Producers of Phonograms, INR/CE/I/2 of March 12, 1993, see para. 28(b).

*Films*

With respect to films, it was appropriate to provide a definition in Article 2(1), fourth indent, because there is no international convention which expressly protects film producers or includes a general definition to give a harmonising effect. The wording of the definition originally proposed by the Commission was approved by the Parliament, but amended by the Council, without changing the meaning. The amended wording has to be explained against the background of the existing legal regimes in Member States. According to the prevailing terminology in one Member State, the term "cinematographic works" includes only cinema films as opposed to films on television or on video cassette. This Member State therefore proposed using the term "audiovisual work" which mirrors its national law and covers all kinds of film works. This term is however not known in most of the other Member States, which employ the traditional term "cinematographic work" for films on television and videocassette as well as for cinema films. The term "cinematographic work" was therefore retained in the text and the term "audiovisual work" was added. The definition of films based on the Commission's original proposal thus became too cumbersome, and the Council decided to use the term "film" and to provide a definition in Article 2(1), fourth indent, which applies throughout the Directive.

The term "moving images" signifies films which do not have a sufficient degree of originality and are therefore not "works," such as reports on sports events or, possibly, the recording of a concert or theatre performance. The producer's protection as first rightholder under Article 2(1), fourth indent, which is provided in recognition of his economic and technical efforts, covers film works as well as moving images. On the other hand, the film director who is considered to be the author of a film enjoys the rental and lending rights only in respect of the cinematographic or audiovisual "work" and not in respect of the moving images.

The phrase "visual recordings, and visual and sound recordings" in the Commission's original proposal corresponds to the finally adopted version ("the original and copies of his film," and "whether or not accompanied by sound").

Accordingly, films are covered by the Directive whether or not they are works, whether or not they are accompanied by sound, and on whatever material object they are fixed, whether prepared for cinema performance, for television broadcasting or on a video cassette, video compact disc or other media. In practice, the rental and lending of films will usually refer to videos, particularly since rental or lending for the purposes of public performance and broadcasting are excluded.[23]

*The exception in Article 2(3)*

The exclusion of certain objects as proposed by the Commission in Article 2(3) was not opposed by the Parliament. In the Council Working Group, however, some Member States initially proposed also excluding works of art

---

[23] See Recital (13) and the comment, pp. 37–38, above.

and photographic and literary works from the application of the Directive because, *inter alia*, these works would in practice be rented or lent to an insignificant extent. This gained no support from the majority of the Member States which insisted on equal treatment for all kinds of works and pointed out that literary, artistic and photographic works are regularly included in films and sound recordings, which are the main objects of rental, and in books, which are the main objects of lending.

One Member State went even further and proposed that works of applied art and works of architecture in two-dimensional form should not be excluded. In the end, Member States did agree that only buildings in three-dimensional form should be excluded from the rental and lending rights, given the intention of avoiding a situation in which the architect could prohibit the rental of living space by the owner of the building. Accordingly, works of architecture in two-dimensional form, for example in the form of a photograph of the building or an architectural drawing which is included in a book, or a building which is included in a film, are protected under the Directive. As far as works of applied art are concerned, it was agreed that these should continue to be excluded. Examples such as the rental of cars and the rental of crockery by caterers were mentioned in the discussions in the Council Working Group.

## 2. ARTICLE 2(4)

*Article 2*

. . .

4.   The rights referred to in paragraph 1 may be transferred, assigned or subject to the granting of contractual licences.

. . .

COMMENTARY

Article 2(4) is intended to make explicit what was implicit in the Commission's original text. Since that text did not expressly deal with the transferability of the exclusive rental and lending rights, it was implied that this question would continue to be governed by national law. As may be seen from the Explanatory Memorandum on Article 3,[24] the Commission started from the assumption that the exclusive rental and lending rights would be transferable. The Parliament did not propose any wording to cover the issue. However, some Member States seemed to assume that the requirement of

---

[24] See para. 3.1.1, p. 45.

unwaivability laid down in Article 4 as regards the right to remuneration also applied to the exclusive rights. They requested clarification, which was initially inserted as a new Article 3(1) and then transferred to form the present Article 2(4).

The wording of Article 2(4) gives Member States the freedom to implement its ideas in a number of different ways. It was intended to cover all kinds of contractual transfer of the exclusive rights which might be permitted under the national laws of the Member States. Accordingly, the Member States may apply the legal regime concerning the transfer of rights which is prevailing under their national systems. The words "transferred," "assigned" and "subject to the granting of contractual licences" are connected by the word "or" and may therefore be applied in the alternative. In particular, it is possible for a Member State to provide that authors' or performers' exclusive rights are not transferable or assignable, but that authors and performers may grant contractual licences or authorise[25] a person to rent or lend a book, phonogram and so on.

It follows from the wording and context of Article 2(4), and from the understanding of the Member States in the Council Working Group, that only contractual transfers, assignments and licenses are permissible, as opposed to any form of legal, or compulsory, non-contractual licence. Even a non-rebuttable presumption of transfer of rights, as exists in a few Member States in relation to performers and film producers, is not allowed under Article 2(4), or elsewhere under the Directive, since it would amount to a legal licence and would be incompatible with the recognition of the exclusive rights of a certain group of right-owners, which as a result would be deprived by law of those rights.[26]

For the sake of consistency, the text of Article 2(4) is repeated in Chapter II in relation to the exclusive rights of reproduction and distribution; as far as the exclusive rights under Articles 6 (fixation rights) and 8 (broadcasting and communication to the public) are concerned, it seems to have been omitted by mistake. However, this should not lead one to the opposite conclusion that the rights under Articles 6 and 8 are non-transferable.

Article 2(4) and the corresponding provisions in Chapter II do not apply to any remuneration rights which may be available, such as a remuneration right for home copying or the right under Article 8(2).

## 3. RECITAL (19) AND ARTICLE 2(5), (6) AND (7)

### Recital

(19) Whereas the provisions of Chapter II do not prevent Member States from extending the presumption set out in Article 2(5) to the exclusive rights included in that chapter; whereas furthermore the provisions of Chapter II do not prevent Member States from providing for a rebuttable presumption of the authorization

---

[25] See the statement made by the Commission on Art. 2(4) for the records of the Council meeting of June 18, 1992: "The Commission considers that Art. 2(4) also covers the case of rightholders giving an authorization."

[26] See, however, in this context the specific regime of assignment of rights under Art. 2(7) and pp. 60–61, below.

of exploitation in respect of the exclusive rights of performers provided for in those Articles, in so far as such presumption is compatible with the International Convention for the Protection of Performers, Producers of Phonograms and Broadcasting Organizations (hereinafter referred to as the Rome Convention);

*Article 2*

...

5.   Without prejudice to paragraph 7, when a contract concerning film production is concluded, individually or collectively, by performers with a film producer, the performer covered by this contract shall be presumed, subject to contractual clauses to the contrary, to have transferred his rental right, subject to Article 4.

6.   Member States may provide for a similar presumption as set out in paragraph 5 with respect to authors.

7.   Member States may provide that the signing of a contract concluded between a performer and a film producer concerning the production of a film has the effect of authorizing rental, provided that such contract provides for an equitable remuneration within the meaning of Article 4. Member States may also provide that this paragraph shall apply *mutatis mutandis* to the rights included in Chapter II.

## Commentary

### (a) The Presumptions of Transfer in General

The provisions of Article 2(5), (6) and (7) refer to the contractual relationship between performers and authors on the one side, and film producers on the other. The Commission's original proposal did not expressly deal with this issue and so its regulation was left to the Member States.

### *Discussions in the European Parliament*

The Parliament, however, proposed adding a provision on the presumption of transfer of the exclusive rental and lending rights. The discussions in the various Committees of the European Parliament which were dealing with the Directive were quite heated on this issue and finding a balanced solution was not easy. The Committee on Economic Affairs rejected a proposed amendment containing a non-rebuttable presumption of transfer, while the Committee on Culture adopted an amendment proposing a rebuttable presumption which would be without prejudice to the participation right under Article 3.[27] Amongst several amendments tabled in the Legal Affairs

---

[27] Reference is made to the Commission's original version.

Committee, the following two amendments were passed and proposed to the plenary of the European Parliament:

An employment contract between a performer and a film producer must be in writing. The signing of such a contract by the artist would lead to a rebuttable presumption of transfer which would be without prejudice to the participation right of Article 3.[28]

A similar provision was proposed in relation to composite and collective works or works of collaboration created for public presentation and performance.

Eventually, the plenary adopted an amendment which was similar to the first of the above amendments. In addition, it proposed the application of this presumption of transfer to the reproduction and distribution rights of Chapter II.

### The Commission's amended proposal

The Commission, in its amended proposal, followed the Opinion of the Parliament at first reading, not least in order to take account of the request of the film industry, which wanted to facilitate the exploitation of films throughout the Community. The Commission also endorsed the Parliament's Opinion concerning the need to compensate performers for the potential weakening of their legal position due to the presumption of transfer. The Commission therefore proposed that the presumption be rebuttable and subject to a written contract, as well as to the economic participation right under Article 3.[29] The Commission extended this provision beyond employment contracts to all contracts between performing artists and film producers concerning film production. In addition, it added corresponding presumptions to Articles 6 and 7 (reproduction and distribution rights).

### Discussions in the Council Working Group

Whereas the European Parliament and the Commission seemed to have found an acceptable balance between the interests of film producers and performers, in the course of the discussions in the Council Working Group several Member States were inclined to favour a mere presumption of transfer, without compensating the performing artists with a certain amount of protection as proposed by the Parliament and the Commission.

In particular, the need for written contracts between performers and film producers, as a precondition for the application of the presumption, was questioned. In the end, the working group preferred to allow Member States to decide whether they wanted to require that contracts be in writing.

At first, some Member States did not agree that the presumption of transfer should be subject to the economic participation right of the artist under Article 3[30]; eventually, however, all Member States agreed that it was necessary to provide performers with compensation and that it had to be linked to the presumption of transfer.

---

[28] The numbering of this Article follows the Commission's original proposal.
[29] See n. 28, above.
[30] See n. 28, above.

There was a similar discussion in the Working Group concerning the provision which stated that the presumption should be rebuttable. In the end, however, not all Member States were convinced by the concept of a rebuttable presumption: one Member State insisted on being able to continue to apply its national law, which amounted to a non-rebuttable presumption. With the need to obtain an overall compromise in mind, this was finally allowed. It is to be found in Article 2(7), which reflects that Member State's national law. However, this concession was only granted to that Member State because of its already well developed regulation of the contractual relationship between performers and film producers – regulation which is rather comprehensive, as it includes several social and financial elements and tries to balance the respective interests of performers and film producers.

The provisions on the presumptions of transfer were amongst the most disputed provisions of the Directive. The insistence of the Commission and some Member States that performers should be given a minimum protection as compensation for the weakening of their position as a result of the presumption of transfer ensured that the legal position of performers was not considerably weakened. The adopted text prescribes a presumption of transfer which is subject to several protective conditions. Member States may not, with respect to the rental right, provide for a presumption which falls outside these conditions. The same is true for presumptions with respect to authors. Member States may provide for presumptions of transfer of an author's rental right to a film producer, but they are bound by the conditions of Article 2(6) and thus by Article 2(5). Some comments on these paragraphs are given below.

## (b) Article 2(5)

*Contract concerning film production*

The presumption of transfer under Article 2(5) applies only to contracts concerning film production. A "contract" must be concluded, whether orally or in writing. Any general conditions on the conclusion of the contracts under Article 2(5), for example as regards the legal capacity of the parties, are governed by national law.

The contract between the performer and the film producer must concern "film production"; this will usually mean that it deals with the performer's artistic participation in, or his contribution to, the film which is to be produced. It does not matter whether the film producer is acting as an employer. Article 2(5) applies equally to employment, service or similar contracts. This is supported by the wording, which does not exclude such contracts, and by the historical development: the Parliament's proposal, which referred only to employment contracts, was extended by the Commission's amended proposal to contracts in general,[31] and the Member States agreed to this broad

---

[31] See p. 56, above.

concept. Accordingly, any national laws on the legal position of employed performers or performers under service or similar contracts will be overruled by the provisions of Article 2(5).

Article 2(5) applies only to contracts "concerning film production." Member States may not apply this presumption, or any other presumption of transfer of the rental right, to other contracts, in particular contracts between a performer and a phonogram producer or broadcasting organisation concerning the production of a phonogram. Article 2(5) to (7) deals with the presumption of transfer of the rental right in a comprehensive and exhaustive way. The provisions deal not only with presumptions which *have to be* provided, but also with those which *may be* provided. If the Member States had wanted to be free to provide further presumptions of transfer, they could have added a provision to make this possible, just as they did with respect to authors in Article 2(6), with respect to the rights of Chapter II in Recital (19) and with respect to the legal regime of a particular Member State in Article 2(7).

This view is supported by the way in which the discussions in the Council Working Group developed. Some Member States wanted to extend, or to leave Member States free to extend, the presumption of Article 2(5) (or a similar presumption) to contracts other than those concerning film production. These proposals were, however, rejected by a majority of the Member States. Accordingly, outside the areas expressly mentioned by the Directive, and beyond the specified conditions, no presumption of transfer of the performer's or author's exclusive rental right may be provided.

*Individually or collectively*

The word "individually" in Article 2(5) refers to contracts which are concluded between individual persons, namely between a performer and a film producer. The word "collectively" refers to contracts one or both parties of which are groups of persons, such as actors' unions or associations of film producers. Whenever, for example, a trade union member participates in a film made by a certain film producer, the contractual provisions agreed upon between the trade union and the producer (or his association) will apply. These and similar collective agreements are covered by Article 2(5) and have been included in order to take account of their wide-spread use in the film industry.

*Contractual clauses to the contrary*

The presumption of transfer of the rental right under Article 2(5) only works on the basis that there are no "contractual clauses to the contrary." Thus, the performer may retain his exclusive rental right and avoid the application of the presumption if he agrees contractually with the producer that the right is not to be transferred to the producer (he might prefer, for example, to transfer it to a collecting society). This may be agreed orally or in writing, and may be express or implied, depending on the applicable national laws on the interpretation of contracts. The word "clause" is not limited to written clauses. If it were so, Article 2(5) would not make sense, in so far as it would require the parties to add a written clause to an oral contract. Furthermore, there is no reason to restrict the variety of means by which the performer can show that he has not transferred the rental right, and thereby rebut the presumption of Article 2(5).

Provisions under which the performer is "deemed" to have transferred his rental right, or the film producer, employer or any other person is "deemed" to be the original right owner or to have the right to exercise the performer's rental right, without the performer having the opportunity to state that he wishes to retain the right, would amount to non-rebuttable presumptions of transfer and would not comply with Article 2(5).

### The application of Article 4 as a pre-condition

The second pre-condition for the operation of the presumption of transfer in Article 2(5) appears in the phrase "subject to Article 4." The phrase "subject to" has to be understood, as in the case of the pre-condition described above, in the sense of "provided that Article 4 is applied." Thus, the presumption only operates if the unwaivable right of the performer to equitable remuneration for rental under Article 4 is recognised in law. This precondition aims to protect performers (in particular where, as is often the case, they are not aware of "losing" their exclusive rights as a result of a legal presumption of transfer) by expressly safeguarding the remuneration right under Article 4. This right is explained in detail below.

### The presumed transfer of the rental right

When the requirements and conditions of Article 2(5) are met, the performer is presumed to have "transferred his rental right" to the film producer. The word "transferred" is not limited to any specific concept of the transfer of rights. As under Article 2(4),[32] the Directive does not wish to interfere with existing national concepts or legal regimes concerning the transmission of rights. Accordingly, in Member States which provide for the non-transferability of rights, it will be sufficient to allow for a presumption of the grant of a licence or of authorisation. The presumption of transfer may be incorporated into national law in the form of a presumption of assignment, grant of a licence, authorisation of rental, authorisation to exercise the exclusive rental right and so on.

### The applicability of Article 2(5) to other rights

Article 2(5) provides for a presumption of transfer of the rental right only. The question arises whether the Member States may, or have to, apply this presumption to the lending right or other rights. As far as its application to the performer's *rights under Chapter II* is concerned, note the provisions of Recital (19) and the second sentence of Article 2(7) and the comments on Article 10, below.[33] With respect to the application of Article 2(5) to the performer's *lending right*, should a Member State decide to grant it as an exclusive right without exercising its right of derogation under Article 5, the

---

[32] See p. 53, above.
[33] See pp. 109–113.

wording and the exhaustive nature of Article 2(5) to (7) seem to favour the view that no presumption of transfer may be applied to the lending right. However, this would lead to the rather doubtful conclusion that, despite the great flexibility which Article 5 offers the Member States, the exclusive lending right once chosen by a Member State would be stronger for its rightholders than the exclusive rental right.

In fact, the way in which the discussions in the Council developed rather suggests that Article 2(5) also applies to the exclusive lending right. According to the Commission's amended proposal and the discussions in the Council, the presumption of transfer, and Article 4 to which the presumption refers, were intended to cover the exclusive lending right as well. At one stage of the discussions, when it was doubtful whether the lending right would remain in the Directive at all, and wide derogations from the exclusive lending right were being conceded under Article 5, it seemed politically advisable to delete the reference to the lending right in Article 4 in order to avoid giving the impression that the derogation options, which favoured a compromise on lending, might be thwarted by the remuneration right in Article 4. Consequently, the lending right was also deleted from Article 2(5), since a presumption of transfer without the guarantee of economic participation under Article 4 was undesirable. When it became clear that the lending right would remain in the Directive after all, no-one wanted to jeopardise this position by any further drafting changes to the lending right, and so the reference to the lending right was not reintroduced in Article 4 or in Article 2(5). This legislative history shows that the Member States did not object in principle to the inclusion of the lending right in these provisions.

Moreover, there is no reason to believe that Member States wanted to regulate the exclusive lending right in a different way from the exclusive rental right, as far as the presumption of transfer is concerned. Rental and lending are similar kinds of exploitation, and the interests of producers and performers are comparable in each case. This reasoning gives rise to an interpretation, which would seem accurately to reflect the Member States' intentions, according to which the Directive at least allows, if not obliges, Member States to include the exclusive lending right in provisions made under Articles 2(5) and 4. Consequently, if a Member State does not make use of the derogation option under Article 5, but provides for an exclusive right, the application of Article 2(5) and Article 4 to this right would be the logical and preferable approach.

### (c) Article 2(7)

The relationship between Article 2(5) and 2(7) is not obvious at first sight. Article 2(5) is mandatory, whereas Article 2(7) is optional. Article 2(7) is an exception to Article 2(5), which is supported by its position *after* Article 2(5). Furthermore, there are substantive differences: although Article 2(7) requires, unlike Article 2(5), a written and signed contract ("the signing of a contract"), it restricts the performer's rights more because it does not allow the performer to rebut the presumption by stipulating that he is not willing to transfer the rental right. In this way, Article 2(7) not only constitutes an exception to Article 2(5) (and, thus, may be applied only in the alternative) but also to Article 2(1) which grants performers an exclusive rental right, presumably not with a view subsequently to deprive them of the ability to exercise it. Accordingly, Articles 2(5) and (7) are alternatives and represent the principle and the exception respectively. The discussions in the Council even lead to a further conclusion: since Article 2(7) was a political concession to one particular Member State, which has a rather balanced, comprehensive regulation of film contracts,[34] the exception in Article 2(7) is of relevance for that Member State only, and is unlikely, and not recommended to be applied by any other Member States.

### (d) Article 2(6)

With respect to authors, the Member States were not in favour of a mandatory presumption of transfer of the rental and lending rights and agreed instead in Article 2(6) on the mere possibility to "provide … for a similar presumption as set out in paragraph 5." The exhaustive nature of the provisions on the presumption of transfer[35] and the fact that the Directive specifies the kind of presumption which may be applied (instead of stating generally that Member States may provide for "a," or "a rebuttable" or other presumption) means that Member States, in relation to a presumption of transfer of authors' exclusive rental rights, may either not provide for any presumption of transfer at all, or provide for a presumption "similar" to that of Article 2(5). "Similar" in Article 2(6) implies that all the requirements and conditions of Article 2(5) have to be fulfilled, except that the term "performer" is to be read as "author" and the reference to paragraph 7 in Article 2(5) obviously does not apply, as may be seen from the position of Article 2(6) in relation to Article 2(7) and from the debates in the Council Working Group.[36]

The term "authors" refers to authors of films such as film directors as well as to authors of underlying works, that is earlier works used as the basis for the film. The Directive does not make any distinction. Furthermore authors of films and of underlying works are not defined by the Directive and these terms are used differently throughout the Community. For example, the screenplay writer/scriptwriter may be a film author in one Member State and an author of an underlying work in another Member State.

The Member States are free to apply the presumption in Article 2(6), or any other presumption with respect to authors' rights, to rights other than the rental and lending rights. The Directive covers, as far as authors are concerned, only those two rights and does not regulate the operation of any other right. However, for the sake of consistency it would be appropriate not to draw a distinction between the various rights in this respect, and instead to apply the same kind of presumption to all rights. Accordingly, if a Member

---

[34] See p. 57, above.
[35] See p. 58, above.
[36] See p. 57, above.

State wants to apply the presumption of transfer of Article 2(6) to the rental and lending rights, it would be advisable to provide, if at all, for the same kind of presumption to apply to other rights.

In the context of the provisions on the application in time of the Directive (Article 13), the Council has considerably weakened the protection afforded to performing artists within the otherwise balanced approach of Article 2(5). In this respect, see the comments below on Article 13(7) to (9).

# Article 3. Rental of Computer Programs

Article 3 refers to the rental of computer programs as covered by the Directive on the protection of computer programs.

*Article 3*

**Rental of Computer Programs**

## ARTICLE 3 (RENTAL DIRECTIVE)

This Directive shall be without prejudice to Article 4(c) of Council Directive 91/250/EEC of 14 May 1991 on the legal protection of computer programs.[37]

## COUNCIL DIRECTIVE 91/250/EEC OF 14 MAY 1991 RECITAL (16) AND ARTICLE 4(c)

*Recital*

(16) Whereas, for the purposes of this Directive, the term "rental" means the making available for use, for a limited period of time and for profit-making purposes, of a computer program or a copy thereof; whereas this term does not include public lending, which, accordingly, remains outside the scope of this Directive.

*Article 4*

**Restricted Acts**

Subject to the provisions of Articles 5 and 6, the exclusive rights of the rightholder within the meaning of Article 2 shall include the right to do or to authorize:

. . .

(c) any form of distribution to the public, including the rental, of the original computer program or of copies thereof. The first sale in the Community of a copy of a program by the rightholder or with his consent shall exhaust the distribution right within the Community of that copy, with the exception of the right to control further rental of the program or a copy thereof.

---

[37] [1991] O.J. L122/42.

Commentary

Since Article 4(c) of the Council Directive on the legal protection of computer programs provides for an exclusive rental right, the rental Directive is without prejudice to that provision.

The Commission's original proposal for the rental Directive employed the same definition of the term "rental" as in the computer Directive,[38] but the Council changed the definition, which raises the question as to whether the change has any bearing on the relationship between the computer program Directive and the present Directive. Since according to Article 3, the rental Directive is without prejudice only to Article 4(c) of the computer Directive, as interpreted by Recital (16) of that Directive, the rental Directive logically applies only to those acts of rental which are not covered by the computer Directive. It seems, however, that the definitions largely mirror one another,[39] so that there will be no room for applying the present Directive to the rental of computer programs.

Article 3 of the rental Directive was included in the Commission's original proposal as Article 2(3). The transfer from Article 2(3) to Article 3 has not resulted in any change of content.

According to Recital (16) of the computer program Directive, public lending is excluded from the scope of that Directive. Consequently, the rental Directive covers the "lending" (within the meaning of Article 1(3)) of computer programs, as may be seen in particular from the wording of Article 5(2), where computer programs are expressly mentioned.

Being a rather technical provision, Article 3 was subject to minimal discussion during the legislative process. It was, however, mentioned in the Council working group in conjunction with the issues concerning Article 5 (derogation from the exclusive lending right).

---

[38] See Art. 1(2) of the Directive and Recital (16) of the Directive on computer programs.
[39] See the comments on Art. 1(2), above.

# Article 4. Unwaivable Right to Equitable Remuneration

Article 4 is one of the main achievements of this Directive and may have repercussions in copyright law in general. It is designed to deal with the situation that authors and performers, due to their weak bargaining position in relation to producers, will often not in practice adequately benefit from their exclusive rental rights. It ensures that in addition to the exclusive right under Article 2(1), authors and performers will actually benefit from the rental right by providing for an unwaivable right to obtain equitable remuneration for the rental. Article 4(3) and (4) deal with the administration of this remuneration right.

## 1. RECITALS (15) TO (17) AND ARTICLE 4(1)

*Recitals*

**Unwaivable right to equitable remuneration**

(15) Whereas it is necessary to introduce arrangements ensuring that an unwaivable equitable remuneration is obtained by authors and performers who must retain the possibility to entrust the administration of this right to collecting societies representing them;

 (16) Whereas the equitable remuneration may be paid on the basis of one or several payments at any time on or after the conclusion of the contract;

(17) Whereas the equitable remuneration must take account of the importance of the contribution of the authors and performers concerned to the phonogram or film;

*Article 4*

1.   Where an author or performer has transferred or assigned his rental right concerning a phonogram or an original or copy of a film to a phonogram or film producer, that author or performer shall retain the right to obtain an equitable remuneration for the rental.

...

COMMENTARY

### (a) The General Background

In the Commission's original proposal, the provision relating to remuneration consisted of one Article (Article 3) with one paragraph only, and was worded differently from the final text. The substance has not fundamentally changed but, in some respects, the wording has become clearer.

The background to this Article, as illustrated in the Explanatory Memorandum to the Commission's original proposal,[40] may be explained as follows. It is usually not sufficient simply to determine who should be the first rightholder of a new right such as the rental right. The legislation must in addition ensure that the first right-owners will actually be able to benefit from their rights. Without specific legislative measures, this would often not be the case because the weaker parties, usually authors and performers as opposed to the producers of sound or video recordings, generally assign their rights to the producers without obtaining separate remuneration for every right or obtaining more than a remuneration on a flat-rate basis. According to the Commission, having regard to the prevailing situation and to the underlying purpose of copyright law, unlimited contractual freedom would not be appropriate because it would not lead to an equitable result. The Commission's proposed solution to this problem was to grant both an assignable exclusive right and a right to obtain an adequate percentage of the revenues flowing from the exploitation of a work by rental or lending by a third person. With this solution, producers would not be fettered in their exploitation of the exclusive rights but all first rightholders were guaranteed an adequate share of the rental and lending revenues.

It should be noted that the European Parliament welcomed, and even reinforced, the Commission's proposal to provide for a specific protection for authors and performers. In particular, it rejected a proposal for a new paragraph which would probably have called the whole Article into question.

On the other hand, the Member States were uncertain about this new concept for some time; some objected to the principle itself and preferred unlimited contractual freedom, while others agreed with the idea underlying Article 4 but were doubtful about the actual wording, the practicalities of administration and whether there was a need to regulate this problem on the Community level. Some Member States questioned whether the Community was competent to deal with issues related to contract law; it was, however, indicative of their genuine concerns that they did not raise the same doubts with respect to the provisions added later dealing with the presumption of the transfer of rights from performing artists and authors to film producers (Article 2(5) to (7)). Before the Member States accepted this Article in a modified form, but without fundamental changes in substance, it was fiercely debated in principle and in detail, and many new versions were proposed and then rejected. The concept has survived, however, and it is fair to say that the

---

[40] See the Explanatory Memorandum to the original proposal, para. 3.1.1, p. 45 et seq.

Commission and the European Parliament have played a vital role in persuading the Member States of the need to include this Article in the Directive.

## (b) Particular Issues

### Scope of the Article

The Commission's original version was phrased in a rather abstract way which gave rise to many questions of understanding. The text of the adopted Directive is clearer but covers the same situation. The original proposal envisaged a situation in which someone (for example a video shop) is given the authorisation to rent or lend a sound or visual recording. This authorisation may logically only be given by all the rightholders concerned, such as the composer, the performer (who will usually have already assigned his rights to the producer) and the producer himself. Accordingly, the original wording read: "If *the rightholders authorize* ..." and as a result, each of the rightholders concerned was to receive an adequate part of the payment for the authorisation of the rental. The rightholders who were expected and intended to benefit from this provision, and whose rights were to be safeguarded, were mainly authors and performing artists.[41]

The adopted version of the Directive expressly refers to the author and performer, thereby indicating that Article 4 is a protective provision in favour of authors and performers, who are typically in the weaker position when negotiating exploitation contracts. Since authors and performers alone are not in a position to authorise the rental[42] and as they usually transfer or assign the rental right (or are presumed by law to do so) the word "authorize" was replaced with the words "transferred" and "assigned." These words have to be broadly interpreted, as in Article 2(4) and (5).[43] They even cover a situation in which an author or performer is presumed by law to transfer or assign his right, as is apparent from Article 2(5) and (6) and from the aim behind Article 4.

The above remarks may also explain why the phrase *"to a third party"* – which caused confusion in some Member States where it is an unknown legal term – was replaced by the words *"to a phonogram or film producer."* The rightholders' common authorisation for rental, to which the original text referred, is usually given to a third party, *i.e.* a person who is not one of the rightholders, such as a video shop whereas authors and performers, to whom the final text refers, after transfer their rental rights to the phonogram or film producer. Consequently, where performers or authors do not transfer their rental rights to the producer, but to some other person or entity, Article 4 in its final form would seem not to apply. However, in view of the purpose of Article 4, the following distinction has to be made: (a) if the exclusive rights are

---

[41] This is evident from the Commission's explanations on Art. 3. See the Explanatory Memorandum, para. 3.1.1, p. 45 *et seq.*

[42] In addition, the producer's consent is necessary to authorise the rental of a phonogram or videogram.

[43] See pp. 53–55, above.

transferred to the performers' or authors' collecting societies, Article 4 will not apply because collecting societies generally strengthen the performers' and authors' bargaining position, and it is the very purpose of a collecting society to distribute the revenues to the rightholders, so that the need for Article 4 to safeguard the interests of the performers and authors will not arise; (b) in cases of attempted avoidance, Article 4 will apply because its protective purpose will not allow the provision to be avoided by using legal structures which are not covered by the precise wording. For example, a producer may ask performers or authors to transfer their exclusive rental rights directly to the distributor or to some other person with whom the producer has business connections. Although strictly this is not covered by the wording of Article 4, the Article would apply because the case represents an obvious attempt to evade the application of the provisions.

### Rental/Lending Right

The Council restricted the scope of the Article to rental, and thereby excluded lending. This occurred in the context of the discussions in the Council Working Group concerning the possible deletion of the lending right from the Directive altogether.[44] The discussions show that the Member States did not object in principle to the inclusion of the lending right in Article 4. It would seem to be an accurate reflection of their intentions and of the legislative history of the Directive to apply Article 4 also to the exclusive[45] lending right,[46] once a Member State has chosen not to apply the derogation in Article 5. Of course, the rightholders are likely to demand only small payments for the lending authorisation from public libraries and other lending institutions, in order not to put these organisations under commercial pressure.

### Phonograms and Films

The scope of Article 4 has always been limited to rental or lending of phonograms and originals or copies of films (this corresponds to the original proposal's terms "sound recording, visual recording or visual and sound recording"). This is due to the fact that the problem dealt with in this Article arises mainly in the context of these items; the rental of books is rare, and the lending of books will probably be covered by remuneration systems under Article 5. The application of Article 4 to other items would certainly reflect the spirit of the Article and Member States should be encouraged to do so.

### Equitable Remuneration for Rental

The Commission's original proposal provided for a right "to obtain *an adequate part of the said payment*," *i.e.* the payment for the authorisation of rental or lending. The Commission wanted to ensure the equitable sharing of the rental revenues.

In the Parliament, many amendments were proposed but rejected at first reading, such as the replacement of "adequate part of the said payment" by

---

[44] For a more detailed explanation, see the comments on Art. 2(5), p. 60, above.
[45] Art. 4 does not apply where a Member State has derogated from the exclusive right under Art. 5.
[46] For a more detailed explanation see the comments on Art. 2(5) to (7), p. 60, above.

"adequate remuneration" (Economic Affairs Committee), and the new wording "the right to obtain a remuneration" (Cultural Affairs Committee) and "the right to negotiate payment" (Legal Affairs Committee). In the end, the plenary did not propose any major amendment to the Commission's first sentence, but adopted an additional sentence in order to define more precisely the term "adequate part": "The adequate part shall be duly proportional to the contribution to the work and its exploitation." According to the Report of the Legal Affairs Committee, this sentence was intended to underline the importance of the creative contributions made by authors and performers and to ensure that, in determining what is "adequate" under Article 4, these contributions would be duly taken into account.

The Commission included this new sentence in its amended proposal in a slightly modified version. For the sake of clarity, it added the word "importance" (of the contribution) and indicated, in accordance with the Parliament's wishes, that the creative and artistic contributions of authors and performers are of major importance in the exploitation of sound recordings or film[47] as may be seen from the great influence their contribution has on the decision of the consumer to rent a particular sound recording or film. The Commission omitted the words "and its exploitation" from the text of the Parliament's opinion because it considered them to be superfluous and even, in this context, ambiguous.

The Member States welcomed the idea of providing a guideline for interpretation of the term "adequate part"[48] and because of its interpretative character, the sentence was turned into a Recital (17). The Member States chose even more precise wording than the Commission: this expressly refers to the importance of the contributions of *authors and performing artists* and thereby reveals its protective nature and implies that their contributions are often underestimated.

Although Recital (17) no longer refers to "adequate part" but to "equitable remuneration," it still impinges on the relationship between the groups of rightholders concerned. It goes without saying that, in determining the shares of authors, performers and producers in the rental revenues, the producer's contribution must also be taken into account. The fact, however, that the recital refers only to authors and performers highlights the importance of their contributions and is intended to strengthen their bargaining position vis-à-vis the producers. This protection of authors and performers was supported by the above-mentioned discussions in the Parliament and in the Council Working Group. Although precise percentages are not indicated, the shares of exploitation revenues which are usually given to authors and performers will have to be increased if they do not meet the text of "equitability." The Member States may fix by law certain percentages or minimum percentages and take account of the authors' and performers' actual contributions; this method will be practical where the right under Article 4 is exercised by a

---

[47] The Commission modified the Parliament's version by replacing "work" with "sound recording, visual recording or visual and sound recording."

[48] The guideline for interpretation was retained even after the replacement of the term "adequate part" with "equitable remuneration."

collecting society and also where a Member State incorporates Article 4 into its contract law and provides for a (minimum) percentage. It may, however, be preferable for Member States not to prescribe certain percentages but simply give some guidelines on the basis of Recital (17) and leave it to the parties and the judges to decide what is equitable in the circumstances.

Some Member States doubted the practicability of the Commission's original version ("adequate part *of the said payment*"). They seemed to assume that the rightholders would physically have to receive an adequate part of every single payment for any rental act; this was not the intention of the original proposal. In addition, several Member States had different views on the meaning of the words "adequate" and "equitable" and some Member States did not even think there was any difference between the terms. In the end, the Member States, mindful of the need for a compromise, adopted the wording "equitable remuneration for rental" instead of "adequate part of the said payment." This new wording is in fact less precise and less technical than the previous wording. In the end, an equitable remuneration for the rental will amount to, and will usually be at least as much as, an adequate part of the rental revenues. The remuneration that "*for*" rental implies that, according to general copyright principles, the remuneration has to be related to the extent of exploitation by rental. Accordingly, the more rentals of a particular videogram or phonogram that take place, the more remuneration that has to be paid. In practice, where this would lead to disproportionate administration costs, payments may be made on the basis of the estimated extent of rental, which may be ascertained by various random tests; collecting societies have been using these and similar methods for some time. In the end, however, the principle itself must always be observed. This is emphasised by the word "equitable," which refers not only to the share in relation to other groups of right-owners,[49] but also to the whole amount in relation to the extent of exploitation. Accordingly, the remuneration will be "equitable" only if both the rental revenues of all exploitation acts and the author's or performer's creative or artistic contribution are taken into account.

In addition, the phrase "remuneration for rental" implies that the remuneration paid for rental must be separate from the remuneration for other forms of exploitation. The right-owners should be able to see clearly which revenues are the result of which type of exploitation. It is to be recommended that Member States bring in appropriate measures in order to ensure a full adoption of Article 4 into national law, for example by imposing on producers and collecting societies the obligation to reveal information on the extent of exploitation or the rental revenues, whether on a regular basis or on demand. This seems particularly important in the case of flat-rate payments.

Several Member States insisted on the clarification that *flat-rate payments* would still be possible. Accordingly, Recital (16) specifies that the "equitable remuneration may be paid on the basis of one or several payments at any time on or after the conclusion of the contract." The recital describes possible methods of payment. The amount, however, must always meet the requirement of Article 4(1) which is repeated in Recital (16), that the remuneration

---

[49] This aspect is dealt with in Recital (17) – see the comments, p. 69, above.

itself has to be *"equitable"* in any event. In addition, the flat-rate payment must relate to rental only and may not include non-specific payments for other kinds of exploitation. Accordingly, one payment on conclusion of the contract or a reasonable time after its conclusion, or several payments the first of which is made on conclusion of the contract or a reasonable time thereafter, may possibly, but will not necessarily, fulfil the criterion of "equitable remuneration." This depends entirely on the total amount which has been paid, which has to represent an "equitable remuneration" within the meaning of Article 4(1), thus taking into account the rental revenues from all exploitation acts which occurred during the existence of the rental right, and the author's and performer's creative and artistic contributions. Consequently, as soon as the flat-rate payment appears insufficient due to, perhaps, the unexpected success of the rental, one or several further payments will have to be made. For example, if the equitable remuneration in a certain case is £8,000 after 40 years of exploitation and £10,000 after 50 years of exploitation of the rental right, and one flat-rate-payment of £8,000 was made on the conclusion of the contract, the remaining £2,000 will have to be paid in one or several payments beginning at the time when the payment of £8,000 no longer covers the ongoing acts of exploitation. Accordingly, the difference between flat-rate payments and percentage payments lies only in the method of payment.

It was never the intention simply by allowing one or several flat-rate payments to be made, thereby to exclude future adjustments and not taking into account ongoing exploitation. If that were the case, Recital (16), which is, by its nature, interpretative in character, would allow Article 4 to be completely undermined.

In practice, Recital (16) will be important where Member States incorporate Article 4 into provisions on the contract between the author or performer and the producer. Producers who do not want to make regular payments based on certain percentages of the rental revenues will be able to make one or several payments up front. Where Member States provide for the administration of the Article 4 right by collecting societies, the recital will not be so important because collecting societies usually distribute the collected revenues once every year in any case.

Since experience has shown that flat-rate payments made by producers to authors and performers carry the risk of depriving authors and performers of their equitable remuneration, and, moreover, might cause administrative problems in the context of the obligation under Article 4, this method of payment may not be the most appropriate way of putting Article 4 into practice.

## 2. ARTICLE 4(2)

*Article 4*

...

2. The right to obtain an equitable remuneration for rental cannot be waived by authors or performers.

...

COMMENTARY

The unwaivability of the right to obtain an equitable remuneration for rental represents an essential element of Article 4. Without this provision, authors and performers would, in practice, run the risk of being forced by the producer to waive the right. The Council placed this provision in a separate paragraph, thereby emphasising its importance.

The Council Working Group discussed whether to use the word "waived" or "assigned." It preferred the word "waived" because it would provide better protection for the authors and performers. In fact, the expression "the right cannot be waived" means that, for example, even its assignment would not be possible, unless the payment of the equitable remuneration were safeguarded. Assignment is however possible for the purpose of administration. Collecting societies often take an assignment from right-owners before conducting the administration of their rights. This possibility is expressly mentioned in Article 4(3) and (4) and Recital (15) and is further explained below. Such an assignment for administration purposes is possible under Article 4(2) because it does not represent a waiver; the rightholder still obtains the payment.

The addition in the final text (compared to the original proposal), according to which this right cannot be waived "by authors or performers," merely reflects the fact that authors and performers are the only rightholders of the remuneration right. No-one else could waive the right. Accordingly, it does not represent any change in substance.

This specific provision has not given rise to any major discussions; as soon as the principle and the need for Article 4 was accepted, it was clear that it would have to include the concept of unwaivability in order to function properly.

## 3. RECITAL (15) AND ARTICLE 4(3) AND (4)

*Recital*

(15) Whereas it is necessary to introduce arrangements ensuring that an unwaivable equitable remuneration is obtained by authors and performers who must retain the possibility to entrust the administration of this right to collecting societies representing them;

*Article 4*

...

3.  The administration of this right to obtain an equitable remuneration may be entrusted to collecting societies representing authors or performers.

4.   Member States may regulate whether and to what extent administration by collecting societies of the right to obtain an equitable remuneration may be imposed, as well as the question from whom this remuneration may be claimed or collected.

## Commentary

### (a) The Legislative Background

In Article 3 of the Commission's original proposal, the second sentence was less clear than the text of the adopted Directive, but attempted to convey the same meaning. It said that the remuneration right "cannot be waived, but its administration may be assigned." The Commission wanted to make it clear that the participation right can be assigned, but only where this is done for administration purposes, in particular by collecting societies.[50] Like its Committees on Cultural and Legal Affairs, the European Parliament in plenary passed amendments to clarify to whom the administration of the participation right may be entrusted, namely "in particular to collective administrative associations representing the *professional categories concerned*." The Commission, in its amended proposal, endorsed and further clarified this amendment by expressly referring to *authors and performers* only, since collective administration was considered to be protection for them, whereas producers were seen to gain little benefit from it.

The Council, having restricted Article 4 to authors and performers, for the sake of clarity replaced the words "representing the professional categories concerned" with the words "representing authors or performing artists." Similarly, it split up the provision into two separate paragraphs.

### (b) Collecting Societies

The term "collecting societies" is not defined in the Directive. Collecting societies are characterised, according to the usual meaning of the term, by their activity, which consists mainly of granting licences and collecting, on behalf of authors or neighbouring right-owners, revenues from certain kinds of copyright and neighbouring right exploitation, and in distributing these revenues to the right-owners according to established distribution schemes. The right-owners who entrust the administration of their rights to collecting societies must retain the right to decide, via their agents, on the administrative details such as the contents of distribution schemes. In order to guarantee efficient and satisfactory administration, legislation should provide for mechanisms ensuring transparency of, and control over the activities of the collecting societies. The Directive does not require any special legal form of

---

[50] See the Explanatory Memorandum, para. 3.1.2, p. 48 and para. 3.2.2, p. 49.

organisation for a collecting society; the word "society" is used in a broad way and includes all organisations which allow right-owners to retain control over the administration of their rights.

### (c) "Representing Authors or Performers"

The phrase "representing authors or performers" in Article 4(3) might seem superfluous, since it is self-evident. The fact that it was expressly included in the text reflects the overall protective nature of Article 4 towards authors and performers. The Member States wanted to make sure that authors and performers did not lose control over the administration of their rights when they entrusted them to collecting societies, but that they were themselves adequately represented, or even participated, in the decision-making process concerning the administration of their rights. In particular, the requirements of Article 4(3) would not be met if producers or other parties with interests at variance with those of authors and performers organised the collective administration of the authors' or performers' rights.

It is not necessary for a collecting society to represent only authors, only performers or only those two, thereby excluding other groups of right-owners such as producers who might adhere to the collecting society in respect of other rights. In fact it is obvious that, in practice, collecting societies often represent several groups of rightholders at the same time, such as authors of musical works and their publishers, or performers and phonogram producers. However, authors and performers, as the only beneficiaries of this unwaivable right, must be able to exclude such other groups of rightholders from the control over its administration.

### (d) Entrusting the Administration of the Right

The expression "the *administration* of this right ... may be *entrusted* to collecting societies" was chosen because it seemed sufficiently broad to cover the various legal ways in which the right may be assigned under the national laws of the Member States. It does not have a strict, technical meaning. "Administration" means primarily the collection of money and its distribution according to copyright principles (basically, distribution according to the extent of exploitation of a certain work or performance). The word "entrusted" does not refer to any specific kind of administration contract, but rather includes an element of trust, which indicates that the right-owner may assign the right, but not the benefit of that right, and thus that the collecting society is bound to hand over the money collected on his behalf.

### (e) Appropriate Ways to Implement Article 4(3) and (4)

Article 4 does not exclude other ways of asserting the unwaivable remuneration right. The word "may" in Article 4(3) indicates that collective administration is only one of several possibilities. However, Article 4 favours collective administration, as may be seen from the fact that this is the only method expressly mentioned in a separate paragraph and that Recital (15) guarantees authors and performers the possibility of taking advantage of this method. Accordingly, no matter how a Member State incorporates Article 4 into its law – for example, by provisions on contract law – the authors and performers must still be guaranteed by law the possibility of entrusting their right under Article 4 to a collecting society. This implies that the laws of the Member States must offer a legal basis for the activities of collecting societies as described above.

Recital (15) does not contradict the provisions of Article 4(4), according to which Member States may regulate the question of from whom the remuneration may be claimed or collected. Even if a Member State provides that the remuneration must be claimed from the producer, collective administration remains possible, because authors and performers would never "claim" the remuneration *from* collecting societies, but *through* their collecting societies from producers or directly from rental outlets.

One of the most appropriate ways to incorporate Article 4 into national law would be by providing a statutory, unwaivable remuneration right in the situation envisaged in Article 4(1). Member States may provide for the possibility of collective administration of this right. Following a proposal by one Member State, which at present provides for a statutory remuneration right for rental which may only be claimed by collecting societies, it was made clear that administration by collecting societies may be imposed (Article 4(4)). Indeed, in a case where the remuneration right under Article 4 is intended to be administered by collecting societies, it is recommended that its administration by collecting societies should be imposed, since this would prevent single right-owners approaching video clubs with a payment claim and would thereby facilitate the administration of rights in practice. Member States are, however, not obliged to provide for a mandatory collective administration.

In addition, it is desirable (but not obligatory) to determine in law from whom the collecting societies (or authors and performers directly) may claim or collect the remuneration, whether from the producer, the rental outlets or their associations. The most appropriate solution, which would best fulfil the aim of Article 4, would be to determine that rental outlets or, preferably, their associations, are the debtors. Producers and the collecting societies (together rather than separately) could then negotiate the entire amount to be paid by the rental outlets, which would be shared between the producers and the collecting societies.

Where a Member State does not make the administration of this right by collecting societies obligatory, and where collecting societies are not sufficiently active or successful in encouraging authors and performers to entrust the administration to them, the requirements of Article 4 may be met in several other ways. In particular, authors and performers may assert their remuneration rights in the context of collective agreements between their trade unions and employers' associations or individual employers. This solution seems advisable in cases where the trade unions enjoy a strong bargaining position compared to the employers. The legislation would have to provide for legal ways to ensure that the right under Article 4 may be actively exercised within such collective agreements.

There is of course another way to exercise the right under Article 4: it involves the individual assertion of the remuneration right by the author or performer against the producer in each individual contract. The law might state, for example, that the producer has to pay an equitable remuneration and specify this remuneration with respect to rental, providing for appropriate legal measures to encourage compliance, such as the producer's obligation to give information on the extent of, and revenues from, rental. In any event, the unwaivability of this right would have to be expressly laid down in the law. However, this would on the whole seem to be a less appropriate way of implementing Article 4. Authors and performers, typically the weaker parties in individual contracts with producers, would again be dependent on producers in their attempts to enforce the right to equitable remuneration. This would hardly reinforce the aim of Article 4, namely to counterbalance the disadvantages typically encountered by authors and performers in their negotiations with producers.

There may be further ways in which Member States can implement Article 4 but, in any event, the most important thing will be to fulfil the purpose behind Article 4 and to ensure that authors and performers effectively obtain an equitable remuneration for the rental of their works and performances. The actual impact of Article 4 has been reduced by the provisions on the application in time which are explained below.[51] The scope and importance of the right will in practice depend to a great extent on initiatives taken by the collecting societies.

---

[51] See the comments on Art. 13(8) and (9), pp. 126–129, below.

# Article 5. Derogation from the Exclusive Public Lending Right

Article 5 outlines how Member States may derogate from the exclusive lending right, in particular by providing a remuneration right, the so-called "public lending right."

## RECITAL (18) AND ARTICLE 5

### Recital

(18) Whereas it is also necessary to protect the rights at least of authors as regards public lending by providing for specific arrangements; whereas, however, any measures based on Article 5 of this Directive have to comply with Community law, in particular with Article 7 of the Treaty;

### Article 5

#### Derogation from the exclusive public lending right

1.    Member States may derogate from the exclusive right provided for in Article 1 in respect of public lending, provided that at least authors obtain a remuneration for such lending. Member States shall be free to determine this remuneration taking account of their cultural promotion objectives.

2.    When Member States do not apply the exclusive lending right provided for in Article 1 as regards phonograms, films and computer programs, they shall introduce, at least for authors, a remuneration.

3.    Member States may exempt certain categories of establishments from the payment of the remuneration referred to in paragraphs 1 and 2.

4.    The Commission, in co-operation with the Member States, shall draw up before July 1, 1997 a report on public lending in the Community. It shall forward this report to the European Parliament and to the Council.

## COMMENTARY

### (a) General

In order to present a realistic proposal, the Commission had originally provided for the possibility of derogating from the exclusive lending right. The original Article 4 had taken account of the fact that national legislators usually want to provide a lending right only in the form of a remuneration right known as public lending right, and outside the framework of copyright laws. Often, they want to permit only remuneration with respect to certain categories, such as books, but are willing to apply an exclusive right with respect to other categories, such as phonograms. In view of the diverse legal situation in the Member States, the Commission's original proposal offered a wide variety of ways in which to implement the lending right. As may be seen from the final version of the Directive, however, even the Commission's proposal was not flexible enough to be acceptable for all Member States.

The European Parliament in its intensive discussions at the first reading of Article 4, focused on two issues; the exclusion of certain items from the possibility of derogation and the reasons for allowing derogations. In particular, in respect of the first issue, the Economic Affairs Committee proposed excluding videograms; Member States would therefore have been obliged to provide for an exclusive lending right with respect to videograms. Similar proposals were made in the Cultural Affairs Committee; in addition, it was proposed that there should be a mandatory exclusive lending right with respect to sound recordings, which could be replaced by a remuneration right only after one year of marketing. The Legal Affairs Committee adopted an amendment under which the exclusive right could be replaced by a remuneration right only with respect to books, periodicals and educational films; this amendment, having been extended to sound recordings and films which had already been on the market for two years, was put to the vote but rejected in the plenary session of the European Parliament.

As far as the second issue was concerned (reasons for derogation), the Committee on Culture and the Legal Affairs Committee adopted amendments restricting the reasons for a derogation to clearly defined cultural or social issues. They were, however, not passed in the plenary session.

Two proposals to delete the lending right completely from the Directive were rejected in the Legal Affairs Committee.

In summary, the European Parliament, after a rather controversial debate, did not adopt any of the proposed amendments and thus did not itself propose any amendment at all to the original Article 4. Accordingly, the Commission in its amended proposal left Article 4 unchanged.

This Article was one of the most controversial Articles discussed in the Council Working Group. For a long time, about a half of the Member States were opposed in principle to its inclusion and even to the inclusion of a lending right at all. The main reasons for this reluctance seemed to be (1) the financial implications for national budgets, in particular where Member States expected to be obliged to pay a considerable amount of remuneration to foreign rightholders, and (2) a lack of practical experience in implementing and managing a public lending right system.

A number of Member States, in favour of a higher level of protection, preferred a provision which would be less flexible than the Commission's proposal. In particular, they favoured a mandatory exclusive lending right with respect to specific items such as phonograms and wanted Member States to be obliged to include performers as beneficiaries of the remuneration right. A great number of different versions were discussed, including one which would only have given the opportunity to derogate from the exclusive lending rights as set out in Article 1(1), without mentioning any remuneration. A compromise was finally achieved at the first meeting of the Internal Market Council on May 14, 1992. It reflects the highly divergent opinions of the Member States and to understand its provisions it must be remembered that it represents an overall compromise.

### (b) Particular Issues

*The Title*

The inclusion of the word "public" in the title of Article 5 is not of particular significance. It was included following a proposal by a Member State which thought it would be more consistent with the text of Article 5(1). Indeed, the exclusive lending right of Article 1, to which Article 5(1) refers, does concern public lending (*i.e.* lending to the public as opposed to lending amongst friends); although this is not expressly stated, it may be gleaned from the definition in Article 1(3). However, the expression "exclusive public lending right" in the title of Article 5 may at first sight seem contradictory, because the term "public lending right" is usually only used in the context of the remuneration right, rather than the exclusive lending right. In fact, the title refers to the exclusive right of lending to the public.

*Article 5(1)*

Article 5(1) allows Member States to provide for *remuneration (at least for authors)*, instead of an exclusive lending right. This derogation may be provided in respect of all types of lending objects or, as follows from Article 5(2), in respect of certain objects only. The derogation will always apply to objects, as opposed to rightholders or others. Thus, Article 5 does not allow the granting of an exclusive right to one group of rightholders and a remuneration right to another group of rightholders in respect of the same item. However, Member States may provide a remuneration right for books and phonograms for example, but an exclusive right with respect to videograms and other specified items. In this case, the remuneration right may be vested in authors only, thereby excluding the performers and phonogram producers who contributed to the phonograms, or in both authors and performers, in which case the phonogram producer would enjoy neither a remuneration right nor an exclusive right, or in authors, performers and phonogram producers. The exclusive right granted, in the above example, in respect of videograms, will have to be vested in all the rightholders concerned (authors, performers and film producers); Articles 1 to 4 will apply in this case.

A Member State may also derogate from the exclusive right only after a certain time, by providing for example that rightowners in relation to phonograms or videograms enjoy an exclusive lending right for, say, two years following publication, and thereafter, for the remaining term of protection, a remuneration right instead of the exclusive right.

The derogation may apply not only to the exclusive nature of the lending right, but also to the *copyright-based nature* of the lending right. This was mentioned both in the Commission's original and in its amended proposal

79

and was not queried by the Parliament or the Council. The deletion of the express reference to "copyright-based" in the adopted version was not intentional; it simply happened during the course of continuous drafting exercises in respect of this Article. It was always understood among Member States that the remuneration under Article 5 could be provided outside the copyright laws, and thus would not have to be "copyright-based." This is supported by a statement by the Commission noted at the Council meeting of June 18, 1992, according to which the existing public lending right system of a particular Member State, which is not based on copyright law, complies with Article 5.[52] The fact that the Commission's statement only refers to one Member State is due to the fact that that Member State was the only one to request such a statement. It cannot lead to the opposite conclusion, namely that other Member States' provisions on public lending right would not comply with Article 5.

The statement by the Commission may also provide some further help with regard to the interpretation of Article 5. Since it refers to the whole regime on public lending right by that Member State, even those provisions which do not comply with copyright principles may be regarded as being in compliance with Article 5, such as the provisions on the eligibility for remuneration of persons after the author's death[53] and on the duration of the public lending right.[54] Again, no contrary conclusion may be drawn with respect to other Member States' provisions. It accords with the spirit of the Article and its nature as a compromise to conclude that similar provisions would still comply with Article 5.

Since Article 5 does not deal with the *administration of the remuneration right*, Member States are free to choose any method, such as administration by collecting societies, ministerial departments or other administrative bodies. Likewise, Member States may determine who should be liable to pay the remuneration, whether the State, the library or other entity. Member States may also determine the detailed criteria according to which the remuneration is to be distributed; these criteria however must reflect the general principle that a considerable part, if not the whole amount, of the remuneration has to be paid according to the extent of lending, as may be seen from the wording "remuneration *for* such lending." The extent of lending of the works concerned and the amounts of the individual payments may be ascertained by random sampling and similar methods which do not give rise to unreasonable administration costs. The Directive does not prevent Member States from providing, in addition to such a remuneration, and whether separately or not, for social, cultural or other funds from which authors or others may obtain social aid, cultural awards or scholarships.

Contrary to the Commission's original proposal, the adopted text of Article 5 does not require that the remuneration be "*equitable.*" This deletion was

---

[52] The Commission statement reads: "The Commission considers that the present Danish law on public lending satisfies the requirements of Article 5."
[53] These are, under Danish law, not the author's heirs, as would be the case under copyright law, but certain persons expressly nominated by law.
[54] In Danish law, it does not correspond to the duration of copyright, but to the duration of the life of the persons eligible after the author's death.

necessary in order to obtain the approval of those Member States which were concerned about the financial impact. The deletion must not be viewed as an indication of a general tendency to deprive authors of an equitable remuneration. Article 5 certainly allows for the provision of an "equitable" remuneration.

The *second sentence of Article 5(1)* was introduced following a proposal by one Member State which is beginning to build up a new library system as a means of cultural promotion, with a view to widening public access to culture. The Member State did not want to endanger this project by payment obligations in respect of the public lending right. The second sentence allows the Member State (or any other Member State which is in a similar situation) to reduce the remuneration which it would normally pay in respect of the public lending right and channel the funds into building up the new library system. This compromise was allowed because the modernisation of library systems will encourage lending activities and is therefore a step towards higher remunerations in the future. Despite its general wording, the sentence accordingly should not be allowed to have too broad an impact, since it was included solely in order to cover the above-mentioned case.

The potential obligation to pay remuneration to *foreign rightholders* was of considerable concern to some Member States. The Directive does not in any way deal with the question of whether and to what extent a national public lending right system is covered by the principle of national treatment under the Berne Convention. A Community Directive cannot have any direct implications for the general interpretation of an International Convention. The fact that the Directive does not oblige the Member States to regulate the remuneration right under Article 5 in the framework of copyright law[55] does not have any implications either, because the applicability of the principle of national treatment depends on the substance of such regulation, and not on its legal form. Even a form of regulation which falls outside the relevant national copyright Act is covered by the principle of national treatment, if as a matter of substance, it is in fact a copyright matter.

The reference in Recital (18) to Article 7 of the EEC Treaty (the principle of non-discrimination on the grounds of nationality) is intended to underline the importance of the Article, which would have to be observed even without this reference. The Directive does not expand on what legal measures as regards the eligibility of nationals of the Community would not comply with Article 7 of the EEC Treaty. However, an indication may be inferred from the Commission's statement mentioned above[56]; the solution adopted by the Member State concerned is regarded by the Commission as complying with Article 7.[57]

## Article 5(2)

Article 5(2) reflects a compromise between two Member States. One of them wanted a mandatory exclusive lending right in respect of computer programs. The other insisted on the possibility of providing for a remuneration

---

[55] See pp. 79–80, above.
[56] See n. 52.
[57] Denmark provides that authors are only eligible if they write in the Danish language; in the case of translated works, only the translator into the Danish language is eligible.

right for computer programs. Article 5(2) is drafted in a way which suggests that the exclusive lending right is considered to be the norm, at least with respect to phonograms, films and computer programs. Of course, this also applies to other items, since the whole of Article 5 is designed to be a derogation from the principle of the exclusive lending right. Accordingly, it is doubtful whether Article 5(2) contains any substantial addition. It simply seems to emphasise that an exclusive right is regarded as particularly important in respect of films, phonograms and computer programs. Indeed, these categories are most susceptible to copying; therefore, the problems are comparable to those in the case of rental, where an exclusive right was considered necessary, *inter alia*, to counteract the copying problem. This interpretation is supported by a statement by the Commission noted at the Internal Market Council meeting of June 18, 1992 – a statement which refers to the contents of its report on public lending, to be drawn up in accordance with Article 5(4).[58] However, Member States remain free to choose either an exclusive right or the remuneration right under Article 5.

Since the second sentence of Article 5(1) has not been repeated in Article 5(2), one may conclude that it does not apply in the case of phonograms, films and computer programs; hence, the remuneration cannot be reduced to take account of cultural promotion objectives.

*Article 5(3)*

Article 5(3) was inserted in order to meet the concerns of two Member States which wanted to be free to exclude libraries at educational establishments and public libraries from public lending right payments.[59] It allows a Member State, which has derogated from the exclusive lending right and provided for a remuneration at least for authors, expressly to exempt certain categories of libraries from the payment. Accordingly, the remuneration will have to be provided for in principle and then certain types of establishment will have to be identified and exempted from the payment obligation. The word "certain" implies not only that the establishments have to be specified, but also that one or several, but not all, categories may be exempted.

The mere fact that Article 5 allows the avoidance of payment of remuneration for lending through public libraries runs the risk of undermining the Directive's provisions on the lending right. Since this provision was drafted mainly to meet the concerns of two Member States, it may be expected (and would conform to the spirit of the compromise) that Member States will exempt, if any, only certain kinds of public libraries from the public lending right payments.

---

[58] The Commission statement reads: "The Commission agrees that its report is to include the question of whether derogations are justified for works other than literature."

[59] See the statement made at the Internal Market Council meeting of June 18, 1992: "The Commission considers that the categories of establishments which may be exempted under Article 5(3) include public libraries, universities and educational establishments."

*Article 5(4)*

In view of the wide scope for exemption and derogation, the Directive will probably result in little harmonisation in the lending right field. It may be seen as a first step. Accordingly, the Commission undertook to draw up a report on public lending in the Community before July 1, 1997, and Article 5(4) sets out the obligation of the Commission in this respect. The statement by the Commission noted at the Internal Market Council meeting of June 18, 1992, specified that this "report is to include its position on further possible legislative initiatives regarding public lending." The fact that Article 5(4) was expressly included in Article 5, although the Commission is entitled to draw up such a report even if it were not mentioned in the Directive, indicates that the Commission has agreed to pay particular attention to developments in the lending market. This is underlined by the fact that the report is to be forwarded to the European Parliament and to the Council.

In addition, Article 5(4) obliges Member States to co-operate with the Commission for the purposes of the report, in particular by providing information, and stresses the importance of the public lending right, thus encouraging Member States to provide for an appropriate public lending right system. The future right-owners themselves will have to take advantage of the fact that the public lending right has been considered of sufficient importance to be included in a Community Directive. It will largely depend on their initiative, in the context of the incorporation of the Directive into national law, whether or not they will finally obtain a right for which they may have struggled on a national level for some time.

# Chapter II of the Directive: Its Title, and the Scope of Protection

Chapter II of the Directive covers the harmonisation of certain neighbouring rights in the field of intellectual property. The term "rights related to copyright" was preferred to the more commonly used term "neighbouring rights" because it seemed to be more neutral. It indicates that the Directive does not impose on Member States the continental legal regime of "authors rights and neighbouring rights" and that it allows Member States to retain their copyright laws, as long as they protect performers, phonogram and film producers, as well as broadcasting organisations and cable distributors, in accordance with the Directive.

*Recital (20)*

(20) Whereas Member States may provide for more far-reaching protection for owners of rights related to copyright than that required by Article 8 of this Directive;

Chapter II provides for complete harmonisation of the fixation, reproduction and distribution rights of performers, phonogram and film producers, broadcasting organisations and cable distributors. This may be deduced from Recital (20) which refers only to Article 8 (Broadcasting and Communication to the Public). The only flexibility with respect to the scope of these rights occurs in Article 10, which enables Member States to provide for certain limitations on the rights, and in the possibility of providing for presumption of transfer of performers' rights; that possibility might be considered as a kind of limitation in a broader sense to performers' rights (Article 2(7), second sentence and Recital (19)). It should be added that, at least for the time being, it is difficult to conceive of any cases of fixation, reproduction and distribution not already covered by the Directive.

However, with respect to the broadcasting and communication rights, Article 8 provides for a minimum protection, as may be seen from Recital (20). Accordingly, Member States may provide for broader protection as regards broadcasting and communication to the public, for example by providing an exclusive right instead of the remuneration right of Article 8(2), or by extending the remuneration right of Article 8(2) to the use of any phonograms, not just commercial ones.[60]

---

[60] For further examples see the comments on Art. 8, pp. 94–98.

Chapter II is without prejudice to the rights of other groups of neighbouring right-owners which are not dealt with at all by Chapter II, such as the rights of publishers of printed works or of organisers of concerts. The Commission has expressly stated this to be the case with respect to publishers of printed works because one Member State insisted on this clarification being made.[61] One should not conclude from this, however, that publishers of printed works are the only group of right-owners to which Chapter II does not apply. Likewise, Recital (20) does not permit such a conclusion because its statement about the minimal nature of Article 8 only refers to the scope of the rights in question, not to the potential right-owners. On the other hand, these are right-owners which are deliberately not allowed to enjoy protection under Chapter II, such as cable distributors or video producers which are not covered by the definitions in Articles 6(2) and (3) and 2(1) respectively.

---

[61] The Commission's statement noted at the Internal Market Council meeting of June 18, 1992 reads: "The Commission states that Chapter II does not apply to publishers of printed works, and that consequently it does not prevent Member States from providing or maintaining in their national law protection of such publishers."

# Article 6. Fixation Right

Article 6 provides for the harmonisation of the fixation right of performers and broadcasting organisations. It contains an indirect definition of "broadcasting organisations."

## 1. ARTICLE 6(1)

*Article 6*

**Fixation right**

1.   Member States shall provide for performers the exclusive right to authorize or prohibit the fixation of their performances.

COMMENTARY

The fixation right of performers was not subject to any criticism or amendment by the European Parliament or by the Council. The fixation of a personal performance represents its first reproduction and is the precursor of all later acts of exploitation. This right is therefore very important, particularly in the war against piracy, such as bootlegging.

For a discussion on the terms "performer" and "performance," see the commentary on Article 2(1).[62]

As in Chapter I of the Directive, the "exclusive right" to authorise or prohibit the fixation of the artist's performance is of the same legal nature as the rights vested in the other groups of rightholders covered by the Directive. It provides a stronger protection than the mere "possibility of preventing" the fixation and other acts as laid down in Article 7 of the Rome Convention. Accordingly, it will not be sufficient for Member States merely to provide protection under criminal law rather than an enforceable right to authorise or prohibit the fixation of the performance; in other words, they must give a statutory civil right of action.

Article 6(1) only covers the first fixation of a personal performance. A fixation of this first fixation represents a reproduction and is covered by Article 7. The fixation right therefore relates only to previously unfixed personal performances. The fixation of a performance means its first fixation on a device from which the performance can repeatedly be reproduced for perception,

---

[62] See p. 45 *et seq.*, above.

such as a phonogram or a film with or without an associated soundtrack. It is irrelevant in terms of the protection whether the performance is given publicly or in a studio.

## 2. ARTICLE 6(2) AND (3)

*Article 6*

...

2.   Member States shall provide for broadcasting organizations the exclusive right to authorize or prohibit the fixation of their broadcasts, whether these broadcasts are transmitted by wire or over the air, including by cable or satellite.

3.   A cable distributor shall not have the right provided for in paragraph 2 where it merely retransmits by cable the broadcasts of broadcasting organizations.

COMMENTARY

The first fixation of a broadcast represents, as in the case of artists' performances, the precursor of all later acts of exploitation; accordingly, it is very important that broadcasting organisations have an exclusive fixation right. Again, Article 6 covers only the first fixation of a broadcast, since the fixation of the first fixation represents a reproduction which is covered by Article 7.

The Commission, in its original proposal, considered that the term "broadcasts" as included broadcasts made via satellites and transmissions by cable services, to the extent that such services made their own broadcasts or programmes in the same way as traditional broadcasting organisations. If such services provided only unaltered and simultaneous retransmissions of received broadcasts, they were considered not to be covered by the proposed Directive. The reasoning behind this distinction was the need to protect broadcasts in general, particularly because of the high organisational, technical and economic expenditure which is necessary for broadcasting own programmes.[63]

The Parliament did not suggest any amendment to the original proposal. In the Council Working Group, certain Member States pointed out that the terms "broadcast" and "broadcasting organisations," at least in the English language, did not cover cable transmissions and cable programme services. They proposed that the Commission's understanding, as laid down in the Explanatory Memorandum, should be expressly mentioned in the text of the Directive. Accordingly, in the course of discussions, the second sentence of the original Article 5 (now 6) was turned into a new paragraph 2 and completed by the words "whether these broadcasts are transmitted by wire or over the air, including by cable or satellite and provided that they are not mere retransmissions of broadcasts of other broadcasting organisations." This solution

---

[63] See the Explanatory Memorandum, para. 5.2, p. 55.

seemed to satisfy all Member States. However, about a year later, one Member State considered that the last part of Article 6(2), beginning with "provided that," would contravene the Rome Convention, which grants broadcasters certain rights with respect to "their broadcasts." According to that Member State, the reference to "their" broadcasts would include rebroadcasts of broadcasts made by another broadcasting organisation. Although this interpretation of the Rome Convention is not the only valid one, the Member State in question stuck to its interpretation and insisted on an amendment of the text. Finally, after the Internal Market Council meeting of May 14, 1992, the section mentioned above was moved to form a new Article 6(3) and restricted to retransmission by cable. Since the Rome Convention does not cover the protection of cable distributors, this provision does not conflict with that Convention. It was accepted by all Member States and became the final text of the Directive.

Both the second half of Article 6(2) and Article 6(3) have to be viewed as an indirect definition of the "broadcasting organisations" in which the rights of Chapter II are vested. In particular, the fixation right is vested in traditional broadcasting organisations, satellite broadcasters and cable distributors. However, cable distributors do not enjoy a fixation right of their own if they "merely retransmit" the broadcasts of other broadcasting organisations. The word "merely" reflects the reasoning behind this exclusion. According to the Member States' deliberations, which followed the Commission's opinion as laid down in the Explanatory Memorandum and referred to section 7(6)(a) of the United Kingdom Copyright, Designs and Patents Act 1988, it was not considered appropriate to grant a proper neighbouring right for cable distributors which only make simultaneous retransmissions of received broadcasts, but cable distributors which make their own programmes enjoy fully the rights of Chapter II.[64]

---

[64] See the Explanatory Memorandum, p. 55.

# Article 7. Reproduction Right

Article 7 provides for an exclusive reproduction right for performers, phonogram and film producers and broadcasting organisations. It makes it clear that this right is transferable.

## ARTICLE 7

*Article 7*

1.   Member States shall provide the exclusive right to authorize or prohibit the direct or indirect reproduction:
- for performers, of fixations of their performances,
- for phonogram producers, of their phonograms,
- for producers of the first fixations of films, in respect of the original and copies of their films, and
- for broadcasting organisations, of fixations of their broadcasts, as set out in Article 6(2).

2.   The reproduction right referred to in paragraph 1 may be transferred, assigned or subject to the granting of contractual licences.

## COMMENTARY

### (a) Legislative background

Since reproduction represents the basic form of material exploitation and is a precondition for material distribution, the Commission considered it an essential component in the war against piracy that all Member States provide an exclusive reproduction right for the main groups of neighbouring rightholders, namely performers, phonogram and film producers and broadcasting organisations. The European Parliament and the Council agreed in principle. The only amendment which was adopted by the Parliament related to the presumption of transfer of the performer's right to the film producer.[65] The Council Working Group discussed, in addition to the question of the presumption of transfer, the question of whether performers should enjoy the reproduction right to the same extent as the other rightholders or whether their right should be limited as set out in Article 7(1)(c) of the Rome Convention. The few Member States which preferred the least protection for performers were, however, asked by the Commission and the other Member

---

[65] See the commentary under Art. 10, pp. 109–110.

States to take into account the fact that most Member States already provided a fuller protection than Article 7(1)(c) and that the Community aims not only at providing minimum rights but at achieving full harmonisation. In addition, it was pointed out that the intention was to achieve a high level of protection across the Community rather than protection on the level of the lowest common denominator, in particular regarding the protection afforded to performers whose legal position has often been neglected compared to other rightholders.

## (b) Rightholders and the subject matter protected

With respect to the rightholders and the subject matter protected, reference is made to the commentary on Article 2(1)[66] and with respect to broadcasting organisations and their broadcasts, reference is made to the commentary on Article 6(2) and (3).[67] That commentary concluded that the reference to Article 6(2) in Article 7(1) fourth indent should be read as referring to Article 6(3) as well. This may be gleaned from the fact that the former Article 6(2), which for a long time during the discussions contained the entire indirect definition of broadcasting organisations, was split up into the separate Articles 6(2) and 6(3) only at a very late stage, namely after the Internal Market Council meeting of May 14, 1992. The reference in Article 7 to the old Article 6(2) has erroneously not been extended to the new Article 6(3). This is confirmed by the fact that it would not be logical to provide for a definition of a rightholder with respect to a specific right, such as the fixation right, but not with respect to other rights. Accordingly, a broadcasting organisation will enjoy the reproduction right, whether its broadcasts are transmitted by wire or over the air, including by cable or satellite; it will, however, not enjoy the reproduction right if it is a cable distributor who merely retransmits the broadcasts of other broadcasting organisations.[68]

## (c) Reproduction

The term "direct ... reproduction," which is also used in Article 10 of the Rome Convention, means reproducing a recording onto the same or a different medium. The main examples are the re-pressing of a phonogram or the reproduction on one film of a performance which has already been recorded on another film, or even the reproduction on a phonogram of a performance which has been recorded on the soundtrack of a film. The term "indirect reproduction" (which is also used in Article 10 of the Rome Convention) means, for example as regards a phonogram, the recording of a broadcast which itself has been made on the basis of a phonogram.

The "reproduction" of any protected subject matter under Article 7 includes the reproduction of part thereof, such as a part of the fixation of a performance or of a phonogram. Accordingly, any person who wants to

---

[66] See pp. 45 *et seq.*, above.
[67] See pp. 87–88, above.
[68] See further comments under the commentary on Art. 6(2) and (3), pp. 87–88, above.

reproduce a song from a protected phonogram for the purposes of the production of a film will need the authorisation of the performer and the phonogram producer (as well as that of the composer). The term "reproduction" also includes reproduction in another format, such as the reproduction of a cinema film on a video cassette or as a film in television format.

Although Article 7 provides for the reproduction right as an exclusive right, this does not prevent Member States from introducing a remuneration right for private copying, as may be seen from Article 10(1)(a) and from the clarification in Article 10(3) of the Directive.

Article 7(2) was added for the purposes of clarification and for consistency with the provisions of Chapter I, to which the same clause had previously been added. It will have to be construed in the same way as Article 2(4).[69]

---

[69] See Art. 2(4) and the comments thereon, pp. 53–54, above.

# Article 8. Broadcasting and Communication to the Public

Article 8 provides for the harmonisation of certain rights with respect to broadcasting and communication to the public for performers, phonogram producers and broadcasting organisations.

Recital (20)

*Recital*

(20) Whereas Member States may provide for more far-reaching protection for owners of rights related to copyright than that required by Article 8 of this Directive;

## 1. General remarks on Article 8 and Recital (20)

### (a) Legislative background

This Article was not part of the original Commission proposal which was limited, in line with Chapter 2 of the Green Paper, to rights of material exploitation, such as reproduction and distribution. Article 8 was introduced as a result of proposals by the European Parliament and the Council Working Group and it was endorsed by the Commission's amended proposal, bearing in mind the lack of progress on the proposal for a Decision of the Council that Member States should adhere to the Berne and Rome Conventions.

Article 8 largely follows the equivalent provisions of the Rome Convention,[70] but provides better protection in several respects. Since the level of protection with respect to broadcasting and communication to the public varies to a considerable extent in different Member States and no consensus on a harmonised level of protection was possible, it was agreed that the rights of broadcasting and communication to the public laid down in Article 8 are

---

[70] Art. 7(1)(a), Art. 12, and Art. 13(a) and (d) of the Rome Convention.

minimum rights and that Member States may provide for wider protection. Examples will be given in the commentaries on the relevant provisions below.

## (b) The cable and satellite proposal

The proposal made by the European Parliament and the Commission's amended proposal (Article 6bis which later became Article 8) contained an additional Article 8(4), according to which the provisions of Article 8 should be without prejudice to the provisions of the proposed cable and satellite Directive,[71] which provided for the harmonisation of satellite broadcasting rights. It subsequently became clear that the rental Directive would be adopted before the proposal on cable and satellite broadcasting and therefore would govern the harmonisation of the rights (and limitations thereon, including possible presumptions of transfer) of broadcasting and communication to the public, including satellite broadcasting. Consequently, Article 8(4) was no longer necessary and was deleted. However, in order to make it clear that a specific issue dealt with by the cable and satellite proposal, namely the definition of "communication to the public by satellite," should be governed by the future cable and satellite Directive, the Council and the Commission made a common statement[72] to the effect that Article 8 is without prejudice to the corresponding provisions of that Directive. In the end, the Commission's amended proposal for the cable and satellite Directive replaced the original provisions on the minimum harmonisation of certain neighbouring rights with a reference to the corresponding provisions under the rental Directive. Accordingly, Article 8 and Recital (20) govern the harmonisation of the broadcasting (including satellite broadcasting) and communication rights of performers, phonogram producers and broadcasting organisations, whereas the cable and satellite Directive will deal with the definition of "communication to the public by satellite."

## (c) The terms used and other general remarks

As far as the terms "performer," "exclusive right" and "phonogram producer" are concerned, as well as the possibility of providing for presumptions of transfer of rights, the reader is referred to the relevant comments above.[73]

Article 8 does not deal with the rights of film producers at all. Hence, Member States are free to grant broadcasting and communication rights to film

---

[71] Proposal for a Council Directive on the coordination of certain rules concerning copyright and neighbouring rights applicable to satellite broadcasting and cable retransmission, COM(91) 276 final – SYN 358.

[72] The statement was noted at the Internal Market Council meeting of June 18, 1992. It reads: "The Council and the Commission agree that the provisions of Article 8 are without prejudice to those provisions of Council Directive ... /EEC of ... on the coordination of certain rules concerning copyright and related rights applicable to satellite broadcasting and retransmission by cable which provide for performing artists and producers of phonograms the right of communication to the public by satellite, and for broadcasting organizations the right of simultaneous retransmission of their broadcasts by satellite."

[73] See pp. 48, 33–34, 109 et seq.

producers. The fact that Article 8, unlike Articles 7 and 9, does not contain any provision on the transferability of the rights, does not mean that the rights under Article 8 are not transferable. Articles 7(2) and 9(4) were introduced in order to be consistent with Article 2(4), which itself was introduced only for clarification. When, later, Article 8 was included in the proposal, the issue of transferability had ceased to be discussed and did not get included in the Article. Member States did not want to provide for the non-transferability of the rights of Article 8 and so this issue is governed by national law, as may be seen from the comments on Article 2(4).[74]

The Directive does not give any definition of the phrase "communication to the public." Accordingly, the national laws of Member States apply, but since Article 8 largely follows the equivalent provisions of the Rome Convention, that Convention may help interpretation. Examples of "communication to the public" will be mentioned in the context of the commentary on each paragraph of Article 8.

## 2. ARTICLE 8(1)

*Article 8*

### Broadcasting and communication to the public

1.   Member States shall provide for performers the exclusive right to authorize or prohibit the broadcasting by wireless means and the communication to the public of their performances, except where the performance is itself already a broadcast performance or is made from a fixation.

. . .

COMMENTARY

### (a) Broadcasting by wireless means or by wire (cable)

On the whole, there was little discussion on Article 8(1) during the legislative procedure. The main controversial issues were whether the broadcasting right should include broadcasting by cable (cable distribution) and whether the rights of Article 8(1) should be recognised only in respect of live performances. The European Parliament, in the proposal submitted at first reading, did not restrict the broadcasting right to broadcasting by wireless means and a number of Member States wanted to include cable distribution. The Commission, as may be seen from its amended proposal, preferred limiting the right to broadcasting by wireless means in order to avoid any conflict with the proposed Directive on satellite broadcasting and cable retransmission.

Since Article 8(1) provides only for a minimum level of protection, Member States may also allow performers an exclusive right to broadcast by cable, as

---

[74] See p. 53 *et seq.*, above.

long as the provisions of the proposed Directive on satellite broadcasting and cable retransmission are respected. Given the fact that the technical means of broadcasting – whether wireless or by cable – may not justify a different regime, it would be preferable to provide for an exclusive broadcasting right which covers broadcasting by wireless means as well as by cable.

### (b) Live performances

One proposal made, but not adopted, in the European Parliament in connection with this provision did not restrict the broadcasting and communication rights to live performances. Similarly, some Member States were opposed to this restriction, which was nevertheless passed by the European Parliament and adopted in the Commission's amended proposal. No consensus was ever reached between the Member States on the deletion of the restriction to live performances.

Since Article 8(1) contains minimum rights, Member States are free to grant performers an exclusive right of broadcasting and of communication to the public, even where the performances are not live performances but have already been broadcast or are fixations of performances. From a commercial point of view, such a right would be relevant in particular in the case of a music video from which a broadcast or communication to the public is made. Under the minimum protection of Article 8(1) the performers would not be entitled to prohibit the broadcasting or communication to the public of such a music video and thus would be deprived of the revenues from an essential form of exploitation.

The restriction to live performances, given in the second half of Article 8(1) (beginning with the word "except") also means that the performer does not have any right to prevent the *repeated broadcasting* of the first broadcast made from his personal performance, because the performance would then already be a broadcast performance and, in addition, the repeated broadcast would necessarily have to be made from the fixation of the first broadcast. The same is true for the *rebroadcasting* of the first broadcast made from a personal performance. Similarly, the performer may not prohibit the communication to the public of his broadcast performance or the fixation of his performance, for example the public playing or showing of a pre-recorded video cassette or sound recording or of a broadcast which has been recorded on tape or video cassette. The public playing or showing may be made, for example, via a loud speaker and a screen from the room where the performance takes place to another room, in order to enable a larger audience to attend the performance. Accordingly, the minimum right of Article 8(1) covers only the broadcasting and communication to the public of the personal performance which has not (yet) been broadcast or fixed (recorded).

### (c) Satellite broadcasting

Article 8(1) includes the exclusive right to broadcast the live performance by satellite, since satellite broadcasting represents a form of broadcasting by wireless means. The fact that Article 8, as opposed to Article 6(2), does not expressly mention the word "satellite," does not mean that Article 8 does not cover satellite broadcasting. The Member States did not want to exclude satellite broadcasting; if they had, they would have excluded it expressly, as they did in respect of broadcasting by cable by limiting the right to "broadcasting by wireless means."

## 3. Article 8(2)

*Article 8*

...

2. Member States shall provide a right in order to ensure that a single equitable remuneration is paid by the user, if a phonogram published for commercial purposes, or a reproduction of such phonogram, is used for broadcasting by wireless means or for any communication to the public, and to ensure that this remuneration is shared between the relevant performers and phonogram producers. Member States may, in the absence of agreement between the performers and phonogram producers, lay down the conditions as to the sharing of this remuneration between them.

...

### Commentary

#### (a) General

Article 8(2) provides for a remuneration right for performers and phonogram producers in the situation where a broadcast is made on the basis of a commercial phonogram or where a commercial phonogram is publicly played or otherwise communicated to the public. This provision gives a wider protection than Article 12 of the Rome Convention, since (1) it does not, unlike Article 16(1)(a) of the Rome Convention, allow any reservations on its application, at least as far as citizens of the Community are concerned, (2) it obliges Member States to provide the remuneration right *both* for phonogram producers *and* performers and (3) it covers not only direct use, but also indirect use, for broadcasting and for any communication to the public.

#### (b) Phonogram published for commercial purposes and its reproduction

"Phonograms published for commercial purposes" within the meaning of Article 8(2) are all kinds of sound recordings which have been published in order to be exploited in the market place, such as pre-recorded music cassettes, LPs and compact discs. "Reproductions" of such phonograms are any copies thereof, in particular private recordings onto tape from pre-recorded cassettes, LPs or compact discs. Other sound recordings, which are not covered by Article 8(2), include recordings made by broadcasting organisations in their recording studios and which are not put on the market but are used for repeat broadcasts. Likewise, Article 8(2) does not cover unpublished phonograms, such as phonograms which have been made by a music group for mere documentation purposes or for distribution as a gift to friends. Other important examples of items not covered by Article 8(2) are visual and sound recordings, such as videograms; accordingly, no remuneration is due under Article 8(2) for broadcasting on the basis of a videogram or for the public showing of such a videogram. Since Article 8(2) provides only minimum protection, Member States may extend the remuneration right to these cases as well as to other similar situations.

### (c) Satellite and cable broadcasting

Broadcasting by cable is not covered by Article 8(2), the wording of which refers expressly to broadcasting "by wireless means" only. Again, however, Article 8(2) provides minimum protection, so that Member States are free to extend the remuneration right to cable broadcasting.

As in Article 8(1), satellite broadcasting is covered by Article 8(2).[75]

### (d) Remuneration right/exclusive right

Since Article 8(2) sets out only the minimum protection, it allows Member States to provide even greater protection by means of an exclusive right.

### (e) Direct and indirect use for broadcasting and public communication

Although several earlier versions drafted in the course of the discussions in the Council Working Group included, after the words "is used", the words "directly or indirectly," these words have disappeared in the final version, as Member States thought it unnecessary to spell out the two forms of "direct" and "indirect" use.

The main example of the direct use of a phonogram for broadcasting is where a broadcast is made directly on the basis of a phonogram. The direct communication of a phonogram to the public is the public playing of a phonogram, for example in a restaurant, supermarket, underground station, discotheque or other public place.

The main example of the indirect use of a phonogram for broadcasting is where a phonogram is used for a broadcast and the broadcast is rebroadcast by another station. Accordingly, Article 8(2) includes a remuneration right for the rebroadcasting of a broadcast made on the basis of a phonogram. The indirect use of a phonogram for public communication occurs, for example, when a broadcast, which has been made on the basis of a phonogram, is communicated to the public by being shown or played in a restaurant, bar, or any other place where it is shown on television or played by radio to the public.

---

[75] See the comments on Art. 8(1), pp. 95–96.

### (f) Single equitable remuneration

Article 8(2) provides, following Article 12 of the Rome Convention, that the user has to pay a single remuneration only, which then has to be shared between two groups of beneficiaries. This wording has been included to help the broadcasting organisation or other user who will be obliged to pay only once. The Member States have several means of implementation. They may provide that (1) the payment has to be made to performers and producers jointly; this applies where performers and producers are represented by a common body or representative, as for example in the case of the German collecting society GVL; or (2) the payment has to be made to performers, who are then obliged to pay a share to the producers; or (3) the payment has to be made to the producers, who are then required to pay a share to the performers. As far as options (2) and (3) are concerned, Member States will have to ensure that the group of rightholders which receives the remuneration is fully accountable to the other group.

Article 8(2) refers only to the payment of a single remuneration and does not include any provision dealing with the question of whether the negotiation with the users on the remuneration must also be restricted to one group of right-owners. Since Article 8(2) provides, unlike Article 12 of the Rome Convention, for a remuneration right for both performers and producers, it would be in line with the spirit of the Article if both groups of right-owners were allowed to join in the negotiations with the user.

As in Article 12 of the Rome Convention, the word "equitable" has not been defined. This word may be dealt with in detail by national laws, or its interpretation may be left to the courts.

### (g) The sharing of the remuneration

The second sentence of Article 8(2) allows Member States to lay down the conditions as to the sharing of the remuneration between performers and producers, when this has not already been agreed. This provision has been taken from Article 12 of the Rome Convention. Since the respective international organisations of phonogram producers and performers have agreed on an equal sharing of this remuneration, there will in practice be no need for further legislation by Member States.

## 4. ARTICLE 8(3)

*Article 8*

...

3. Member States shall provide for broadcasting organizations the exclusive right to authorize or prohibit the rebroadcasting of their broadcasts by wireless means, as well as the communication to the public of their broadcasts if such communication is made in places accessible to the public against payment of an entrance fee.

COMMENTARY

Article 8(3) provides for the exclusive rights of rebroadcasting and communication to the public for broadcasting organisations.

## (a) Broadcasting organisations

"Broadcasting organisations" within the meaning of Article 8(3) include organisations broadcasting over the air, satellite broadcasters, and cable distributors which do not merely simultaneously retransmit by cable the broadcasts of other broadcasting organisations. This follows from Article 6(2) and (3), which contain an indirect definition of broadcasting organisations. The definition applies to the whole Directive, even if this is not immediately obvious. It is true that Article 8(3), unlike Articles 7(1) fourth indent and 9(1) fourth indent, does not refer to this definition[76]; this may be explained by the fact that the rights of broadcasting organisations were introduced into the proposal at a time when the references to the definition in Article 6 had already been included in Articles 7 and 9 and were no longer being discussed. Accordingly, it must be assumed that the definition in Article 6(2) and (3) is also valid in the context of Article 8(3). This is confirmed by the fact that it would not make sense, under any law or Directive, to provide several rights for a particular group of right-owners, such as broadcasting organisations, but to define that group only in respect of some of the rights in question. Furthermore, if the definitions in Article 6(2) and (3) were not to apply, cable distributors would not be granted the rights of rebroadcasting and communication to the public at all, since the word "broadcasting" does not in itself, at least in the English language, cover cable distribution.[77]

## (b) Rebroadcasting

Since Article 8(3) was modelled on the equivalent provisions of the Rome Convention,[78] the "rebroadcasting" of a broadcast includes only the simultaneous broadcasting by one broadcasting organisation of the broadcast of another. Protection against deferred retransmission is given by the fixation right under Article 6(2), since the broadcast must be fixed before such a retransmission can take place.

"Rebroadcasting" under Article 8(3) does not cover any retransmission by wire or cable but only rebroadcasting by wireless means, in particular by satellite or some other means over the air. Again, the fact that satellite is expressly mentioned in Article 6(2) but not in Article 8(3) does not mean that transmission by satellite is not included in that provision.[79]

Accordingly, under Article 8(3) a traditional broadcasting organisation, a satellite broadcaster or a cable distributor must be given the exclusive right to

---

[76] See, however, the comments on the incompleteness of these references, pp. 89–91, 102.
[77] See the comments on Art. 6(2) and (3) for the definition of a broadcasting organization within the meaning of Art. 8(3), p. 88.
[78] Art. 13(a) and Art. 3(d) of the Rome Convention.
[79] See the comments on Art. 8(1), pp. 95–96.

prevent another broadcasting organisation from simultaneously broadcasting over the air, (by satellite or otherwise), their broadcasts, satellite broadcasts and cable programs (as long as the cable programs themselves have not merely been simultaneously retransmitted).[80]

Since Article 8(3) sets out only the minimum protection, Member States may extend this protection, for example to retransmission by cable or non-simultaneous rebroadcasting by another broadcaster, *i.e.* deferred retransmission; in the last example, protection against deferred retransmission by another broadcaster would be ensured both by the fixation right and by a separate rebroadcasting right.

### (c) Communication to the public

Under Article 8(3), broadcasting organisations within the meaning of Article 6(2) and (3) have the right to prohibit the public showing, playing or other communication to the public of their television or radio broadcasts, if this communication is made in places accessible to the public against payment of an entrance fee. The last condition originates in Article 13(d) of the Rome Convention and refers to the time when few households had their own television sets and broadcasts of sports events or plays were often communicated in public places against payment of an entrance fee.

This situation is rare these days and so the European Parliament at first reading proposed granting broadcasting organisations the rebroadcasting right, but not the right of communication to the public. In the Council Working Group, several Member States preferred a limited communication right, as found in Article 13(d) of the Rome Convention, but others were in favour of a broader right. In the end, a majority of Member States decided that it was not appropriate to grant broadcasting organisations a broad exclusive right to prohibit the public showing or playing of their broadcasts. Thus, the communication right was limited to the situation covered by Article 13(d) of the Rome convention.

Since Article 8(3) lays down only the minimum protection, Member States are free to grant a communication right without the condition that the communication be made in places accessible to the public against payment of an entrance fee. Such a broader right would cover, in particular, the showing or playing of television or radio broadcasts in bars, restaurants, supermarkets and so on.

The Council Working Group also discussed the question of whether the communication right should be restricted to television broadcasts, as it is in Article 13(d) of the Rome Convention. The Member States eventually decided also to include radio broadcasts and so the restriction to television broadcasts contained in the Commission's amended proposal was deleted.

---

[80] See Art. 6(3).

# Article 9. Distribution Right

Article 9 provides for an exclusive distribution right, and its exhaustion, for performers, phonogram and film producers and broadcasting organisations. It makes it clear that the right is transferable.

## 1. ARTICLE 9(1) AND (3)

*Article 9*

**Distribution right**

1.   Member States shall provide
- for performers, in respect of fixations of their performances,
- for phonogram producers, in respect of their phonograms,
- for producers of the first fixations of films, in respect of the original and copies of their films,
- for broadcasting organizations, in respect of fixations of their broadcasts as set out in Article 6(2),

the exclusive right to make available these objects, including copies thereof, to the public by sale or otherwise, hereafter referred to as the "distribution right."

...

3.   The distribution right shall be without prejudice to the specific provisions of Chapter I, in particular Article 1(4).

...

COMMENTARY

### (a) Legislative background

The Commission's original proposal was not called into question by the Parliament or the Council. It provided for an exclusive distribution right for performers, phonogram and film producers and broadcasting organisations and reaffirmed the European Court's rule of exhaustion based on Community law. The European Parliament adopted only one amendment which related to the presumption of transfer of performers' rights to film producers; this is dealt with under the commentary on Article 10.[81] In the Council Working

---

[81] See p. 110.

Group, a few minor problems arose which were solved without a major debate. In particular, one or two Member States were not inclined to recognise a distribution right for performers. However, the neglect of this group of important contributors to cultural productions would not have been justified, and the majority of the Member States, following the Commission's reasoning, considered the recognition of a distribution right for performers to be essential, not only in terms of the fight against piracy, but also with a view to providing equal treatment for all contributors to sound recordings, films and broadcasts.

### (b) Objects

The wording "their respective subject matter" in the Commission's original proposal has been replaced by "these objects, including copies thereof." This change has not altered the meaning. A performer still has the exclusive right to distribute the fixations of his performance, such as compact discs, the soundtrack of a film, the tape on which his musical or other performance has been recorded by a broadcasting organisation, or a video cassette showing his performance as an actor. Such fixations include the first fixation and all copies thereof. This was already clear in the Commission's original proposal. Similar considerations apply to phonogram producers, who have the exclusive right to distribute their music tapes, compact discs and so on, as well as to film producers and broadcasting organisations. The word "objects" seems to be even more precise than the word "subject matter," since the protected subject matter is the performance, the phonogram, the film and the broadcast, whereas the distribution right exists in respect of the objects incorporating the intangible subject matter, namely the fixations of the performances, broadcasts, phonograms and films.

### (c) Rightholders and protected subject matter; the exclusive right

For explanations on the rightholders and their protected subject matter see the relevant comments under Article 2(1)[82] and, with respect to broadcasting organisations and broadcasts, under Article 6(2) and (3)[83]; for the fact that the reference to Article 6(2) has to be read as a reference to Article 6(2) and (3), see the commentary on Article 7.[84] Accordingly, cable distributors which merely retransmit broadcasts of other broadcasting organisations do not enjoy the distribution right.

The fact that Article 9 uses the phrase "the exclusive right" without adding the words "to authorise or prohibit" and thus reads differently from Articles 2, 6, 7 and 8, does not signify any difference in meaning. It is simply a question of syntax.

---

[82] See p. 45 *et seq.*
[83] See p. 87.
[84] See pp. 89–91.

## (d) Distribution to the public

The phrase "to the public" has deliberately not been defined, since international experience has shown the problems of finding an appropriate definition. Moreover, the word "public" is often used in connection with various aspects of national copyright laws and not only with respect to the distribution right. Given the lack of definition, Member States are free to determine the meaning of the word "public." As the purpose of the Directive is to secure a high level of protection, the word "public" should be understood in a broad sense, excluding only acts of distribution such as private gifts which are made within a group of personally connected persons, such as between friends.

## (e) By sale or otherwise

The Commission's original proposal defined the distribution right as the exclusive right "to make available, *for an unlimited period of time*, ... by sale or otherwise." The words "for an unlimited period of time" excluded other forms of distribution, such as rental and lending. These forms of distribution are characterised by the fact that objects are made available for a limited period of time and therefore must be returned, whereas objects under the provision of the distribution right were meant to be made available without a time limitation (for example by sale).

Some Member States, although not against the idea in theory, thought that the expression "for an unlimited period of time" might be ambiguous, in so far as it could be deemed to allude to the duration of the right itself. It was agreed that these words should be deleted, so that the wording covered all forms of making available, including rental and lending. Consequently, it was necessary to ensure that the provisions on the distribution right, including its exhaustion, would not adversely affect the provisions dealing with the rental and lending rights. Accordingly, a new Article 9(3) was added in order to make it clear that the distribution right was without prejudice to the rental and lending rights; the express reference to Article 1(4) means that, in particular, the exhaustion of the distribution right does not affect the continuation of the rental and lending rights. For example, when a phonogram is sold in the Community by, or with the consent of, the rightholder and the distribution right has been exhausted, his exclusive rental and lending rights under Article 1 with respect to that particular phonogram continue to exist.

Since the omission of the words "for an unlimited period of time" was not intended to change the scope of the distribution right, it will still be possible for a Member State to provide separate rights for rental and lending on the one hand, and for distribution in a narrow sense on the other. It was not intended to lay down how Member States shape the legal structure of the distribution right in relation to the rental and lending rights. It may be expected, however, that most Member States will adopt the most commonly accepted solution, under which the distribution right covers rental and lending, and its exhaustion is without prejudice to the continued existence of the rental and lending rights.[85]

---

[85] See also the comments on Art. 1(4), p. 43.

## 2. ARTICLE 9(2)

*Article 9*

...

2. The distribution right shall not be exhausted within the Community in respect of an object as referred to in paragraph 1, except where the first sale in the Community of that object is made by the rightholder or with his consent.[86]

...

## COMMENTARY

### (a) Legislative background

The Commission's original proposal reflected the established jurisprudence of the Court of Justice of the European Communities, according to which the first putting into circulation of copies of works within the Community by the rightholder, or with his consent, results in the Community-wide exhaustion[87] of the distribution right with respect to those copies. This rule, which applies also to the distribution right of neighbouring rightholders, is based on Articles 30 *et seq.* and 36 of the EEC Treaty and resolves the conflict between a national, exclusive right on the one hand, and the aim of the free movement of goods within the Community on the other. Article 7(2) of the original proposal, and the version of it which was finally adopted as Article 9(2), guarantee that the distribution right will not create new barriers to trade in the Internal Market. The wording of Article 9(2) has been changed as a result of a proposal by one Member State, which wanted to bring the wording closer to that of Article 4(c) of the Directive on the legal protection of computer programs. The text has not, however, been copied word for word.

### (b) Community exhaustion[88]

The main example of the application of Article 9(2) is as follows. The holder of, for example, all rights with respect to a phonogram (he may be a phonogram producer to whom the composer of the music and the musicians

---

[86] When the Treaty on the European Economic Area (EEA) comes into force, the E.C. rules on free movement of goods and exhaustion of distribution rights will apply throughout the EEA, and the relevant EFTA countries will have to implement the existing Community law ("*acquis communautaire*") relating to the single market. Thus, when the EEA treaty is in force, the word "Community" in this paragraph (and in the Commentary below) will have to be read as extending to the whole EEA. Equally, references to "Member States" in the following Commentary will have to be read as including all EEA Member States.

[87] See n. 86, above.

[88] See n. 86, above.

have assigned their distribution rights), or the rightholder's licensee, has sold a certain copy of a phonogram within the Community for the first time. In this case – and only in this case – the distribution rights of the phonogram producer, the composer and the musicians are exhausted within the Community in respect of the particular copy of the phonogram. This means that these rightholders are no longer able to prohibit, on the basis of an exclusive right, its further distribution within the Community (except by way of rental and, possibly, lending).

### (c) International exhaustion

Article 9(2) does not expressly address "international exhaustion." Nevertheless, Member States[89] are prohibited under this paragraph from applying international exhaustion. Consequently, a Member State may not provide that the first sale in any country outside the Community[90] results in the exhaustion of the distribution right within its territory (and thus within the Community).

This follows from the wording ("except where") which only allows for *one* type of exhaustion: it occurs *only* where an object has been first sold in the Community with the consent of the rightholder, but not in other situations, such as the situation where an object is first sold outside the Community. No different interpretation is possible. Under the Directive, Member States are not allowed to introduce further exceptions other than those explicitly stated. International exhaustion would be an additional exception which is consequently not allowed.

This prohibition follows on from Article 9(1) which would be of little significance if a Member State could allow for the exhaustion of the distribution right within the Community once an object has been put into circulation with the consent of the rightholder anywhere in the world. The purpose of Article 9(1) is to harmonise the distribution right by providing that right-owners must be entitled to prohibit distribution within the Community at least once, namely before the Community exhaustion (see (b) above) applies. International exhaustion would undermine the harmonisation of the distribution right in the Community.

In summary, where an object has been first sold within the Community by or with the consent of the rightholder, intra-Community exhaustion applies. Where an object has been first sold outside the Community (by or with the consent of the rightholder) no exhaustion applies to the right within the Community; hence, the distribution right within the Community continues to exist.

---

[89] See n. 86, above.
[90] See n. 86, above.

## 3. Article 9(4)

*Article 9*

...

4.   The distribution right may be transferred, assigned or subject to the granting of contractual licences.

### Commentary

Reference is made to the comments on Article 2(4) and Article 7(2).[91]

---

[91] See pp. 53, 91, above.

# Article 10. Limitations to Rights; and Recital (19): Presumption of Transfer

Article 10 lays down the possible limitations to the rights referred to in Chapter II of the Directive. Recital (19) deals with possible presumptions of transfer in respect of the rights in Chapter II; since presumptions of transfer may be thought of as a form of limitation on the respective rights, Recital (19) is commented on at the end of the comments on Article 10.

## 1. ARTICLE 10

*Article 10*

### Limitations to rights

1.   Member States may provide for limitations to the rights referred to in Chapter II in respect of:

(a)   private use;
(b)   use of short excerpts in connection with the reporting of current events;
(c)   ephemeral fixation by a broadcasting organization by means of its own facilities and for its own broadcasts;
(d)   use solely for the purposes of teaching or scientific research.

2.   Irrespective of paragraph 1, any Member State may provide for the same kinds of limitations with regard to the protection of performers, producers of phonograms, broadcasting organisations and of producers of the first fixations of films, as it provides for in connection with the protection of copyright in literary and artistic works. However, compulsory licences may be provided for only to the extent to which they are compatible with the Rome Convention.

3.   Paragraph 1(a) shall be without prejudice to any existing or future legislation on remuneration for reproduction for private use.

### COMMENTARY

Article 10 was modelled on Article 15 of the Rome Convention and contains the limitations which Member States are allowed to impose with respect to the rights of fixation, reproduction, broadcasting, communication to the public and distribution of performers, phonogram and film producers and broadcasting organisations, as set out in Articles 6 to 9 of the Directive. These limitations do not have to be imposed; however, broader limitations would not comply with the Article.[92] A closer harmonisation of the limitations to the neighbouring rights of Chapter II did not seem to be appropriate at the time and would probably have caused a number of new fundamental problems, thus delaying the adoption of the Directive. Since the text of Article 10 in the Commission's original proposal followed the wording of Article 15 of the Rome Convention, neither the Parliament nor the Council Working Group proposed any amendments. There were also very few comments by Member States on its provisions, so that this Article will have to be interpreted in a similar way to Article 15 (Rome). A few basic remarks and examples will therefore suffice as a comment.

### (a) Article 10(1)(a)

The private copying of audiovisual material is an example of the situation envisaged under Article 10(1)(a). Member States may provide that the exclusive reproduction rights of performers, phonogram and film producers and broadcasting organisations do not cover home taping (reproduction for private use) or that home taping is legally licensed and therefore may be undertaken without the consent of the right-owners. At the same time, the possibility of limiting the exclusive reproduction right does not prevent Member States from providing for a remuneration right for home taping, as has been made clear in Article 10(3). The limitation of the exclusive right to a remuneration right is also possible in all the other cases in which limitations are allowed under Article 10.

### (b) Article 10(1)(b)

An example of an Article 10(1)(b) situation is the broadcasting of a short excerpt from the performance of an opera within a television program on recent, or forthcoming, cultural events in an area.

### (c) Article 10(1)(c)

Article 10(1)(c) takes account of the current practice of broadcasting organisations, which do not usually broadcast live but from tapes which they produce for the purpose of broadcasting. Even a broadcast made on the basis of a phonogram is often made from a reproduction of that phonogram on a tape made for the purpose of broadcasting. Member States may allow such fixations made by a broadcasting organisation in its own facilities and for its own purposes only when they are made for a limited period of time and subsequently erased.

---

[92] See, however, the express possibility of providing for presumptions of transfer in Recital (19) p. 110 *et seq.*, below.

**(d) Article 10(1)(d)**

Examples of acts of exploitation which may be permitted under Article 10(1)(d) are the fixation or reproduction of a broadcast by an educational establishment for educational purposes and the reproduction of a film in order to replace an old copy in an archive collection.

**(e) Article 10(2)**

Article 10(2) allows Member States to provide for the same limitations in respect of neighbouring rights dealt with in Chapter II as they provide in respect of authors' rights.[93] The laws of the Member States already largely contain, as regards the limitations on neighbouring rights, references to the limitations provided in respect of authors' rights in their own laws. The second sentence of Article 10(2) also has to be understood in the same way as Article 15(2), second sentence, of the Rome Convention. In particular, compulsory licences are allowed under the provisions of Article 7(2) and Article 13(d) of the Rome Convention.

## 2. THE PRESUMPTION OF TRANSFER OF RIGHTS ADDRESSED IN RECITAL (19) (FIRST PART)

## RECITAL (19) (FIRST PART)

*Recital*

(19) Whereas the provisions of Chapter II do not prevent Member States from extending the presumption set out in Article 2(5) to the exclusive rights included in that Chapter; ...

COMMENTARY

**(a) Legislative Background**

The possibility of providing for a presumption of transfer was one of the main issues discussed in the course of the legislative procedure, not only with respect to the rental right, but also with respect to the exclusive rights provided for in Chapter II. The original Commission proposal had not included any presumption of transfer but the European Parliament proposed, with respect to the reproduction and distribution rights, the same kind of presumption as it had proposed with respect to the rental right, namely a rebuttable presumption of transfer of the performer's right to the film producer, without prejudice to the remuneration right under Article 4 (Article 3 of the original

---

[93] In this context, a statement made by the Commission and noted at the Internal Market Council meeting of June 18, 1992 with a view to safeguarding Art. 2(7) is worth mentioning: "The Commission considers that Article 10(2) is without prejudice to the provisions of Article 2(7)."

proposal). The Commission, in its amended proposal, endorsed the idea of a rebuttable presumption of transfer which would be subject to the *mutatis mutandis* application of the remuneration right under Article 4.

In the Council Working Group, many Member States were opposed to the mandatory imposition of such a presumption; some did not want to include any presumption of transfer in Chapter II of the Directive, while others preferred different kinds of presumptions. As an initial compromise, the group agreed to delete the presumptions from the Articles on the reproduction and distribution rights, and to include the possibility of a rebuttable presumption in respect of the rights of Chapter II in a new recital. Eventually, a compromise was reached involving the acceptance of the potential weakening of the performer's protection under the new Article 2(7) as against the reinforcement of the performer's protection in Recital (19); the rebuttable presumption in that Recital was replaced by a reference to the presumption as set out in Article 2(5).

### (b) The Reference to Article 2(5)

This means that the whole of Article 2(5) has to be applied to any presumption of transfer which a Member State might provide, in respect of any exclusive right of a performer under Chapter II, in his relationship with a film producer. Since Article 2(5) itself, as well as Article 4 referred to in it, are directly applicable only to the rental right, it is clear that the extension of the presumption set out in Article 2(5) to the exclusive rights included in Chapter II, as provided for in Recital (19), necessarily entails the application of Article 2(5), including the reference to Article 4, by analogy (*mutatis mutandis*). Otherwise, the amendment made to Recital (19) in the context of the final compromise mentioned above would be inconsistent with its purpose and meaningless. This is confirmed by the Council's comments to the European Parliament on the Common Position,[94] according to which Recital (19) reflects the substance of Amendment Nos. 19 and 21 of the European Parliament. These amendments refer to the presumption of transfer of the rental right, a rebuttable presumption linked to the equitable remuneration right of Article 4, and expressly state that the Article containing this presumption "applies accordingly" in the case of the reproduction and distribution rights.

### (c) Alternatives for Implementation

Leaving aside Article 2(7), which is based on the legal position in one particular Member State,[95] and the second part of Recital (19), which is commented on below,[96] the alternative ways of providing for a presumption of

---

[94] Document dated June 30, 1992, p. 8.
[95] See the comments on Art. 2(5), (6) and (7), pp. 56 60, 61 above, and p. 111, below.
[96] See p. 112 *et seq.*

transfer with respect to the rights under Chapter II are as follows: (1) Member States may refrain from providing any presumption of transfer with respect to the rights under Chapter II. (2) If Member States intend to provide for a presumption, they are bound to provide for a presumption as set out in Article 2(5), namely a presumption which is notable for its rebuttable nature and for the condition of equitable remuneration for the exploitation of the respective right. This means that Article 2(5), and Article 4, apply *mutatis mutandis* to any presumption of transfer which a Member State may provide with respect to any right covered by Chapter II.

Accordingly, a presumption of transfer may be provided for only in a situation where a contract concerning film production is concluded, individually or collectively, by a performer with a film producer.[97] The presumption may refer to the performer's exclusive rights of fixation, reproduction, broadcasting, communication to the public and distribution. Member States may provide for such a presumption only under the two conditions mentioned in Article 2(5), namely (1) the presumption must be subject to contractual clauses to the contrary—thus, it is a rebuttable presumption and the performer must be able to retain, by contractual stipulations, his distribution or other rights to which the presumption applies, and (2) the presumption of transfer must be subject to Article 4, which applies *mutatis mutandis*. Consequently, the presumption of transfer of, for example, the performer's distribution right to the film producer is only valid if the performer retains an unwaivable right to obtain an equitable remuneration for the distribution. According to the underlying concept, the performer is guaranteed an equitable remuneration for every kind of exploitation of his performance as compensation for the weakening of his position by the presumption of transfer. This remuneration may be stipulated in the contract and paid by the producer; it may also, however, be administered by collecting societies under the provisions of Article 4(3) and (4).[98]

It should be noted that the second sentence of Article 2(7) allows another form of presumption with respect to Chapter II of the Directive. Member States may provide that the signing of a contract concluded between a performer and a film producer concerning the production of a film has the effect of authorising the fixation, reproduction, broadcasting, communication to the public and/or distribution, provided that such contract provides for an equitable remuneration in respect of all those rights. Since reference is made in the second sentence of Article 2(7) (via its first sentence) to the whole Article 4, this remuneration right must be unwaivable, and the collective administration of the right is possible under Article 4(3) and (4). Since Article 2(7) was introduced to take account of the legal situation in a particular Member State as a part of an overall compromise, it may be understood that the exception in Article 2(7) is designed to be applied by that Member State only.[99]

---

[97] See however the comments below on the second part of Recital (19), p. 112.
[98] For more details on Arts. 2(5) and 4, which apply *mutatis mutandis*, see the comments thereon, pp. 55, 74.
[99] See also the comments, pp. 56/60 *et seq.*

## 3. The Presumption of Transfer of Rights Addressed in Recital (19) (Second Part)

## Recital (19) (Second Part)

*Recital*

(19) ... Whereas furthermore the provisions of Chapter II do not prevent Member States from providing for a rebuttable presumption of the authorization of exploitation in respect of the exclusive rights of performers provided for in those Articles, insofar as such presumption is compatible with the International Convention for the Protection of Performers, Producers of Phonograms and Broadcasting Organisations (hereinafter referred to as the Rome Convention).

## Commentary

The second part of Recital (19) appeared at a very late stage in the discussions of the Council Working Group. It was introduced as a result of a divergence of opinion on the question of whether Member States would be permitted, under Chapter II, to provide for a presumption of transfer from performers to phonogram producers or broadcasting organisations. One Member State insisted on having this option, whereas most of the other Member States rejected it and were of the opinion that the Directive excludes such a presumption because it regulates exhaustively the issue of presumption of transfer.[1] One even considered that such a presumption would limit performers' rights in such a way as would not comply with the Rome Convention and would, merely for that reason, not be allowed under the Directive. The Member State which had insisted on having the presumption also argued that such a presumption would comply with the Rome Convention and thus would be allowed under the Directive. Finally, a compromise in the form of the second part of Recital (19) was found. It leaves open the question of compatibility with the Rome Convention and reflects the open disagreement between Member States, which continued to have different opinions on the subject. This part of the Recital does not therefore seem to provide Member States with a reliable guide to interpretation and it may be best if Member States were to disregard the second part of the recital.

In regard to the question of whether the Directive permits a legal presumption of transfer of a performer's rights under Chapter II outside of a contract concerning film production, it appears that the Directive does not allow such a presumption. The regulation of the presumptions of transfer under the Directive is exhaustive.[2] In addition, it would not make sense to provide a presumption of transfer of the rental right exclusively with respect to

---

[1] See also p. 58, above.
[2] See p. 58, above.

contracts concerning film production, but to allow further presumptions in respect of the rights under Chapter II. Furthermore, it would be inconsistent to require the conditions of Article 2(5) to be met for a presumption in the case of film production, but to allow further presumptions without those conditions. Finally, since the second part of the recital is of little use, one may conclude from the first part that presumptions of transfer are allowed under Chapter II only under the conditions specified in Article 2(5), that is in respect of the relationship between a performer and a film producer.

# Article 11. Duration of Authors' Rights

Article 11 determines the minimum duration of the rental and lending rights provided for authors under the Directive.

## ARTICLE 11

### Article 11

#### Duration of authors' rights

Without prejudice to further harmonization, the authors' rights referred to in this Directive shall not expire before the end of the term provided by the Berne Convention for the Protection of Literary and Artistic Works.

## COMMENTARY

According to Article 11, the minimum terms of protection laid down in the Berne Convention are to apply to the authors' rental and lending rights covered by the Directive. Thus, the usual term of protection will, in accordance with Article 7(1) of the Berne Convention, be at least the life of the author plus 50 years. In respect of cinematographic works, anonymous, pseudonymous works and photographic works, the minimum terms of protection laid down in Articles 7(2) to 7(4) of the Berne Convention apply. Further special terms of protection which exist in some Member States, for example in respect of posthumous works, collective works or official publications, and which are not covered by the Berne Convention, continue to be governed by national law; this followed on from the second part of Article 9 of the Commission's original proposal which was later deleted, as the Member States did not consider it to be necessary.

As shown by the opening words of Article 11 ("without prejudice to further harmonization"), the duration of the protection of authors' rights and neighbouring rights in general will be harmonised in the near future by a Directive which is already under discussion.[3]

---

[3] See the Proposal for a Council Directive on the term of protection of copyright and certain related rights, COM (92) 33 final – SYN 395, [1992] O.J. C92/6; and the Commission's Amended Proposal, [1993] O.J. C27/7.

# Article 12. Duration of Related Rights

Article 12 determines the minimum duration of the rights of performers, phonogram and film producers and broadcasting organisations.

## ARTICLE 12

### Article 12

#### Duration of related rights

Without prejudice to further harmonization, the rights referred to in this Directive of performers, phonogram producers and broadcasting organizations shall not expire before the end of the respective terms provided by the Rome Convention. The rights referred to in this Directive for producers of the first fixations of films shall not expire before the end of a period of 20 years computed from the end of the year in which the fixation was made.

## COMMENTARY

Article 12 provides for a minimum duration for "related rights" dealt with in the Directive, by way of reference to the respective terms of protection provided in Article 14 of the Rome Convention. Accordingly, the rental and lending rights of performers, as well as their rights under Chapter II, will last at least until the end of a period of 20 years computed from the end of the year in which the performance took place or was fixed on a visual or sound recording. The rights of phonogram producers will last at least until the end of a period of 20 years computed from the end of the year in which the fixation of the phonogram was made. The rights of broadcasting organisations (as defined in Article 6(2) and (3)) will last at least until the end of a period of 20 years computed from the end of the year in which the broadcast or cable distribution took place. As far as the rights of film producers (as defined in Article 2(1)) are concerned, the Commission's original proposal provided for the application of the Rome Convention *mutatis mutandis*. Following the suggestion of some Member States, this reference to the Rome Convention was clarified in the final version by the second sentence of Article 12, which corresponds to the minimum protection provided for in Article 14 of the Rome Convention in respect of phonograms.

As with authors' rights, the duration of neighbouring rights is expected to be comprehensively harmonised in the future Directive referred to above.[4]

---

[4] See n. 3, above.

Member States which are to introduce neighbouring rights into their legislation for the first time, and only pursuant to the Directive, will have to decide to what extent the protection should be made retrospective. In this respect, reference is made to Article 13(1) and to the comments thereon.[5]

---

[5] See pp. 119–120, below.

# Article 13. Application in Time

Article 13 deals with the application in time of the provisions of the Directive, that is the question of when and to what extent they apply. The general rule is contained in Article 13(1) and (2), while Article 13(3) to (9) refer to various specific situations.

## 1. GENERAL REMARKS

This Article, of rather marginal interest at the outset, became one of the central issues at a very late stage of the legislative procedure. In fact, provisions on the application in time of any piece of legislation are usually little noticed but extremely important, because they may minimise or even neutralise the effects of certain operative provisions. Often, as in the case of this Directive, the provisions on the application in time have a crucial effect on the economic implications of the legislation. Accordingly, the discussions on this issue strongly reflected the opposing and rather fixed positions of interested parties.

### (a) The legislative background

The Commission originally proposed to apply the Directive to all works and subject matter protected at the required date of implementation. It aimed at the widest possible scope of application in order to achieve the greatest harmonisation. The Committees on Economic and on Cultural Affairs of the European Parliament, in the course of the first reading, both rejected proposals which would have exempted all existing contracts from the application of the Directive. The Legal Affairs Committee, however, passed such a proposal, rejecting at the same time a less rigid proposal under which existing contracts were not completely exempted, but the parties to such contracts were granted a period of three years after the Directive came into force in which to modify the contracts to comply with the Directive. This intermediate solution was then re-introduced and finally adopted by the European Parliament in plenary session at first reading.

The Commission, in its amended proposal, endorsed this proposal in clear wording. In addition, it introduced a new provision exempting the existing stock of rental outlets and lending establishments from the exclusive rental and lending rights.

### (b) Protection for existing stock

The Council Working Group discussed, amongst other issues, two main problems. First, the Member States wanted to protect rental outlets and lending establishments in respect of their existing stocks. Without any specific provision, it would have been possible for right-owners, such as phonogram producers, entirely to prohibit the rental of compact discs and other phonograms. In that case, rental outlets which were only renting phonograms would have had to shut down, even if they, as usual, had acquired the phonograms for the purpose of renting and had been relying on being able to rent them to the public. Member States agreed that rental outlets and lending establishments should be protected from the rigid application of the rental right (Article 13(3)) in respect of their existing stocks.

### (c) Protection for existing contracts

Secondly, the Member States were concerned about existing contracts. Most Member States wanted to exempt existing contracts from the application of the Directive. They wanted to avoid the situation where existing contracts, for example between actors and film producers, would have to be renegotiated, which would often not be practicable and would hinder the producer or distributor in his exploitation of the film. Even the intermediate solution, which would grant the right-owners three years in which to adapt their contracts to the Directive, found little support among the Member States, although it had been passed by the European Parliament.

During the discussions, some Member States were reminded of the fact that the complete exemption of existing contracts would have been unduly favourable to producers and at the expense of authors and performers. Indeed, the complete exemption of existing contracts would have meant that authors and performers who contributed or were to contribute to a phonogram or film on the basis of a contract concluded before the date of adoption of the Directive would not have obtained any of those revenues from the rental and other rights which they should have acquired as a result of the Directive. This would have been true even if their entire repertoire was on the market at the date of adoption, or came on the market thereafter, if the contract was concluded before the date of adoption. At the same time, producers would not only have been exempted from having to acquire the rental or other rights of authors and performers, but they would also have been the only rightholders to benefit from revenues from the future exploitation of the author's or performer's works. In other words, with respect to the future exploitation of existing repertoires, the Directive would have benefited solely those who exploited the works and performances, in particular phonogram and film producers.

During the discussions in the Council Working Group the Commission suggested to Member States a more balanced approach which, on the one hand, would take account of the producers' concerns not to be hindered in their exploitation by the need to acquire the new rights which authors and performers enjoyed as a result of the Directive, and which, on the other hand, would take account of the demands of authors and performers at least to benefit adequately from the future revenues from the exploitation of their works and performances. Accordingly, "old" contracts should in principle not be affected by the Directive and Member States should be permitted to provide for a non-rebuttable presumption of transfer of the new rights. At the same time, Member States would be obliged to provide authors and performers with the equitable remuneration referred to in Article 4. Many Member States did not even want to apply this remuneration right in respect of works and performances covered by "old" contracts, because they claimed that it would be too complicated to find and pay all the actors from old films and other right-owners. In the end, consensus was reached on a provision which allowed Member States to apply the remuneration right only from July 1, 1997 and on a provision under which the remuneration right applies to "old" contracts only if the authors and performers assert their right before January 1, 1997 (Article 13(8) and (9)).

## 2. ARTICLE 13(1)

*Article 13*

### Application in time

1.    This Directive shall apply in respect of all copyright works, performances, phonograms, broadcasts and first fixations of films referred to in this Directive which are, on 1 July 1994, still protected by the legislation of the Member States in the field of copyright and related rights or meet the criteria for protection under the provisions of this Directive on that date.

...

COMMENTARY

### (a) "Still protected"

Article 13(1) sets out the two alternative conditions under which copyright works, performances, phonograms, broadcasts and films[6] are covered by the Directive. The first is that all copyright works and other subject matter referred to in the Directive which, on July 1, 1994, still enjoy copyright or neighbouring rights protection under national law are covered by the Directive. For example, if the copyright in a work in a Member State expires on December 31, 1993, the work will not be protected in that Member State on July 1, 1994 and therefore does not fall under the Directive. If, however, the same work enjoys protection in another Member State until December 31,

---

[6] For discussions on these terms see the comments, pp. 50–52, above.

2013, it is still protected by the copyright law of that Member State and will be covered by the Directive there; thus, its author has to be granted a rental and lending right in that Member State.

### (b) "Meet(ing) the criteria for protection"

The second (alternative) condition is that the subject matter must "meet the criteria for protection under the provisions of this Directive" on July 1, 1994. This requirement, which has its twin provision in Article 70 of the Dunkel text of December 1991 on GATT/TRIPs, is designed to cover all subject matter which is not protected under the national law of a Member State because that particular Member State does not provide any protection for that subject matter at all. This provision is aimed, therefore, at those Member States which do not yet have any legislation on neighbouring rights.

In some cases, the Directive itself states quite specific "criteria for protection." For example, a film producer, in order to qualify for protection under the Directive, must meet the criteria for protection under Article 2(1), fourth indent. Even if the Directive does not specify any particular requirements, as in the case of phonogram producers, they nevertheless have to meet the implicit and general criteria for protection contained in the Directive.

One such general requirement is duration (Article 12). For example, a phonogram is protected under the Directive for at least 20 years from the end of the year of its fixation. If a phonogram was made during 1974, it would therefore have to enjoy protection at least until the end of 1994 and would meet the criteria for protection on July 1, 1994. If, however, it was made during 1973, then the phonogram would only enjoy protection under the Directive until at least the end of 1993 and the "criteria for protection" on July 1, 1994 would not be met. If this were not the case, the Directive would provide protection for any phonograms, films and so on without any limit on duration. It is the Member States which have to decide what length of protection they want to provide and the period beyond 20 years for which they want to introduce protection for already existing phonograms, films and so on. Accordingly, Member States are obliged to apply the rights set out in the Directive to pre-existing performances, phonograms, films and broadcasts if they meet the criteria for protection under the Directive and, in particular, if they are less than 20 years old (Article 12). If they are older, Member States are free to decide whether or not to grant protection.

## 3. Article 13(2)

*Article 13*

. . .

2.    This Directive shall apply without prejudice to any acts of exploitation performed before 1 July 1994.

. . .

COMMENTARY

Article 13(2) was included in order to emphasise the fact that the Directive does not apply retrospectively, but only to future acts of exploitation. It does not refer to the works and subject matter (unlike Article 13(1)), nor to any contracts (unlike Article 13(3) and (6) to (9)), but to "acts" of exploitation, such as the rental or lending of a phonogram, the fixation of a performance, the making of a reproduction of a film, or the broadcasting or public playing of a concert. The Directive does not affect such acts if they were performed before 1 July 1994. In this context, "performed" means "come to an end" or "concluded."

In the case of rental and lending, it would be appropriate to consider the act as "performed" at the moment of rental or lending to the user, rather than at the moment of returning the phonogram. In cases where the act is of a long duration, as for example the fixation of an actor's performance in a film or film series over several months, the fixation would be "performed" (concluded) before July 1, 1994 only if the whole or almost the whole film, or one part of a series, were fixed before July 1, 1994.

# 4. ARTICLE 13(3)

*Article 13*

. . .

3.   Member States may provide that the rightholders are deemed to have given their authorization to the rental or lending of an object referred to in Article 2(1) which is proven to have been made available to third parties for this purpose or to have been acquired before 1 July 1994. However, in particular where such an object is a digital recording, Member States may provide that rightholders shall have a right to obtain an adequate remuneration for the rental or lending of that object.

. . .

COMMENTARY[7]

## (a) The scope of the possible exception

Article 13(3) envisages the protection of rental outlets and lending establishments which have, before July 1, 1994, purchased or otherwise legally obtained compact discs or other objects for the purpose of renting or lending. Member States may provide that these outlets and establishments, which have already been relying on being able continuously to rent or lend the items which they obtained for that purpose, need not suddenly be faced with rightowners prohibiting the rental or lending of items which they have in stock on

---

[7] See also the general remarks, p. 118, above.

July 1, 1994 by providing that the rightholders are deemed to have authorised the rental or lending.

"The rightholders" means all rightholders involved in a particular case, for example the composer, performer and phonogram producer in the case of the rental of a compact disc. The phrase "the rightholders are deemed to have given their authorisation" amounts to a fictitious authorisation, or a non-rebuttable presumption of authorisation.

This fictitious authorisation may apply only to the rental or lending of such objects which are shown (1) to have been acquired before July 1, 1994 or (2) to have been made available to third parties for this purpose before July 1, 1994. Usually, rental outlets or lending institutions buy compact discs, books and so on in order to rent or lend them. It is, however, also possible that they themselves rent them from distributors, or that they receive books as donations, as often happens with public libraries. The second alternative, above, was included to cover such cases. The term "third party" simply means any person who is not one of the rightholders concerned, in particular in this context a rental outlet or lending institution.

The fact that the object was obtained before July 1, 1994 must be "proven." The Directive leaves it to the Member States to regulate the details concerning the proof, such as the rules of evidence and the burden of proof which are to be applied. In practice, there will be several ways of ascertaining whether an object was obtained before or after July 1, 1994, for instance by the labelling of all cassettes which are made available for rental or lending after July 1, 1994, or by means of the written orders or invoices showing the date of delivery of the cassettes or other items to the rental outlets.

The date of July 1, 1994 was controversial in the Council Working Group. Some Member States wanted to be able to protect existing rental and lending institutions by allowing them to continue renting or lending their stock up to the date of the actual (as opposed to required) implementation of the Directive in each Member State. On the other hand, other Member States pointed out that any date after the adoption of the Directive could not be justified, since the reason for such protection was the reliance of rental and lending institutions on the continuation of the existing legal regime. In addition, they saw that the longer period could easily be abused: rental outlets and libraries would enlarge their stocks of compact discs, etc., as much as possible before the required or actual date of implementation in order to avoid the application of the exclusive rental right to the greatest possible extent. Finally, a majority of the Member States accepted the date of July 1, 1994.

However, if a Member State decides to apply this optional Article 13(3), it may determine a date earlier than July 1, 1994. Since the Member States are free not to limit the application of the exclusive rental and lending rights, and thus not to apply Article 13(3) at all but to provide for the full exclusive rights even with respect to existing stocks, they are clearly permitted to apply this limitation of the exclusive rights in a less limitative way, namely by specifying a date earlier than July 1, 1994.

## (b) Remuneration

The second sentence of Article 13(3) was introduced at a late stage in the discussions in the Council Working Group at the request of one particular Member State, which asked for a more balanced solution. The interests of rental outlets and lending institutions were taken into account in the first sentence, and so the interests of rightholders should be taken into account by the provision of a remuneration right in the second sentence. The rental and lending institutions could continue their activities in respect of their existing stocks but they should pay an adequate remuneration to the rightholders, who would suffer from the usual copying activities occurring in connection with the rental or lending, particularly in the case of digital recordings which do not deteriorate with frequent use.

Accordingly, Member States may, having applied the exception under Article 13(3), provide for the rightholders as set out in Article 2(1) a right to obtain an adequate remuneration for the rental or lending. This right will in practice probably best be administered by collecting societies. It will apply, according to the general rule in Article 13(2), to rental and lending acts performed after July 1, 1994. The second sentence of Article 13(3) underlines the importance of providing such a remuneration, particularly in the case of digital recordings. Member States are, however, free to provide such a remuneration right either with respect to all recordings and copies of works, to digital or other recordings only, or not at all.

## 5. ARTICLE 13(4) AND (5)

*Article 13*

. . .

4.   Member States need not apply the provisions of Article 2(2) to cinematographic or audiovisual works created before 1 July 1994.

5.   Member States may determine the date as from which the Article 2(2) shall apply, provided that that date is no later than 1 July 1997.

. . .

COMMENTARY

### (a) Article 13(4): Exception to authorship rule in respect of old films

Article 13(4) provides that Article 2(2), according to which film directors have to be considered as authors of films, need not be applied to existing films, that is those created before July 1, 1994. The purpose of this is to facilitate the application of the Directive in those countries where film directors do not yet enjoy any copyright protection. Accordingly, those Member States would not have to provide for rental and lending rights for directors of films created before July 1, 1994, and as a result, directors of such "old" films would never obtain any rental or lending rights, not even in respect of future exploitation.

Since Article 13(4) is not a mandatory rule, film directors may be able to persuade their national legislators of the need to apply Article 2(2) also to existing films. If so, the Member State is free to apply either the general rule in Article 13(1), in particular by including all films which are still covered by copyright protection, according to the term provided under Article 11 of the Directive – and Article 7(1) or (2) of the Berne Convention – or it may choose any date between that determined according to Article 7(1) or (2) of the Berne Convention and July 1, 1994, thus covering all films which are created after that chosen date.

### (b) Article 13(5): Transitional period

Article 13(5) unlike Article 13(4), does not allow Member States to exclude entire categories of "old" films from the application of the Directive, but provides for a transitional period. Accordingly, film directors may be granted rental and lending rights only with respect to rental and lending acts occurring after July 1, 1997, even if the film is created after July 1, 1994.

### (c) Ways of applying Article 13(4) and (5)

Member States may apply Article 13(4) and (5) in the following ways:

(a) If a Member State does not apply either Article 13(4) or (5), film directors will enjoy the rental and lending rights in respect of rental and lending acts occurring from July 1, 1994 and concerning "old" as well as "new" films.

(b) If a Member State applies Article 13(4), but not (5), film directors may enjoy the rental and lending rights with respect to rental and lending activities occurring from July 1, 1994, but only in respect of "new" films created after July 1, 1994.

(c) If a Member State applies Article 13(5) only, film directors will enjoy the rental and lending rights for rental and lending acts occurring from July 1, 1997 (or from another date chosen between July 1, 1994 and July 1, 1997) in respect of "old" as well as "new" films.

(d) If a Member State decides to apply both provisions, film directors will enjoy the rental and lending rights with respect to rental and lending acts occurring from July 1, 1997 and only in respect of films created after July 1, 1994.

## 6. Article 13(6) and (7)

*Article 13*

...

6. This Directive shall, without prejudice to paragraph 3 and subject to paragraphs 8 and 9, not affect any contracts concluded before the date of its adoption.

7.   Member States may provide, subject to the provisions of paragraphs 8 and 9, that when rightholders who acquire new rights under the national provisions adopted in implementation of this Directive have, before 1 July 1994, given their consent for exploitation, they shall be presumed to have transferred the new exclusive rights.

. . .

## COMMENTARY

Article 13(6) and (7) deals with the application of the Directive to "old" contracts; however, the application in time of the unwaivable remuneration right referred to in Article 4 is exclusively dealt with in Article 13(8) and (9) (in respect of both "old" and "new" contracts), while the relationship between rightholders and rental outlets or lending establishments is dealt with in Article 13(3).

### (a) The scope of Article 13(6)

Article 13(6) is, unlike Article 13(7), mandatory. In principle, the Directive does not affect contracts concluded before the date of its adoption, November 19, 1992. Such "contracts" are, according to the wording ("any" contracts), contracts concluded between rightholders and users, and those concluded between different rightholders, such as authors and performers on the one hand and producers on the other. The discussions in the Council Working Group focused, however, on contracts concluded between different rightholders.

### (b) The scope of Article 13(7)

Article 13(7) is intended to facilitate the exploitation by producers of new rights acquired as a result of the Directive in their capacity as assignees, in cases where "old" contracts (contracts concluded before July 1, 1994) were silent on such new rights but included the general consent of the author or performer for exploitation. For example, performers will in future enjoy, as a result of the Directive, their own rental right which they did not have before in a certain Member State. The contracts which they concluded with film or phonogram producers before July 1, 1994 would have included the performers' consent to the exploitation, either generally or by specifying the rights transferred, such as the fixation and reproduction rights. In so far as these contracts did not deal with the rental right (which will almost always be the case, since a rental right did not exist), the Member State may provide that the performers are presumed to have transferred the exclusive rental right to the producer.

Article 13(7) is only an enabling provision; some Member States did not want to be obliged to apply this presumption and were opposed to its mandatory application. Accordingly, a Member State may provide that the new rights are not presumed to have been transferred, but must be acquired by producers from authors and performers, or it may provide that new rights are

125

presumed to have been transferred only if certain conditions are fulfilled, for example if the rental of video cassettes, compact discs or other kinds of exploitation were not unknown at the time when the author or performer gave consent for exploitation.

### (c) The "consent for exploitation"

The "consent for exploitation" will usually have been given in a written or oral contract; however, a contract is not required and simple consent for the film or other work to be exploited is sufficient.

### (d) The "new rights"

The "new rights under the national provisions adopted in implementation of this Directive" are the rental and lending rights and all the exclusive rights under Chapter II, in so far as a Member State introduces them for the first time for certain rightholders as a result of the Directive, thus fulfilling the requirement of incorporating the Directive into national law. Only the exclusive rights and not the remuneration rights are covered by Article 13(7). This may be seen from the purpose of the provision, which is to exempt producers from the need to acquire the new rights before they can proceed to exploit the films or phonograms.

## 7. ARTICLE 13(8) AND (9)

*Article 13*

. . .

8.   Member States may determine the date as from which the unwaivable right to an equitable remuneration referred to in Article 4 exists, provided that that date is no later than 1 July 1997.

9.   For contracts concluded before 1 July 1994, the unwaivable right to an equitable remuneration provided for in Article 4 shall apply only where authors or performers or those representing them have submitted a request to that effect before 1 January 1997. In the absence of agreement between rightholders concerning the level of remuneration, Member States may fix the level of equitable remuneration.

### COMMENTARY

### (a) The scope of Article 13(8)

Article 13(8) offers Member States a transitional period within which to apply Article 4. It allows Member States to provide for the remuneration right under Article 4 to take effect on any date after the required implementation date (July 1, 1994), provided that that date is no later than July 1, 1997.

Article 13(8) is not restricted to "old" contracts. Member States wanted to be able to grant the remuneration right only three years after the required implementation of the Directive, whether "old" or "new" contracts were concerned. Accordingly, Member States may apply Article 4 at the date of implementation of the Directive or at any date thereafter, but no later than July 1, 1997, to "old" and "new" contracts, only to "old" or only to "new" contracts or not at all. After July 1, 1997, however, they have to provide the remuneration right in respect of "old" and "new" contracts. If a Member State decides to apply Article 13(8) to its fullest extent, the right-owners can claim the remuneration under Article 4 only for acts of exploitation occurring after July 1, 1997.

## (b) The scope of Article 13(9)

The purpose of Article 13(9) is to facilitate the application of Article 4 in respect of contracts concluded before July 1, 1994, in particular for producers. Producers and others from whom the remuneration may be claimed under national law[8] will not have to go through the possibly cumbersome process of looking for actors, musicians, composers and others who contributed to films or phonograms made under "old" contracts, or their heirs, in order to pay them the remuneration under Article 4. Under Article 13(9), authors and performers themselves, or their representatives, have to submit a request before January 1, 1997. If they do not do so, they cannot claim any remuneration under Article 4 for any future exploitation of works and performances covered by "old" contracts. This provision is mandatory.

"Those representing" authors and performers will in practice usually be their collecting societies. The term "representing" should be understood in a broad sense. It is not a technical term which would have to be construed according to national rules of civil law concerning representation.

Authors and performers or their representatives must have "submitted a request to that effect before January 1, 1997." For the sake of clarity and legal certainty, Member States will have to regulate in more detail in which ways and to whom such a request has to be submitted. Otherwise, the rule that an equitable remuneration has to be paid for the future exploitation of works and performances covered by "old" contracts might lose its effect. Authors and performers must be provided with the ability to know under what conditions their requests are valid, and must be able to rely on such information. If a Member State does not provide for rules governing this area, any type of request which may be interpreted as a request to obtain remuneration under Article 4 will have to be admitted as being valid.

The need to regulate the preconditions of a valid request becomes particularly obvious in view of Article 13(8). It allows Member States to implement the right established by Article 4 as late as July 1, 1997. Authors and performers, however, have only until December 31, 1996 to claim the remuneration. Thus, they would have to claim remuneration in respect of a right which does not even exist at the time of the request. In this situation it is therefore

---

[8] See the comments under Art. 4, p. 74 et seq., above.

127

particularly important to provide legal certainty with respect to the preconditions of a valid request.

Since the Directive does not specify to whom the request has to be made, Member States are free to regulate this question. The most obvious way would be to specify that the request should be made to the debtor under national law, usually the producer or rental outlet. However, authors and performers or their representatives may not be able to find out who the individual debtors are, in particular where, for instance, a film or phonogram producer with whom the "old" contract was concluded has become bankrupt or has given up its business and sold the rights with respect to the film or phonogram to another company. In view of this, Member States might be well advised to provide that authors and performers or their representatives may make the request not to a particular producer or exploiter, but by giving notice in a specified publication or to a certain authority specified by law. Similarly, Member States should determine at least the main elements of such requests, in particular an indication of the producer with whom the original contract was concluded, the title, number or other identification of the individual recording, the works and performances included in the film or phonogram and so on.

Authors and performers should make their requests in respect of all recordings to which they have contributed, even if they are, at the time of the request, no longer on the market. They may be put on the market again in the future; if no request has been made by December 31, 1996, no remuneration for these future exploitations by rental will be able to be claimed.

In practice, the extent to which authors and performers will obtain remuneration for the rental of existing recordings in the future will largely depend on the activities of collecting societies, who should at least draw the authors' and performers' attention to the preclusive period of, two-and-a half-years under Article 13(9) and, with a view to efficiency, ask them to instruct the collecting societies to submit the request on their behalf. They will have to do so anyway where a Member State provides for the mandatory collective administration of the right under Article 4. Where a Member State incorporates Article 4 by means of contract law, it will usually be authors and performers themselves who submit the requests; however, collecting societies will still be free to request the remuneration right on behalf of their authors and performers[9] and to administer this right at least with respect to "old" contracts.[10]

If the request is submitted and no agreement can be reached on the amount of the remuneration to be paid, Member States may decide on the amount. "Member States" in this context covers all administrative, judicial and

---

[9] See Recital (15) and the comment, p. 74 et seq., above.

[10] The Commission made the following statement at the Internal Market Council meeting of June 18, 1992 in respect of the application of Article 13(9) in France: "The Commission considers that the provisions of Article 13(9) may be satisfied by the extension of the agreement that has existed in France since June 1990, which is to be re-negotiated within five years, to all films which fulfill the criteria for protection under the provisions of this Directive at that time, provided that the renewed agreement complies, as from the date set under Article 13(8), with the provisions of Article 4 of this Directive."

legislative authorities. The amount to be paid can, for example, be fixed by law at a certain level, or the decision can be entrusted to a nominated arbitrator or to the courts, which may decide on the amount in the circumstances of each individual case.[11]

---

[11] See also the following statement made by the Commission at the Internal Market Council meeting of June 18, 1992: "The Commission considers that, for the implementation of the last sentence of Article 13(9), Member States are free to use their administrative or judicial authorities or both."

# Article 14. Relation Between Copyright and Related Rights

Article 14 ensures that the protection granted to neighbouring right-owners under the Directive does not affect the protection of copyright.

ARTICLE 14

*Article 14*

**Relation between copyright and related rights**

Protection of copyright-related rights under this Directive shall leave intact and shall in no way affect the protection of copyright.

COMMENTARY

The Commission, in its original proposal, did not consider it necessary to include any provision on the relationship between copyright and related rights, since it was expected that those Member States which had not yet adhered to the Rome Convention would do so in the near future – not least as an indirect result of the present Directive. Accordingly, they would have to comply with Article 1 of the Rome Convention, which regulates this relationship.

In the course of the discussions on the proposal at first reading in the European Parliament, however, several versions of a new Article dealing with this relationship were proposed. The version proposed in the Cultural Committee corresponded largely to a previous version of Article 1 of the Rome Convention which had finally been rejected in the negotiations on that Convention because it would have limited the protection of neighbouring rights to too great an extent. According to that proposal, not only the protection but also the exercise of authors' rights should be unaffected by the neighbouring rights. This means that, for example, a performer could not prohibit the broadcasting of his musical performance, if the composer of the music wanted to authorise the broadcasting. In the end, the European Parliament in plenary session adopted a proposal which corresponded with Article 1 of the Rome Convention and thus referred only to the *protection* of copyright.[12] The Commission adopted this proposal in Article 11bis of its amended proposal and

---

[12] See Amendments voted by the Parliament, Art. 4(a) (new).

adapted the wording to that of the first sentence of Article 1 of the Rome Convention. It underlined the clarificatory character of this Article, the substance of which may shortly be expected to apply, through Article 1 of the Rome Convention, in all Member States. Accordingly, authors and neighbouring right-owners must have parallel rights; all rightholders concerned in a particular case must consent to the exploitation, and the refusal to give consent by one rightholder – be it the author or a neighbouring right-owner – would prevent the exploitation.

# Article 15. Final Provisions

*Article 15*

### Final provisions

1.   Member States shall bring into force the laws, regulations and administrative provisions necessary to comply with this Directive not later than 1 July 1994. They shall forthwith inform the Commission thereof. When Member States adopt these measures, they shall contain a reference to this Directive or shall be accompanied by such reference at the time of their official publication. The methods of making such a reference shall be laid down by the Member States.

2.   Member States shall communicate to the Commission the main provisions of domestic law which they adopt in the field covered by this Directive.

## Commentary

Article 15 requires Member States to implement the Directive by July 1, 1994, to include a reference to the Directive in their adopted measures and to communicate to the Commission the main adopted provisions. The text of this Article corresponds to a model used in all comparable Directives. The date (July 1, 1994) is also decisive for the application in time of the Directive (Article 13).

# Further Issues Dealt With in the Context of the Legislative Procedure

Two further issues which are not closely related to any of the Articles were discussed, but do not appear in the Directive.

## 1. Moral Rights

There was a new Article 4(b) passed by the European Parliament which stated, with respect to the rental and lending rights, that "no changes, cuts or additions may be made to a work by the letter (*sic*),[13] the hirer, the lender or borrower." This amendment introduced a new element which could be seen as protection of an author's moral rights or an adaptation right. It was intended particularly to prevent, for example, rental outlets or libraries or even the hirers or borrowers from cutting or otherwise modifying the tape of a music recording or video cassette without the consent of the author. The Commission endorsed this new Article, in somewhat clearer drafting, in its amended proposal and called it "Moral Rights." However, the Member States considered it to be unnecessary, since it was already covered, if not by their own laws on moral rights, then by those on the adaptation right. Consequently, it was deleted from the Directive.

## 2. The Relation to Third Countries

The second issue concerned the relationship of Member States to third countries. The European Parliament at first reading passed a new Recital (16a), according to which the implementation of the Directive would create a new situation with regard to Member States' relations with third countries and it would be necessary to negotiate with those countries in order to secure reciprocal protection. The Commission endorsed the "underlying idea" of this proposal and accepted this recital in a clarified form in the amended proposal. Since the relationship between Member States and most third countries is governed by the principle of national treatment contained in the Berne Convention, the Universal Copyright Convention and most (wrong) bilateral agreements, and since the principle of national treatment at least under the Berne Convention covers future rights such as, for example, the rental right, the implementation of the Directive will not create a new situation with

---

[13] Intended to mean "lessor."

regard to the relationship with most third countries. There may, however, be some bilateral agreements which are limited to a specific level of protection and which would have to be renegotiated if new rights were introduced by a party to the agreement. In such a case, Recital (16a) would have recommended negotiation with a view to securing at least reciprocal protection. The Commission added the words "at least" in order to indicate that in most cases national treatment applied anyway, and that recourse to reciprocity would normally only be necessary where national treatment was not achievable.

Since Member States did not consider that the Directive would have any direct impact on their relations with third countries, they agreed to delete the recital. Even the fact that the European Parliament, at second reading, passed the new recital again – this time as the only proposed amendment to the Common Position – did not persuade the Member States that it should be included.

SECTION III

# THE POSITION IN THE MEMBER STATES

# 1. Belgium

## 1. THE PRESENT LEGAL SITUATION

The Belgian Copyright Act of March 22, 1886 does not explicitly provide for rental and lending rights for authors and other rightholders, nor for any neighbouring rights protection as such. It is arguable that the concept of "droit de destination," which has been developed by jurisprudence on the basis of the reproduction right, includes exclusive rights of rental and lending for authors. However, these rights do not seem to be exercised in practice.

### (a) Rental and Lending Rights

A draft for a completely new copyright act ("the draft Act") is currently being discussed. The basis for the following comments will be the version which was adopted by the Belgian Senate on May 22, 1992.[1] According to Articles 2, 48(1), 53(1) and 58(b) of the draft Act, authors, performers, phonogram and videogram producers and broadcasting organisations enjoy an exclusive distribution right which covers rental and lending and which is not exhausted after the first sale or other acts. There are two circumstances in which the exclusive rental and lending rights are intended to be replaced by a mere remuneration right: (1) in the case of "rental or lending of literary works and sheet music for non-commercial, educational and cultural purposes by officially recognised institutions" and (2) in the case of similar "non-commercial rental or lending of phonograms and videograms" which takes place at least six months after their first distribution. Authors, performers and producers obtain the remuneration right in case (2); however, under (1) above only authors of literary and musical works are intended to obtain the right (Articles 13(7) and (8), 18(2) and (3) and 54 of the draft Act).

### (b) Presumptions of Transfer and Unwaivable Remuneration Right

Article 30 of the draft Act provides for a rebuttable presumption of transfer of authors' exploitation rights to film producers. Article 31 of the draft is intended to ensure that separate remuneration is made for every kind of exploitation and that any remuneration which was agreed on a flat-rate basis can be modified on the application of the author, if this amount has become manifestly disproportionate in relation to the profit. The author cannot waive this right in advance. A similar presumption of transfer and similar provisions of contract law are proposed for performers who take part in films (Article 50 of the draft Act).

---

[1] Chambre des Représentants de Belgique 473/1, 91/92 (S.E.).

### (c) Rights of the type dealt with in Chapter II of the Directive

*Performers*

The draft Act contains a broad list of exclusive rights for performers: the rights of fixation, reproduction, publication, distribution (without exhaustion), communication to the public (including broadcasting and transmission by cable) as well as every separate use of sounds and images, if they have been simultaneously fixed. If commercial phonograms are used for broadcasting and retransmission by cable, and communication to the public except in the situation of a spectacle, the exclusive rights of performers (as well as those of phonogram producers) are proposed to be replaced with a right to an equitable remuneration (Articles 55 and 56 of the draft Act).

*Producers*

Phonogram and videogram producers will be granted, according to the draft Act, exclusive rights of fixation, reproduction, publication, communication to the public (including broadcasting and transmission by cable) as well as distribution (without exhaustion) and importation; a remuneration right is intended to be granted for certain uses of commercial phonograms (*cf.* the corresponding performers' rights, Articles 55 and 56 of the draft Act).

*Broadcasters*

According to the draft Act, broadcasting organisations will be granted exclusive rights of rebroadcasting, fixation, reproduction, distribution (without exhaustion), communication to the public and communication at a place which is accessible to the public on payment of an entrance fee (Article 58 of the draft Act). The draft Act does not make clear whether cable distributors are intended to enjoy neighbouring rights just like broadcasting organisations.

## 2. The Position under the Directive

It is obvious that the existing Copyright Act of 1886 does not meet the requirements of the Directive; even rental and lending rights would have to be clearly established.

### (a) Rental and Lending Rights

The draft law, however, seems to comply to a large extent with the provisions of the Directive. In particular, the right to remuneration for "rental for non-commercial purposes" (Articles 13, 18 and 54 of the draft Act) only seems to contravene Article 1 of the Directive, which requires an exclusive rental right. In fact, the notion of "rental for non-commercial purposes" may be taken to fall within the definition of "lending," in respect of which Article 5 of the Directive allows a remuneration right. This right, however, has to be granted to all groups of authors who contribute, say, to a book. Accordingly, not only authors of literary works, but photographers or artists and others, whose works are contained in the book, will have to be granted a right to remuneration.

## (b) Presumptions of Transfer and Unwaivable Remuneration Right

The draft Act does not fulfil the requirements of Articles 2(5), 2(6) and 4 of the Directive. In particular, Articles 30, 31 and 50 of the draft Act will need to provide for a right to *equitable* remuneration. This right must not be capable of waiver in any respect. In addition, the condition contained in Articles 31(2) and 50(6) of the draft Act requiring a manifest disproportion between the flat-rate remuneration and the profits actually made will have to be deleted if these Articles are to fulfil the requirements of Article 4; the amount of remuneration must always be equitable, even in the case of flat-rate payments. The amount is governed by *all* acts of rental carried out in relation to a protected work but may not depend on any such "manifest disproportion."

## (c) Performers', Producers' and Broadcasters' Rights in the light of Chapter II of the Directive

With respect to Chapter II of the Directive, the Belgian legislation should make clear that reproduction rights include indirect reproduction, and that the right to remuneration for the use of commercial phonograms includes the use of copies thereof (Articles 55 and 56 of the draft Act). Likewise, this right should clearly include the *indirect* use of commercial phonograms for broadcasting and communication to the public, in so far as these forms of exploitation are not covered by the exclusive rights provided for in the draft Act. The distribution rights of performers, phonogram and videogram producers and broadcasting organisations will have to be amended by a provision for exhaustion of such rights in accordance with Article 9(2) and (3) of the Directive. There will need to be clarification that, in addition to broadcasting organisations, cable distributors, as set out in Article 6(2) and (3) of the Directive, will also enjoy the rights provided by the Directive.

# 2. Denmark

## 1. THE PRESENT LEGAL SITUATION

### (a) Rental and Lending Rights

Under the Danish Copyright Act[2] ("the Act") only authors of musical works, cinematographic works and computer programs in machine-readable form enjoy an exclusive rental right. The legal technique chosen is by way of a limitation on the exhaustion of the exclusive distribution right (Articles 2(1) and (3), and 23(1) to (3) of the Act).

With respect to lending, authors of computer programs and of cinematographic works enjoy an exclusive lending right (see Articles 2(1) and (3) and 23(3) of the Act). Pursuant to a specific law on public lending rights (Act No. 354 of June 6, 1991), authors of all kinds and performers may obtain a remuneration for the lending in public and other libraries, except research libraries, of their works and performances recorded on sound recordings. The Danish system has some particular features of note. For example, the remuneration right is not assignable, nor can it be transmitted on death; instead, surviving dependents, who are explicitly designated by the law, are granted a public lending right of their own for the entirety of their respective lives. In addition, authors obtain the public lending right only if a book is written in the Danish language; in the case of a translation, only the translator into the Danish language is entitled to the public lending right. Likewise, performances only qualify if they are recorded in Denmark.

### (b) Presumptions of Transfer and Unwaivable Remuneration Right

Sections 42 and 27(2) of the Act provide a rebuttable presumption that an author of a pre-existing literary or artistic work who assigns his or her rights to use the work for or in a film at the same time assigns, *inter alia*, his or her right to make such a film available to the public. Neither a presumption of transfer of performers' rights, nor an unwaivable right to remuneration as required by Article 4 of the Directive, exists under Danish law.

---

[2] Copyright Act 1961, No. 158 of May 31, 1961.

## (c) Rights of the type dealt with in Chapter II of the Directive

### Performers

Performers enjoy the exclusive rights of fixation, reproduction and broadcasting (by wireless means and by cable), and of communication to the public of their live-performances (Articles 45(1)(a)-(c) and 45(2) of the Act). With respect to distribution, performers are protected only under Article 55(1)3 of the Act, pursuant to which the distribution of illegally fixed or reproduced copies of performances is a criminal act. The distribution of such copies, which would be illegal under Danish law, which are produced in a foreign country and imported into Denmark with a view to public showing or communication to the public (Article 55b(1) of the Act) is also a criminal act. In addition, the Danish law provides a remuneration right for the use of a phonogram incorporating a performance for broadcasting and simultaneous and unchanged rebroadcasting (Articles 47(1), 45(3) and 22a of the Act), as well as, for commercial purposes, for communication to the public (Article 47(1) of the Act).

As a specific limitation to the exclusive broadcasting right, Article 45(4) of the Act provides that the Royal Theatre is permitted by law to broadcast, via "Danmarks Radio," festival performances of the theatre or performances which are given on the occasion of official visits.

### Phonogram Producers

Phonogram producers enjoy an exclusive right of reproduction (Article 46 of the Act), and a protection by criminal law against the distribution of illegally reproduced phonograms (Article 55(1)3 of the Act). In addition, the same protection as for performers with respect to phonograms produced in foreign countries is provided by Article 55b of the Act. Phonogram producers enjoy a right to remuneration for the use of phonograms for broadcasting and, for commercial purposes, communication to the public (Article 47(1) of the Act); unlike performers, they do not, however, enjoy a remuneration right for simultaneous and unchanged rebroadcasting on the basis of phonograms.

### Broadcasters

Broadcasting organisations are granted an exclusive fixation right, reproduction right, rebroadcasting right and right of communication to the public for commercial purposes (Article 48 of the Act). In addition, the same protection under criminal law as is accorded to performers and phonogram producers, with respect to the distribution of fixed broadcasts, is available under Articles 55(1)3 and 55d of the Act.

### Film Producers

Film producers do not enjoy any rights as first right-owners. They benefit only from a presumption of transfer of certain author's rights (Article 42 of the Act).

## 2. The Position under the Directive

### (a) Rental and Lending Rights

In order to comply with the Directive, the exclusive rental rights under Danish law will have to be extended to all kinds of works, except buildings in three-dimensional form and works of applied art. This could be achieved by a corresponding limitation of the exhaustion of the distribution right. In addition, performers and phonogram and film producers within the meaning of Article 2(1) of the Directive will have to be granted exclusive rental rights.

The Danish provisions on public lending in their present form comply with the Directive. This has been confirmed with respect to the public lending right by a statement made by the Commission for the Council records in relation to Article 5.[3] If the exclusive lending right for authors of cinematographic works is to be preserved, it will need to be extended to performers contributing to a film, and film producers.

### (b) Presumptions of Transfer and Unwaivable Remuneration Right

In order to comply with Article 2(6) of the Directive the presumption of transfer of authors' rights under Article 42 of the Act, if it is to be preserved at all (the Directive does not require any presumption of transfer of authors' rights), will need to be made subject to the remuneration right as contained in Article 4 of the Directive, as far as the rental right is concerned.

A rebuttable presumption of transfer of a performer's rental right to a film producer under the provisions of Article 2(5) of the Directive, in particular subject to an unwaivable right to equitable remuneration in accordance with Article 4 of the Directive, will need to be incorporated into Danish law.

The right of authors and performers to obtain equitable remuneration for the rental of their works and of phonograms and films incorporating their performances (Article 4 of the Directive) will have to be provided for. It would be possible to implement this by way of a statutory right to remuneration which could be administered by collecting societies.

### (c) Performers', Producers' and Broadcasters' Rights in the light of Chapter II of the Directive

In the light of Chapter II of the Directive, Danish law will need to make clear that the reproduction right of performers, phonogram producers and broadcasting organisations includes indirect reproduction. In addition, performers and phonogram producers must be granted a remuneration right for *indirect* use of phonograms for broadcasting and communication to the public (unless this use is covered by an exclusive right); the existing Danish law does not entirely fulfil these requirements. Likewise, the rights of communication to

---

[3] This statement reads: "The Commission considers that the present Danish law on public lending satisfies the requirements of Article 5."

the public of performers, phonogram producers and broadcasting organisations (Articles 47, 48 of the Act) must not be restricted to communication "for commercial purposes"; however, communication "for private use" may be excluded from the right (see Article 10(1)(a) of the Directive). In addition, there will need to be clarification that right-owners under Article 48 of the Act include cable distributors as defined in Article 6(2) and (3) of the Directive. Furthermore, an exclusive distribution right complying with Article 9 of the Directive will need to be provided for performers, phonogram and film producers and broadcasting organisations; the existing protection by provisions of the criminal law does not satisfy the requirements of the Directive. Film producers will, in addition, have to be granted an exclusive reproduction right. In the light of Article 10 of the Directive, it is doubtful whether the limitation on the performer's broadcasting right by Article 45(4) of the Act can continue to subsist.

# 3. France

## 1. The Present Legal Situation

### (a) Rental and Lending Rights

According to French jurisprudence, authors enjoy the so-called "droit de destination," which was developed on the basis of the reproduction right and of provisions of contract law. This right enables the author to control the exploitation of his work even after it has been first put into circulation. Therefore it is arguable that authors enjoy, according to the French law, an exclusive rental and lending right. Phonogram and film producers as well as broadcasting organisations enjoy an exclusive rental right which is explicitly stated in the French Intellectual Property Code[4] ("the Code") (Articles L. 213–1.(2), L. 215–1.(2) and L. 216–1.(1) of the Code).

### (b) Presumptions of Transfer and Unwaivable Remuneration Right

The provisions on contracts between a film producer and an author (Article L. 132–24. *et seq.* of the Code) include a rebuttable presumption of transfer of the author's exclusive exploitation rights and the obligation to pay remuneration for every kind of exploitation of the author's work. The relationship between a film producer and a performer has largely been regulated by specific provisions which introduce, *inter alia*, a non-rebuttable presumption of transfer of the performer's rights to the producer and require separate remuneration for every kind of exploitation of the performance (Article L. 212–3. *et seq.* of the Code).

### (c) Rights of the type dealt with in Chapter II of the Directive

*Performers*

Performers enjoy an exclusive fixation right, reproduction right and right of communication to the public, which includes broadcasting (Articles L. 212–3.(1), 122–2. and 122–3. of the Code). With respect to the use of performances incorporated in commercial phonograms, performers enjoy a

---

[4] Law No. 92–597 of July 1, 1992 relating to the intellectual property code (legislative part).

remuneration right for the direct communication of the performance at a public place, if it is not used in the situation of a spectacle, and for the broadcasting of the phonogram and any simultaneous and entire cable distribution of such broadcast (Article L. 214–1.(1) of the Code). The non-rebuttable presumption of transfer mentioned under (b) above applies to these exclusive rights.

Performers cannot restrict the reproduction or communication to the public of their performance if that performance is minor within the film (Article L. 212–10. of the Code). Such a limitation does not exist with respect to author's rights.

### Producers

Phonogram producers are granted an exclusive right of any form of reproduction (*"toute" reproduction*), distribution by selling, exchange and rental (without any provision on exhaustion of the distribution right). In addition, they are granted an exclusive right of communication to the public, including broadcasting (Article L. 213–1.(2) of the Code) which is reduced to a remuneration right in certain cases (Article L. 214–1.(1) of the Code).

Film producers enjoy the same rights as phonogram producers, with the exception of the remuneration right for communication and broadcasting (Article L. 215–1.(2) of the Code).

### Broadcasters

Broadcasting organisations are granted exclusive rights of reproduction, distribution (being defined in the same way as phonogram and film producers' rights), broadcasting and communication to the public, if such communication is made in a place which is accessible to the public on which payment of an entrance fee (Article L. 216–1.(1) of the Code).

## 2. The Position under the Directive

### (a) Rental and Lending Rights

Since a rental or lending right is rarely exercised in practice by authors, it is recommended that the law be clarified so that either the "droit de destination" includes an exclusive rental right, or specific provision is made, in accordance with the provisions of the Directive, for an exclusive rental right for authors. With respect to the authors' lending right, either the same changes can be made, or a remuneration right will have to be provided complying with Article 5 of the Directive and allowing for several limitations and exceptions.

Performers will need to be granted an exclusive rental right and lending right; derogations from the lending right can be provided for in accordance with Article 5 of the Directive.

Since broadcasting organisations are able to enjoy a rental and lending right under the Directive only in so far as they qualify as "film producers" or "phonogram producers," French law will need to make clear that

145

broadcasting organisations have to qualify as film or phonogram producers in order to be granted rental and lending rights. Phonogram and film producers will need to be granted exclusive lending rights, unless derogations are made according to Article 5(1) and (2) of the Directive.

### (b) Presumptions of Transfer and Unwaivable Remuneration Right

The existing provision relating to authors' contracts regarding film production (Article L. 132–25 of the Code) does not satisfy the requirements of Article 4 of the Directive, since it does not cover all kinds of authors and does not provide for an *equitable* remuneration, or a bar on waiver of the remuneration right. In addition, authors have to be guaranteed such a remuneration right in the case of phonogram rental.

With respect to the relationship between performers and film producers, the French solution (in particular Article L. 212–4. of the Code) has finally been accepted as complying with the Directive and is reflected in Article 2(7) of the Directive. It will, however, be necessary to take into account all the provisions of Article 4 of the Directive, in particular the requirement for *equitable* remuneration and a specific bar on waiver of the right to such remuneration. It will also be necessary to provide performers with a right to an equitable remuneration for the rental of phonograms, as set out in Article 4 of the Directive. As in the case of authors, one way of complying with Article 4 is to entrust the respective collecting societies with the exercise of these rights. With regard to the time of application of Article 4 of the Directive, the Commission made a statement on Article 13(9) of the Directive for the Council records.[5]

### (c) Performers' Rights in the Light of Chapter II of the Directive

With respect to performers' rights under Chapter II of the Directive, the French law should make clear that the reproduction right covers *indirect* reproduction. It would also seem advisable to clarify that the exclusive communication right includes *indirect* use for broadcasting and communication to the public in the circumstances set out in Article 8(2) of the Directive. Alternatively, indirect uses for broadcasting and communication to the public should be explicitly covered by the remuneration right contained in Article L. 214–1. of the Code, but subject to the conditions set out in Article 8(2) of the Directive. Likewise, an exclusive distribution right in accordance with Article 9 of the Directive will have to be introduced for performers. The non-rebuttable presumption of transfer of the performers' rights to film producers (Article L. 212–4. of the Code) may be deemed to comply with Article 2(7) of the Directive, provided however that performers are ensured an *unwaivable* right to *equitable* remuneration for every kind of exploitation of their performances.

---

[5] The statement reads: "The Commission considers that the provisions of Article 13(9) may be satisfied by the extension of the agreement that has existed in France since June 1990, which is to be renegotiated within five years, to all films which fulfil the criteria for protection under the provisions under this Directive at that time, provided that the renewed agreement complies, as from the date set under Article 13(8), with the provisions of Article 4 of this Directive."

It is doubtful whether the limitation on performers' rights under Article L. 212–10. of the Code complies with Article 10 of the Directive.

## (d) Producers' and Broadcasters' Rights in the Light of Chapter II of the Directive

Provision for exhaustion of the exclusive distribution right of phonogram producers, as well as of film producers and broadcasting organisations will have to be made if French law is to satisfy the requirements of Article 9(2) of the Directive. With respect to the phonogram producers' right of public communication, reference should be made to the above comments on performers' communication rights.

There will need to be clarification that broadcasting organisations include cable distributors as defined in Article 6(3) of the Directive.

# 4. Germany

## 1. The Present Legal Situation

### (a) Rental and Lending Rights

By Article 17 of the German Law on Authors' Rights and Neighbouring Rights[6] ("the Law") authors, scientific editors and photographers enjoy, once the exclusive distribution right is exhausted, a right to an equitable remuneration for the rental and lending of copies of their works. The Law imposes the administration of this right upon collecting societies (Article 27(1) of the Law). Germany is the only E.C. Member State where a remuneration right for rental exists.

### (b) Presumptions of Transfer and Unwaivable Remuneration Right

With respect to the relationship between authors of pre-existing works, such as novels used as the basis for films, and film producers, the Law provides for a rebuttable presumption of transfer ("Einräumung") of certain exclusive rights, in particular a distribution right (Article 88). As regards film authors such as film directors there is a rebuttable presumption of transfer of the exclusive right to exploit the work in all known forms to the film producer (Article 89 of the Law).

With respect to the relationship between performers and film producers, the German law provides for the following regulation. As soon as a performer participates in the making of a film or consents to the use of his performance in the film, the law deprives him of most of his rights (Article 92 of the Law).

The law grants a statutory right to remuneration to authors for rental as indicated under (a).

### (c) Rights of the type dealt with in Chapter II of the Directive

*Performers*

Performers enjoy exclusive rights of fixation of their live performances, of reproduction (Article 75 of the Law), of public communication of their live performances (Article 74 of the Law) and of broadcasting and rebroadcasting

---

[6] Law of September 9, 1965 on Authors' Rights and Neighbouring Rights.

(Article 76(1) of the Law). Only in the case of a performance which has been fixed, with the performer's consent, on a visual or sound recording which itself has been published with the performer's consent, does the performer enjoy in place of the exclusive right a right to remuneration for the broadcasting and rebroadcasting of the fixed performance (Article 76(2) of the Law). Likewise, the performer enjoys a remuneration right for the public communication of his/her fixed and/or broadcast performance (Article 77 of the Law).

Performers are granted a certain protection against the distribution of fixed performances by Article 96(1) of the Law, pursuant to which illegally produced copies of such fixations may not be distributed. Any violation of this provision has the same legal effects as an infringement of exclusive rights.

Performers taking part in a film are, in accordance with the conditions set out in (b) above, deprived by Article 92 of the Law of their exclusive rights of reproduction, (re-)broadcasting and communication to the public as well as their right to remuneration for the broadcasting of their performances.

German law provides for a specific limitation on performers' rights: the performer may only exercise his exclusive rights under Articles 74, 75 and 76(1) of the Law by authorising the manner of exploitation of the performance if the person organising the event for its part also agrees to that form of exploitation (Article 81 of the Law, which grants the organiser a neighbouring right).

## Phonogram Producers

Phonogram producers enjoy exclusive rights of reproduction, distribution (Article 85(1) of the Law) and, in the case of a published phonogram incorporating a performance, a right to claim an adequate part of the remuneration granted to performers for the broadcasting, rebroadcasting and public communication of the fixed and/or broadcast performance (Articles 86, 76(2) and 77 of the Law).

## Broadcasters

Broadcasting organisations enjoy exclusive rights of fixation, reproduction and rebroadcasting of their broadcasts, and communication to the public of their television broadcasts if such communication is made in places accessible to the public on payment of an entrance fee (Article 87(1) of the Law). Article 87 of the Law does not provide a definition of "broadcasting organisations." However, according to the prevailing opinion, organisations which merely retransmit broadcasts of other broadcasting organisations are not protected under the Law.

## Film Producers

Film producers enjoy exclusive rights of reproduction, distribution, broadcasting and public communication (Article 94(1) and (4) of the Law). The Law does not offer any definition of a "film producer."

## 2. The Position under the Directive

### (a) Rental and Lending Rights

Provision will need to be made for an exclusive rental right for authors, performers and phonogram and film producers; one way of implementing this would be to introduce a limitation on the exhaustion of the distribution right. Since the right to remuneration for rental has in practice been successfully administered by collecting societies for the benefit of authors, this right (laid down in Article 27 of the Law) could be preserved, in a modified form, with a view to incorporating Article 4 of the Directive into national law, as mentioned in (b) below.

The rental of three-dimensional buildings and works of applied art would have to be exempted from the rental right.

With respect to lending, it will largely be possible to retain the existing system on the basis of Article 27 of the Law. It will, however, be necessary to specifically include *originals* of works and to exclude three-dimensional buildings and works of applied art. It will not be necessary to repeal the rights of scientific editors and photographers.[7] Since all groups of authors of all kinds of lending objects, such as phonograms, are covered by Article 27 of the Law, the requirements of the Directive are satisfied; however, the Directive additionally allows for the vesting of a lending right in performers and/or producers.

### (b) Transfer, Presumption of Transfer and Unwaivable Remuneration Right

The rules on the transfer ("Einräumung") of rights satisfy the requirements of Article 2(4) of the Directive.[8]

With regard to the presumption of transfer of authors' rights, it will be necessary to add to Article 89 of the Law, as regards the rental right, a reference to the equitable remuneration right under Article 4 of the Directive, as set out in Article 2(6) and (5) of the Directive. The same will be true if the presumption of transfer under Article 88 of the Law is extended to the exclusive rental right.

With respect to the performers' exclusive rental right, provision will have to be made for a rebuttable presumption of transfer in accordance with Article 2(5) of the Directive. In particular, the presumption must be subject to the unwaivable remuneration right under Article 4 of the Directive.

One way in which Article 4 of the Directive might best be implemented would be by the continued application of Article 27 of the Law, which would have to be amended in only limited respects so as to comply with Article 4. The remuneration right granted to authors would only need to be extended to performers. In addition, with regard to rental, the new Article 27 of the Law would need to incorporate the requirements of Article 4 of the Directive, in particular the transfer (including the presumed transfer) of exclusive rental

---

[7] See the comments on Art. 2(1) of the Directive, p. 45.
[8] See the comments on Art. 2(4) of the Directive, p. 53.

rights, and the bar on waiver of the remuneration right. Consequently, producers could continue to license the rental of video cassettes and compact discs to rental outlets and, at the same time, collecting societies could obtain, on the basis of general agreements with the associations of rental outlets, remuneration for authors and performers.

### (c) Rights in the Light of Chapter II and Limitations on Performers' Rights

With respect to Chapter II, there will need to be clarification that the reproduction right of performers, phonogram and film producers and broadcasting organisations includes indirect reproduction; this is not clear from the law and may only be presumed from general opinion. An exclusive distribution right will need to be granted to performers and broadcasting organisations. The exhaustion of the distribution right, including that of phonogram and film producers, must comply with Article 9(2) of the Directive; there will need to be a clear statement that the distribution right is not exhausted within the Community in the case of first distribution outside the Community.[9]

The limitation on the broadcaster's communication right under Article 87(1), 3. of the Law to *television* broadcasts will need to be removed. It may be useful to clarify that cable distributors which merely retransmit by cable the broadcasts of broadcasting organisations do not enjoy the rights set out in the Directive.

It will have to be made clear that the film producers who will enjoy the rights set out in the Directive are, under Article 2(1), fourth indent, of the Directive, only those producers who make the first fixation of a film. Therefore those who edit, for example, existing cinema films into a videogram format are not included.

The position of performers participating in the making of a film will need to be altered. One method would be to retain the non-rebuttable presumption of transfer, but only if the conditions precedent set out in Article 2(7) of the Directive are satisfied, in particular the signature of a contract and payment of equitable remuneration (within the meaning of Article 4 of the Directive) in respect of each right which is presumed to have been transferred. However, in view of the particular background to the inclusion of Article 2(7),[10] the incorporation of its provisions into national law is not recommended. Rather, instead of the loss of rights under Article 92 of the Law, either a rebuttable presumption of transfer of the exclusive rights provided for under Chapter II of the Directive should be introduced in accordance with Article 2(5) and Recital (19), first sentence, of the Directive, or no presumption of transfer need be provided at all. If a presumption under Article 2(5) of the Directive is incorporated, it will operate only where a contract, as set out in Article 2(5) of the Directive, is concluded and where the performer is granted an unwaivable right to equitable remuneration for the reproduction or other rights of exploitation included within the presumption. Moreover, the presumption of transfer may not be extended to the remuneration rights set out in Articles

---

[9] See the comments on Art. 9(2) of the Directive, p. 104.
[10] See the comments on Art. 2(7), p. 60.

76(2) and 77 of the Law because the Directive allows for a presumption of transfer only with respect to the exclusive rights covered by the Directive.

In addition it would seem necessary to amend Article 81 of the Law so as to ensure that the organising person thereunder will not be in a position to hinder the exploitation of rights under Articles 74, 75 and 76(1) of the Law if the performer wishes to authorise any such exploitation. This would mean that the person would be unable to prevent these acts of exploitation, once the performer has consented to them.[11]

---

[11] See the comments on Art. 10 of the Directive, p. 107.

# 5. Greece

## 1. THE PRESENT LEGAL SITUATION[12]

The Greek Copyright Act of 1920 does not provide for a rental or lending right. Despite this lack of explicit statutory provision it would seem that authors enjoy, on the basis of the concept of "droit de destination," an exclusive rental and lending right. However, these rights do not seem to be exercised in practice.

Protection for performers, phonogram and film producers and broadcasting organisations does not exist in the form of exclusive rights, but is granted only on the basis of specific terms in contractual agreements, provisions on unfair competition, the privacy right or general civil law rules. A law on the protection of performers has been of no effect since the regulations implementing the law (*cf.* Article 12(2) of the Law) have not been adopted.[13]

## 2. THE POSITION UNDER THE DIRECTIVE

The law will need to be clarified so that authors are entitled to enjoy an exclusive rental right, be it on the basis of "droit de destination" or of an explicit provision and, subject to the derogation offered by Article 5 of the Directive, an exclusive lending right. Aside from these two particular issues, all other provisions of the Directive will have to be introduced into the Greek law.

---

[12] The new Greek Copyright Law No. 2121/1993 which came into force on April 3, 1993 has not been taken into account for the purposes of this work, as a translation was not available at the time of writing. A useful article on "The New Greek Copyright Law" by Maniatis and Zannos is to be found at [1993] 8 E.I.P.R. 296.

[13] Law 1075/80, Official Gazette of the Government of the Hellenic Republic No. 218 of September 25, 1980.

# 6. Ireland

## 1. THE PRESENT LEGAL SITUATION

### (a) Rental and Lending Rights

The Irish Copyright Act 1963 ("the Act") and the Performers' Protection Act 1968[14] do not provide for an exclusive rental right, nor for a lending right in any form. Authors, phonogram and film producers and broadcasting organisations as well as performers enjoy certain protection, but this is limited to the situation of rental of an article the making of which constituted an infringement of copyright or of the performer's right; moreover, this protection depends on the satisfaction of further pre-conditions and does not amount to protection by way of an exclusive rental right (Sections 11(2)(b) and 21(6) of the Act; 2(1)(b) and 3(1)(b) of the Performers' Protection Act 1968).

### (b) Author of a Film, Presumptions of Transfer and Unwaivable Remuneration Right

Under Irish law, the principal director of a film is not recognised as being its author or one of its authors; it is only the maker or the commissioner who is entitled to copyright in the film (Section 18(3) and (10) of the Act).

Section 10(4) and (5) of the Act provides for a rebuttable presumption that an author's employer is entitled to the copyright in the author's work created in the course of employment.

Since performers do not enjoy exclusive rights, the Irish law does not provide for presumption of transfer of their rights.

Provision is not made for an unwaivable right to remuneration as set out in Article 4 of the Directive.

### (c) Rights of the type dealt with in Chapter II of the Directive

*Performers*

The Performers' Protection Act 1968 provides for criminal offences in the case of the unauthorised making of a record or film, the distribution of a record or film made in violation of the Act, the broadcasting and communication to the public of such a record or film and the broadcasting and communication to the public of a performance itself (Sections 2(1), 3(1) and 5

---

[14] Copyright Act No. 10 of April 8, 1963, and Performers' Protection Act No. 19 of July 2, 1968.

154

Performers' Protection Act 1968). According to certain court decisions, these criminal offences may also amount to a tort, thus giving rise to civil liability, so that the performer may be entitled to obtain relief such as an injunction and damages. The case law only refers, however, to particular criminal offences and, in addition, is somewhat controversial.

*Producers*

Phonogram producers are granted an exclusive right of reproduction and, in the case of an unpublished recording, an exclusive right of broadcasting and public communication thereof, or of a copy thereof. In the case of a published recording, the broadcasting and communication right amounts to a remuneration right, since the exclusive right subsists only for so long as equitable remuneration remains unpaid (Section 17(4) of the Act). According to Section 52(1) of the Act, the public communication of a sound recording broadcast by Radio Éireann does not constitute copyright infringement of that recording. Certain protection, which does not amount to an exclusive right, is afforded by Section 21(6) of the Act against different forms of distribution (for example sale, letting for hire) with respect to infringing copies.

The exclusive rights granted to a film producer include rights of reproduction, communication to the public and broadcasting (Section 18(4) of the Act). As in the case of phonogram producers, certain protection against different forms of distribution with respect to infringing copies is provided by Section 21(6) of the Act.

*Broadcasters*

Broadcasts are protected under Irish law only when they are made by Radio Éireann and transmitted from a place in Ireland. Radio Éireann enjoys exclusive rights of fixation (otherwise than for private purposes), reproduction, communication to the public (if the broadcast is seen or heard by a paying audience) and rebroadcasting (Section 19(5) of the Act). The protection mentioned under (d) above against different forms of distribution with respect to infringing copies is also provided for broadcasts by Section 21(6) of the Act.

## 2. THE POSITION UNDER THE DIRECTIVE

### (a) Rental and Lending Rights

An exclusive rental right (also called "restricted act") which is not limited to infringing copies will need to be introduced for authors, phonogram and film producers and performers. Broadcasting organisations may only enjoy a rental right in so far as they qualify as film or phonogram producers.

Provision will need to be made for a lending right if not in the form of an exclusive right in accordance with Article 1 of the Directive, then, at least for authors, as a remuneration right in accordance with Article 5 of the Directive.

155

## (b) Author of a Film, Presumptions of Transfer and Unwaivable Remuneration Right

With respect to rental and lending rights, the principal director of a cinematographic work must be deemed to be its author or one of its co-authors. Irish law is free to consider as co-author along with the principal director any other creative natural person contributing to the film or even the film producer. For consistency, it would seem sensible to consider the principal director of a film as the author or one of its authors on a more general basis, rather than limited to rental and lending rights only.

Together with the exclusive rental right, the unwaivable right to remuneration for authors and performers under Article 4 of the Directive will need to be introduced. Although the Directive would permit Irish law to designate the producer of a film as its co-author, it is clear from the structure of the Directive that "author" (as used in the *Directive*) does not include a performer or producer.[15] This is particularly relevant under Article 4 of the Directive, the purpose of which is to protect the typically weaker parties in a contract, namely performers and authors, as opposed to producers. Thus, the right to remuneration set out in Article 4 of the Directive may not be granted to film producers, even if they are to be considered co-authors under Irish law.

Likewise, a presumption of transfer of the performers' rental right in accordance with Article 2(5) of the Directive will need to be introduced. Certainly as regards the rental right and contracts relating to film producers, the rebuttable presumption in favour of the authors' employer (Section 10(4) and (5) of the Act) will have to be made subject to the unwaivable remuneration right in Article 4 of the Directive (see Article 2(6) of the Directive). With respect to the rental right under other contracts this presumption will have to be removed.

## (c) Performers' Rights in the Light of Chapter II of the Directive

With respect to the protection of performers, the existing case law, which grants civil remedies in certain cases, does not seem to be adequate. The law should make clear that performers enjoy, in addition to the rental and lending right, exclusive rights of fixation, direct and indirect reproduction, distribution in accordance with Article 9(1) and (2) of the Directive and, at least as far as their live performances are concerned, an exclusive right of broadcasting (including via satellite) and communication to the public, whether or not the record or film incorporating their performance was made in violation of the Act. With respect to the direct and indirect use of phonograms published for commercial purposes and of copies thereof for broadcasting and communication to the public, performers must be granted at least a remuneration right (or possibly even an exclusive right) within the terms of Article 8(2) of the Directive.

---

[15] See the comments on Art. 2(1) of the Directive, p. 45, where a similar argument is used in relation to the term "work."

### (d) Producers' Rights in the Light of Chapter II of the Directive

With respect to the existing rights of phonogram producers, it will have to be clarified under Irish law that the reproduction right includes indirect reproduction and that rights of broadcasting and public communication of published phonograms include indirect use for broadcasting and communication to the public. There will need to be clarification that the provisions of Section 52(1) of the Act are without prejudice to the remuneration right for indirect use of commercial phonograms for public communication. Also, it would be advisable to make specific mention in the law that broadcasting includes broadcasting via satellite. In addition, phonogram producers will need to be granted a distribution right subject to exhaustion according to Article 9(1) and (2) of the Directive; the protection accorded by Section 21(6) of the Act does not satisfy the requirements of the Directive.

Such a distribution right will also have to be granted to film producers. Their reproduction right must include indirect reproduction. Furthermore, in order to avoid misunderstandings it would be useful to clarify in Section 18(10) of the Act that film producers include only those who produce the first fixation of a film.

### (e) Broadcasters' Rights in the Light of Chapter II of the Directive

Section 19(5)(d) of the Act concerning the rebroadcasting right of broadcasting organisations should be amended so as to explicitly include broadcasting via satellite. As in the case of phonogram and film producers, broadcasting organisations must be granted a distribution right complying with Article 9 of the Directive. The broadcasting organisations entitled to this right should not be limited to Radio Éireann and must include cable distributors as defined in Article 6(2) and (3) of the Directive.

# 7. Italy

## 1. THE PRESENT LEGAL SITUATION

### (a) Rental and Lending Rights

In Italy, an exclusive rental right is provided by the Copyright Law of 1941[16] ("the Law"), but only for authors whose works have been recorded "on phonograph records, cinematographic films, metal tapes, or any analogous material or mechanical contrivance for reproducing sound or voices" (Article 61(1)1. and 2. of the Law.

Article 69 provides that the lending of protected works to the public for personal use is not covered by copyright.

### (b) Author of a Film, Presumptions of Transfer and Unwaivable Remuneration Right

As regards a film, the co-authors are the author of the literary work upon which the film is based, of the screenplay, of the music and the artistic director. However, it is only the producer of a film who is entitled to exercise the economic rights of the authors of the film. This may be regarded as a non-rebuttable presumption of transfer of such rights. A separate remuneration right for authors is provided only in specific cases (Articles 45(1) and 46(4) of the Act).

With respect to performers there is no presumption of transfer of rights. Italian law does not make provision for a remuneration right satisfying the requirements of Article 4 of the Directive.

### (c) Rights of the type dealt with in Chapter II of the Directive

*Performers*

Performers do not enjoy any exclusive rights, but only rights to remuneration for the fixation, reproduction and broadcasting of their live performances (Article 80(1) of the Law). In addition, a remuneration right is granted for the broadcasting and reproduction of performances that have already been broadcast, fixed or reproduced; however, these rights do not exist where the performance was made for the purposes of broadcasting or reproduction and where a remuneration has been paid for these purposes (Article 80(2) and (3) of the Law). Performers also enjoy a remuneration right in respect

---

[16] Law No. 633 of April 22, 1941.

of the "for-profit" use of a phonogram for broadcasting, films and communication to the public. Under Article 2(2) of Law No. 93 of February 5, 1992, this use of phonograms may be forbidden for a period of 15 to 180 days, if the remuneration is not paid.

*Phonogram Producers*

Phonogram producers enjoy the same rights as do performers with respect to the use of phonograms for broadcasting, films and public communication (Article 73 of the Law). In addition, they are granted exclusive rights of reproduction and distribution (Article 72 of the Law).

*Broadcasters*

Broadcasting organisations enjoy exclusive rights of fixation of their broadcasts and rebroadcasts for "purposes of profit," as well as exclusive rights of reproduction and of rebroadcasting. Unlike the other neighbouring rights, the law does not lay down a fixed duration for the broadcaster's rights.

*Film Producers*

Film producers are entitled to exercise the authors' economic rights. They do not, however, enjoy separate rights as first rightholders, with the exception of the remuneration right for the private copying of videograms (Article 3 of Law No. 93 of February 5, 1992). In addition to film producers, producers of videograms enjoy this right.

## 2. THE POSITION UNDER THE DIRECTIVE

### (a) Rental and Lending Rights

The existing rental right for authors will need to be extended to all media, with the exception of three-dimensional buildings and works of applied art. The right will also have to be extended to performers, and phonogram and film producers.

A lending right will need to be incorporated into the law, even if the exemptions allowed under Article 5 of the Directive are employed. Consequently, Article 69(1) of the Law will have to be modified. If the intention is to provide that lending to the public is free of charge, this would still not necessarily exclude the eventual obligation of libraries and public authorities to pay a remuneration, at least to authors.

### (b) Author of a Film, Presumption of Transfer and Unwaivable Remuneration Right

Article 45(1) of the Law, which has the same effect as a non-rebuttable presumption of transfer of economic rights to the film producer, will, as regards the rental right, either have to be made into a presumption which operates subject to contractual clauses to the contrary and to the unwaivable

159

remuneration right for rental in accordance with Article 4 of the Directive (Article 2(6) of the Directive), or it will have to be deleted.

A rebuttable presumption of transfer of the performer's exclusive rental right to the film producer, a presumption which is subject to the remuneration right of Article 4 of the Directive, will have to be added so as to comply with Article 2(5) of the Directive.

In addition, authors and performers must be assured of an unwaivable right of remuneration for rental in accordance with Article 4 of the Directive.

### (c) Performers' Rights in the Light of Chapter II of the Directive

The performers' remuneration rights, with the exception of the rights under Article 73(1) of the Law, will have to be transformed into exclusive rights. In addition, it would be useful to clarify that reproduction includes the recording of a performance which was broadcast, for example, on the basis of a phonogram ("indirect reproduction"), and that the remuneration right under Article 73(1) of the Law includes indirect use of phonograms, *i.e.* the rebroadcasting and the public showing or playing of a broadcast made on the basis of a phonogram. This remuneration right will also have to be extended to copies of phonograms and the restriction to use "for profit-making purposes" will have to be deleted. It will have to be made clear that the broadcasting and rebroadcasting rights include the (re-)broadcasting via satellite. An exclusive distribution right within the meaning of Article 9 of the Directive will also have to be added. Furthermore, there must be clarification that Article 80(3) of the Law is without prejudice to the reproduction and broadcasting rights provided for under Articles 7 and 8(1) and (2) of the Directive.

### (d) Phonogram Producers' Rights in the Light of Chapter II of the Directive

The phonogram producers' reproduction right should explicitly include indirect reproduction. The distribution right will have to be made subject to exhaustion in accordance with Article 9(2) of the Directive. With respect to the remuneration for broadcasting, which will clearly have to include satellite broadcasting, and communication to the public, the above comments on Article 73(1) of the Law in connection with the performers' rights should be taken into account.

### (e) Broadcasters' Rights in the Light of Chapter II of the Directive

The broadcasters' fixation right must not be restricted to fixation for the purposes of profit; however, this right may be limited in respect of private use (Article 10(1)(a) of the Directive). In addition, a distribution right subject to exhaustion in accordance with Article 9 of the Directive will have to be added. A limit on the duration of the broadcasters' rights, under Article 12 of the Directive, of at least 20 years following first broadcasting should be expressly provided for. It will have to be made clear that the rebroadcasting right includes rebroadcasting via satellite and that the broadcasting organisations who are entitled to the rights provided under the Directive are defined in accordance with Article 6(2) and (3) of the Directive.

## (f) Film Producers' Rights in the Light of Chapter II of the Directive

Film producers must be granted exclusive rights of reproduction and distribution, and those who qualify as "film producers" will have to be defined according to Article 2(1) of the Directive. Accordingly, producers of videograms can only be considered as right-owners in the case where they *first* fix moving images; this is not the case when they copy and, possibly, also edit the cinematographic film for the purposes of a videogram.

# 8. Luxembourg

## 1. THE PRESENT LEGAL SITUATION

### (a) Rental and Lending Rights

The situation with respect to the rental and lending rights is not clear. Article 3(1) of the Copyright Law 1972 ("the 1972 Law")[17] provides for a wide exploitation right for authors; a specific distribution right is granted only to authors of pre-existing works used in films (Article 26(1) of the 1972 Law). It may be assumed that, as under French law, a "droit de destination" has been developed by jurisprudence, which would include, at least in theory, exclusive rights of rental and lending for authors.

### (b) Author of a Film, Presumptions of Transfer and Unwaivable Remuneration Right

Under Article 27(1), first sentence, of the 1972 Law, the producer of a film is considered to be its author.

In addition, the producer of a film benefits from a rebuttable presumption of transfer of the rights of authors of pre-existing works (except musical works) to exploit the film in any form (Article 28 of the 1972 Law).

Performers who have consented to the inclusion of their performance in a film have no further enjoyment of their legal rights (Article 6, Law of September 23, 1975).

An unwaivable remuneration right as required by Article 4 of the Directive is not granted under Luxembourg law.

### (c) Rights of the type dealt with in Chapter II of the Directive

*Performers*

Under the Law of September 23, 1975 ("the 1975 Law") concerning the protection of performers, phonogram producers and broadcasting organisations, performers enjoy exclusive rights of fixation, reproduction (in the cases mentioned in Article 7(1)(c) Rome Convention) and broadcasting and communication to the public (Article 3 of the 1975 Law). Performers do not, however, enjoy these rights once they have consented to the inclusion of the performance in a film, whether or not accompanied by sound (Article 6 of the 1975 Law).

---

[17] Copyright Law of March 29, 1972.

*Phonogram Producers*

Phonogram producers enjoy exclusive rights of reproduction, importation (as regards unauthorised phonograms imported for the purpose of distribution) and distribution of unauthorised phonograms (Article 8 of the 1975 Law).

*Broadcasters*

Broadcasting organisations enjoy exclusive rights of rebroadcasting, fixation and, subject to certain conditions, of reproduction (Article 10 of the 1975 Law).

*Film Producers*

The copyright in a film, and hence, *inter alia*, an exclusive reproduction and distribution right, vest first in the film producer (Article 27(1), first sentence, of the 1975 Law).

## 2. THE POSITION UNDER THE DIRECTIVE

### (a) Rental and Lending Rights

Since the situation with respect to the rental and lending rights is unclear – in any case, these rights seem to be rarely exercised in practice – these rights must be explicitly provided for authors; in addition, the same rights must be provided for performers, phonogram and film producers.

With respect to lending, the derogations under Article 5 of the Directive may be applied.

### (b) Author of a Film, Presumption of Transfer and Unwaivable Remuneration Right

With respect to the rental and lending right, the principal director of a film must be its author. Other individuals, for example the screen-writers, or even the film producer may be considered as co-authors. For consistency, it would be advisable to consider the principal director of a film as the sole, or one of its, author(s) on a general basis, rather than with respect to the rental and lending right only.

The rebuttable presumption contained in Article 28 of the 1972 Law will either have to be made subject to an unwaivable remuneration right as set out in Article 4 of the Directive, or it will have to be deleted.

Article 6 of the 1975 Law may be extended to the performers' rental right, but only if the preconditions of Article 2(7) of the Directive are satisfied, in particular the existence of a signed contract and provision for payment of an equitable remuneration within the terms of Article 4 of the Directive. However, given the content of the discussions among the Member States and the background behind the inclusion of Article 2(7) (it was effectively a concession to one Member State in view of its rather comprehensive regulation of

163

the relationship between performers and film producers, with the aim of providing a balance between the interests of performers and film producers), it would be advisable not to apply Article 2(7) of the Directive, but rather to provide for a rebuttable presumption as set out in Article 2(5) of the Directive.[18]

An unwaivable remuneration right under Article 4 of the Directive will need to be provided for authors and performers. Although the Directive allows Luxembourg law to designate the producer of a film as its co-author, it is clear from the structure of the Directive that the term "author" (as used in the Directive) does not include a performer or producer.[19] This is particularly evident in the case of Article 4 of the Directive, the purpose of which is the protection of weaker parties to contracts, namely performers and authors, as opposed to producers. Thus, the remuneration right in Article 4 of the Directive may not be granted to film producers, even if they are considered to be co-authors under Luxembourg law.

### (c) Performers' Rights in the Light of Chapter II of the Directive

The performers' reproduction right will have to be extended to cover indirect reproduction, and conditions corresponding to those of Article 7(1) (c) of the Rome Convention will have to be deleted. In addition, an exclusive distribution right and a remuneration right for direct and indirect use of phonograms in accordance with Article 8(2) of the Directive must be granted; wider protection than that provided by Article 8(2) of the Directive may be given. In this context, it would be useful to state clearly that broadcasting and rebroadcasting cover satellite broadcasting. Article 6 of the 1975 Law, which takes rights away from the performer once he consents to the inclusion of his performance in a film, will have to be either deleted (the Directive does not require any presumption of transfer with respect to the rights of Chapter II), or modified in order to comply with the conditions of Article 2(7) or, preferably, Article 2(5) of the Directive (see also comments under (b) above in connection with the rental right).

### (d) Phonogram Producers' Rights in the Light of Chapter II of the Directive

With respect to the phonogram producers' reproduction right there will need to be clarification that it covers indirect reproduction. Their distribution right will have to be extended to the distribution of authorised phonograms. There will have to be provision made for the exhaustion of this distribution right in accordance with Article 9(2) of the Directive. Remuneration for direct and indirect use for broadcasting (including satellite broadcasting) and public communication under Article 8(2) of the Directive will also have to be included.

---

[18] See the comments on Art. 2(5) to 2(7), p. 54 et seq.
[19] See the comments on Art. 2(1) of the Directive, p. 45, referring to a similar argument in relation to the term "work". See also n. 15 above, and the relevant text.

### (e) Broadcasters' Rights in the Light of Chapter II of the Directive

The broadcasters' reproduction right will have to include indirect reproduction and must not be restricted to the three situations covered by Luxembourg law. An exclusive right of communication to the public under the circumstances of Article 8(3) of the Directive, and a distribution right under Article 9 of the Directive will have to be added. Broadcasting organisations will have to be defined in accordance with Article 6(2) and (3) of the Directive.

### (f) Film Producers' Rights in the Light of Chapter II of the Directive

If authors' rights are to continue to vest in the first event in film producers, it will not be necessary to create separate neighbouring rights. However, it is recommended that the rights of film directors as authors' rights on the one hand, and the rights of film producers as neighbouring rights on the other hand be clearly separated. In any case, the producers' rights will have to extend to films, which are not protected as works because of lack of originality.

# 9. The Netherlands

## 1. THE PRESENT LEGAL SITUATION

### (a) Rental and Lending Rights

The Dutch Copyright Act ("the 1912 Act") and the Dutch Act on Neighbouring Rights[20] do not provide for a rental right at all.

The Dutch Welfare Act[21] contains provisions for a remuneration right with respect to the lending of works in printed form by public libraries for the most important groups of authors, and publishers. The remuneration right expires with the death of the author. Foreign authors are entitled to the right only if they are resident in The Netherlands, and publishing houses have to exercise their business activities in The Netherlands. In all cases, a work qualifies for a public lending right only if its text is written in the Dutch or Frisian language.

### (b) Presumptions of Transfer and Unwaivable Remuneration Right

Under Dutch law, film producers benefit from a rebuttable presumption of transfer of certain rights of authors of a film such as the right to make the work available to the public. In certain cases, in particular in the case of exploitation in a form that did not exist or was not reasonably foreseeable at the time of completion of the film, the author is explicitly entitled to equitable remuneration (Article 45(d) of the 1912 Act). In addition, according to a recent amendment to Article 45(d) of the 1912 Act,[22] the producer is required to pay an equitable remuneration to the authors of the film for every kind of exploitation; the remuneration has to be agreed between the parties in writing.

With respect to employed authors, Article 7 of the 1912 Act provides for a rebuttable presumption of the authorship in favour of the employer. A similar presumption is provided by Article 8 of the 1912 Act in favour of public bodies, associations, foundations and companies which publish a work as their own work without indicating the name of a natural person as its author.

The relationship between performers and film producers is intended to be regulated in the same way as the respective relationship between authors and film producers (Article 4 of the Act on Neighbouring Rights, see the comment above on Article 45(d) of the 1912 Act).

---

[20] Copyright Act of September 23, 1912 and Act on Neighbouring Rights, Dutch Official Journal 1993, 178; in force July 1, 1993.

[21] Act of February 14, 1987; Dutch Official Journal, 1987, 73.

[22] A new 3rd sentence to Article 45(d) of the Act has been inserted by Art. 35 of the Act.

As far as the performers' position vis-à-vis their employer is concerned, the Act on Neighbouring Rights provides that the employer is authorised to exercise the exclusive rights of the performer, if the parties agreed thereon or if it follows from the type of the contract, from custom or from principles of loyalty and good faith. If the parties agreed otherwise or a different conclusion follows from the contract, custom or principles of loyalty and good faith, the employer must pay an equitable remuneration for every kind of exploitation of these rights (Article 3 of the Act on Neighbouring Rights).

### (c) Rights of the type dealt with in Chapter II of the Directive

According to the Act on Neighbouring Rights ("the 1993 Act"), performers enjoy exclusive rights of fixation, reproduction and distribution as well as broadcasting, rebroadcasting and public communication of live performances or fixed performances. With respect to the use of commercial phonograms for broadcasting and public communication, the exclusive right is reduced to a right to an equitable remuneration (Articles 2 and 7 of the 1993 Act). The relationship between performers and film producers or employers is regulated by Articles 3 and 4 of the 1993 Act (see comments under (b) above).

Phonogram producers are granted exclusive rights of reproduction, distribution, broadcasting, rebroadcasting and public communication; in the case of commercial phonograms, the exclusive right is replaced with a remuneration right for broadcasting and public communication (Articles 6 and 7 of the 1993 Act).

Broadcasting organisations benefit from exclusive rights of fixation, reproduction, distribution, rebroadcasting and public communication (Article 8 of the 1993 Act). No rights vest in film producers as first right-owners.

## 2. THE POSITION UNDER THE DIRECTIVE

### (a) Rental and Lending Rights

An exclusive rental right will need to vest in authors, performers and phonogram and film producers.

Broadcasting organisations may enjoy a rental right only in so far as they are, at the same time, phonogram or film producers.

The existing public lending right will have to be expanded. The principle behind Article 1 of the Directive, *i.e.* an exclusive lending right for all groups of authors, performers, phonogram and film producers, will need to be stated in the law. A derogation from this right may be made in accordance with Article 5 of the Directive, whether it be in respect of books or printed material only, or several kinds of lending objects or even all kinds of lending objects. To the extent that the exclusive right is replaced with a remuneration right, all groups of authors must benefit, and performers, phonogram or film producers may also be granted this right. Broadcasting organisations may, however, only be entitled to the lending right – either in the form of an exclusive right or a remuneration right – in so far as they are, at the same time, phonogram or film producers. If an exclusive right in respect of phonograms or films is to be provided in The Netherlands, Article 4 of the Directive should, following the spirit of the Directive, be applied in favour of authors and performers.

As far as the existing public lending right is concerned, it would seem possible to retain certain specific provisions, such as the short duration of the remuneration right and the entitlement of publishers, since Article 5 of the Directive does not require a copyright-based public lending right[23]; in addition, the discussions on Article 5 of the Directive were characterised by the Commission's offer of flexibility in respect of individual elements of existing public lending right schemes. This can be seen in particular in the Commission statement for the records of the Council on the Danish public lending right scheme.[24]

### (b) Presumptions of Transfer and Unwaivable Remuneration Right

The presumption of transfer of the rights of authors of a film under Article 45(d) of the 1912 Act will, in so far as it includes exclusive rental or, possibly, lending rights, only comply with the Directive if the presumption is made subject to an *unwaivable* right to obtain an equitable remuneration for the rental (or lending) in accordance with Article 4 of the Directive (see Article 2(6) of the Directive). One possible solution would be to modify the recent amendment to Article 45(d) of the 1912 Act accordingly.[25] It seems, however, more advisable to provide that the requirement for an unwaivable right to equitable remuneration is satisfied by a remuneration right administered by collecting societies (as indicated in this work in the context of Article 4 of the Directive).

It seems doubtful whether Articles 7 and 8 of the 1912 Act, which provide for rebuttable presumptions of authorship for employers and certain other bodies, comply with the provisions of the Directive. In respect of rental and lending rights and the author's relationship with a film producer (who may be an employer or other body), Article 2(2) of the Directive does not allow the authorship to be taken away from the principal film director. Consequently, Articles 7 and 8 of the 1912 Act will have to be modified so as to comply with Article 2(2) of the Directive. This may be achieved, for example, by exempting the film director from the application of Articles 7 and 8 of the 1912 Act with respect to his rental or lending rights, or by transforming these Articles into a rebuttable presumption of transfer under Article 2(6) of the Directive which, in turn, would have to be made subject to the remuneration right under Article 4 of the Directive.

The existing rebuttable presumption of transfer of performers' rights to a film producer will need to be extended to the exclusive rental right and made subject to the unwaivable remuneration right under Article 4 of the Directive.[26] Article 3 of the 1993 Act concerning employed performers must clearly be made without prejudice to this rebuttable presumption in accordance with Article 2(5) of the Directive (described above).

---

[23] See the comments on Art. 5, p. 77.
[24] See n. 3.
[25] See n. 18.
[26] For possible solutions see the comments on the authors' presumption of transfer under 2(b), above.

Article 4 of the Directive may be implemented by way of contractual provisions, in particular by amending Article 45(d) of the 1912 Act in order to ensure that it complies with Article 4 of the Directive. However, it would be more in line with the purpose of Article 4 of the Directive[27] to provide that authors and performers, once they have assigned (explicitly or because of a presumption of transfer) their exclusive rental rights, are entitled to an unwaivable statutory right to obtain equitable remuneration for any such rental, and that this right would be exercised by the competent collecting societies. These collecting societies could negotiate, together with the producers and rental outlets, the amounts to be paid to producers and collecting societies respectively.

### (c) Rights in the Light of Chapter II of the Directive

With respect to the Act on Neighbouring Rights, it will have to be made clear that reproduction rights include indirect reproduction and that the remuneration right of performers and phonogram producers under Article 7 includes *indirect* use of commercial phonograms for broadcasting and public communication (unless these uses are covered by the respective exclusive rights). The rebuttable presumption of transfer of performers' rights to a film producer (Article 4 of the 1993 Act) will either have to be made subject to an unwaivable right to obtain an equitable remuneration for every kind of exploitation (and Article 3 of the 1993 Act will have to be without prejudice to this rule) or it will have to be deleted with respect to those rights granted in Chapter II of the Directive (see Recital (19) of the Directive).

Producers of films must enjoy reproduction and distribution rights as first rightholders. The presumption of transfer of authors' rights does not satisfy this requirement. Film producers' rights will need to be extended to cover films which are not protected as works because they do not meet the required standard of originality.

The exhaustion of the distribution rights of performers, phonogram and film producers and broadcasting organisations under the 1993 Act will have to be adapted so as to comply with Article 9(2) of the Directive, in particular as regards the precondition that the first sale be made in the "Community."

---

[27] See the respective comments on Art. 4, p. 66.

# 10. Portugal

## 1. THE PRESENT LEGAL SITUATION

### (a) Rental and Lending Rights

The Portuguese Copyright Act[28] ("the Act") provides, *inter alia*, an exclusive right for authors to sell and rent copies of their works (Article 68(2)(f) of the Act), and an exclusive right of distribution including rental for phonogram and videogram producers (Articles 184(1) and 176(8) of the Act). This distribution right is not subject to exhaustion, so that it is arguable that phonogram and videogram producers enjoy an exclusive rental right.

With respect to lending, the law is less clear and could be interpreted in various ways. Either no lending right exists or there is an exclusive lending right forming part of a broad distribution right of authors, phonogram and videogram producers.

### (b) Presumptions of Transfer and Unwaivable Remuneration Right

When the author of a film authorises, even implicitly, the projection of the film, he is no longer entitled to exercise the rights of economic exploitation of that film; the right to exercise these rights then belongs solely to the producer (Article 125(2) of the Act). In addition, Article 127(2) of the Act provides a rebuttable presumption that the author, who agrees to the production of a film, automatically authorises certain acts, such as distribution of the film, "without prejudice to payment of the agreed remuneration." With respect to employed or commissioned authors, the ownership of copyright is determined in accordance with the relevant agreement (Article 14(1) of the Act). In the absence of any agreement, such ownership is presumed to belong to the intellectual creator (Article 14(2) of the Act).

Performers do not enjoy any rights with respect to performances arising from official functions or pursuant to employment contracts which they have entered into (Article 189(2) of the Act).

### (c) Rights of the type dealt with in Chapter II of the Directive

*Performers*

Performers "may refuse" the fixation, broadcasting and communication to the public of their live performances and, subject to conditions which correspond to those mentioned in Article 7(1)(c) of the Rome Convention, the

---

[28] Act No. 63 of March 14, 1985, as amended by Acts No. 45 of September 17, 1985 and No. 114 of September 3, 1991.

reproduction of fixations of their performances (Article 178 of the Act). They are granted a right to remuneration for the "public communication" of the commercially published phonograms or videograms (Article 184(3) of the Act).

Performers do not enjoy any rights with respect to performances arising from official functions or pursuant to employment contracts (Article 189(2) of the Act).

### Producers

Producers of phonograms and videograms are granted exclusive rights of reproduction, distribution, import and export, dissemination by any means and public performance as well as a right to remuneration with respect to the public communication of commercially published phonograms and videograms (Article 184 of the Act).

The term "videogram producers" appears to include producers of mere copies of cinematographic works on video cassettes (Article 176(3), (5) of the Act).

### Broadcasters

Broadcasting organisations enjoy exclusive rights of fixation, rebroadcasting and, under certain conditions, reproduction (Article 187 of the Act). The definition of "broadcasting organisation" includes, *inter alia*, bodies which effect the diffusion of sounds and/or images by cable (Article 176(9) of the Act).

## 2. THE POSITION UNDER THE DIRECTIVE

### (a) Rental and Lending Rights

It would be useful to state explicitly in the Portuguese law that an exclusive rental right exists for authors, phonogram and film producers, and that the possible exhaustion of the distribution right does not affect the subsistence of the rental right. In addition, an exclusive rental right has to vest in performers.

The above comments on the rental right apply also to the lending right. However, derogations from the exclusive lending right under Article 5 of the Directive may be made so long as at least authors obtain a remuneration.

### (b) Presumptions of Transfer and Unwaivable Remuneration Right

As explained earlier, Article 125(2) of the Act takes away from the author the ability to exercise his rights of economic exploitation of the film; this amounts to a non-rebuttable presumption of transfer of rights from the author to the producer. As this does not comply with Article 2(6) of the Directive it will have to be amended, either by excluding the rental and, possibly, lending right from the application of this provision, or by introducing a rebuttable presumption of transfer in accordance with Article 2(5) of the Directive. Likewise, the presumption in Article 127(2) of the Act will have to be made subject to the unwaivable right to obtain equitable remuneration in accordance with Article 4 of the Directive; the reference in Article 127(2) of the Act to the "agreed remuneration" does not satisfy the requirements of the Directive, since any, even a very low, remuneration may be agreed on. Furthermore, Article 127(2) of the Act does not provide for separate remuneration for every kind of exploitation. It seems appropriate to ensure that, at least with respect to the rental and lending right, the initial ownership of copyright for films is not at the disposal of the parties to an employment or other contract. Accordingly, it will have to be specified that Article 14(1) of the Act does not allow the parties to agree on the initial ownership of copyright of the employer or similar person. Such an agreement would be in contravention of Article 2(2) of the Directive.

Since the rental and lending rights are vested in all groups of performers, including employed performers, Article 189(2) of the Act will have to be deleted. A rebuttable presumption of transfer in favour of film producers in accordance with Article 2(5) of the Directive has to be provided.

With respect to the exclusive rental right (and, as the case may be, lending right), authors and performers will have to be assured of an unwaivable right to obtain equitable remuneration for rental (or lending) in accordance with Article 4 of the Directive.

### (c) Performers' Rights in the Light of Chapter II of the Directive

With respect to performers' rights the words "may refuse" will have to be replaced with the corresponding terms used in connection with the rights of other neighbouring rightholders under Portuguese law so as to clarify that performers will enjoy exclusive rights authorising and prohibiting certain acts.

The conditions under which the performers' reproduction right is granted, will need to be deleted, and the (unconditional) reproduction right will have to include indirect reproduction, in so far as this is not provided for under Article 176(6) of the Act. With respect to remuneration for the public communication of phonograms (Article 184(3) of the Act) there will need to be clarification that this provision also covers broadcasting (including satellite broadcasting), as well as indirect use for broadcasting and communication to the public. A distribution right in accordance with Article 9 of the Directive will need to be granted.

The rights covered by the Directive which are provided for performers will need to vest in all groups of performers, including employed performers. Accordingly, Article 189(2) of the Act will have to be deleted.

### (d) Producers' Rights in the Light of Chapter II of the Directive

With respect to the remuneration right for phonogram producers under Article 184(3) of the Act, the above comments under (c) apply.

The definition of the distribution right of phonogram and film producers will have to be modified so as to accord with the definition in Article 9 of the Directive and will have to be subject to exhaustion in accordance with Article 9(2) of the Directive.

There will need to be clarification under Articles 176(3) and 176(5) of the Act, that rights under the Directive only vest in the first event in film producers if they first fix images on any material whatsoever, and that the mere copying, with or without adaptation, of cinematographic or other films for the purposes of exploitation by videogram does not entitle them to any rights (see Article 2(1), fourth indent, of the Directive).

### (e) Broadcasters' Rights in the Light of Chapter II of the Directive

The protection of broadcasting organisations will have to be completed by an exclusive right of communication to the public in the circumstances envisaged by Article 8(3) of the Directive and by an exclusive distribution right in accordance with Article 9 of the Directive.

The rebroadcasting right will have specifically to include broadcasting by satellite; the definition in Article 176(9) of the Act only refers to broadcasting organisations, but not to the activity of broadcasting. With respect to the reproduction right, the above comments under (c) concerning the performers' reproduction right apply.

The definition of "broadcasting organisations" will have to make clear that cable (re)-distributors within the meaning of Article 6(3) of the Directive are not included.

# 11. Spain

## 1. THE PRESENT LEGAL SITUATION

### (a) Rental and Lending Rights

Authors, phonogram producers and film producers enjoy an exclusive right of distribution, *inter alia*, by rental and lending. This right seems to be exhausted only with respect to sale as set out in the Act Spanish Intellectual Property[29] ("the Act") (Articles 17, 19; 109(1), 113, 122 of the Act). Thus it is arguable that exclusive rental and lending rights exist under Spanish law. However, these rights do not seem to be exercised in practice.

### (b) Presumptions of Transfer and Unwaivable Remuneration Right

With respect to a film production contract, a non-rebuttable presumption of transfer of certain rights, including the distribution right, of authors in favour of film producers is provided by Article 88(1) of the Act; this presumption does not, however, cover exploitation by making available to the public copies of the film for the purpose of use within the family circle, *i.e.* presumably, exploitation by rental and lending.

With respect to contracts between performers and film producers, Article 102(3) of the Act provides for a non-rebuttable presumption of authorisation of reproduction, broadcasting and public communication; in addition, Article 104 of the Act provides a rebuttable presumption of transfer of certain rights to the performer's employer. No remuneration right, as required by Article 4 of the Directive, exists under Spanish law.

### (c) Rights of the type dealt with in Chapter II of the Directive

*Performers*

Performers enjoy exclusive rights of fixation, reproduction, communication to the public and broadcasting, as well as a remuneration right for the use of commercial phonograms for broadcasting and communication to the public (Articles 102(1), 103, 122, 18, 20(1) of the Act). With respect to

---

[29] Act No. 22 of November 11, 1987.

174

presumptions of transfer of performers' rights, the comments above under (b) apply.

*Producers*

Phonogram and film producers enjoy exclusive rights of reproduction, broadcasting, communication to the public and distribution (Articles 109 and 113 of the Act).

*Broadcasters*

Broadcasting organisations are granted exclusive rights of fixation, reproduction, rebroadcasting and of communication to the public at places accessible to the public on payment of an entrance fee (Article 116 of the Act). Broadcasting organisations appear to include cable distributors; it is not clear from Article 116(1) of the Act whether the protection extends to cable distributors which merely retransmit the broadcasts of other broadcasting organisations.

## 2. THE POSITION UNDER THE DIRECTIVE

### (a) Rental and Lending Rights

Given the lack of exercise of a rental and lending right in Spain, it would be advisable to clarify that the exhaustion of the distribution right does not affect rental and lending rights. In addition, an exclusive rental and lending right will have to be provided for performers. Derogations from the exclusive lending right, as set out in Article 5 of the Directive, may be incorporated.

### (b) Presumptions of Transfer and Unwaivable Remuneration Right

If rental and lending are covered by the presumption of transfer of authors' rights in Article 88(1) of the Act and do not fall under the above-mentioned exception, the presumption of transfer will need to be changed to a rebuttable presumption which is subject to the unwaivable right to equitable remuneration under Article 4 of the Directive.

A presumption of transfer of the performer's rental and, as the case may be, exclusive lending right will have to be provided in accordance with Article 2(5) of the Directive; it is possible, but less advisable[30] to introduce a presumption under Article 2(7) of the Directive. The existing presumption in the case of film productions of a performer's authorisation under Article 102(3) of the Act will have to be made subject to an unwaivable right to obtain equitable remuneration in consideration for the resulting exploitation, and subject to a signed contract in accordance with Article 2(7) of the Directive. As an alternative, it would be preferable to change the presumption into a rebuttable presumption subject to the unwaivable remuneration right under Article 4 of the

---

[30] See the comments on Art. 2(5) to 2(7) of the Directive, p. 54.

Directive, in accordance with Article 2(5) of the Directive.[31] In so far as the presumption refers to phonograms, it cannot be retained under the terms of the Directive.[32] The presumption in Article 104 of the Act, to the extent that it covers the relationship between performers and film producers, will have to be completed by a reference to the unwaivable right of equitable remuneration for those kinds of exploitation which are covered by the presumption.[33]

The unwaivable right to equitable remuneration in accordance with Article 4 of the Directive will have to be implemented.

### (c) Rights in the Light of Chapter II of the Directive

There will need to be clarification that the reproduction rights of performers, film producers and broadcasting organisations include indirect reproduction. Performers as well as broadcasters will have to be granted an exclusive distribution right within the meaning of Article 9 of the Directive. Article 103 of the Act will have to explicitly refer to *copies* of commercial phonograms and, like Article 109(1) of the Act, explicitly refer to *indirect* use of phonograms for broadcasting and public communication.

Provisions for exhaustion of the distribution rights of phonogram and film producers will need to comply with Article 9(2) of the Directive. This is not clear from the existing law.

It will have to be made clear that cable distributors which merely retransmit the broadcasts of other broadcasting organisations are not covered by the broadcasting organisations mentioned in Article 116 of the Act (see Article 6(3) of the Directive).

---

[31] See the comments on Art. 2(5) to 2(7) of the Directive, p. 54.
[32] See the comments on Recital (19), phrase 2, p. 112.
[33] See Art. 2(5), 4 and Recital (19) of the Directive and the comments thereon, pp. 54, 112.

# 12. United Kingdom

## 1. THE PRESENT LEGAL SITUATION

### (a) Rental and Lending Rights

Section 18(2) of the Copyright, Designs and Patents Act[34] ("the Act") grants an exclusive rental right to authors of computer programs only and producers of phonograms and films. The same groups of rightholders are granted an exclusive lending right (Schedule 7(8)). Section 66 of the Act empowers the Secretary of State to provide by way of order that, in certain cases, the rental shall be treated as licensed by the copyright owner, if no certified licensing scheme exists.

Performers enjoy an exclusive right of distribution which explicitly covers rental and, as may be assumed, implicitly (as a form of distribution) lending. This right, however, refers only to illicit recordings and applies only if the infringer knows or has reason to believe that the recording is illicit (Section 184(1)(b) of the Act).

Apart from the exclusive lending right, a public lending right exists on the basis of a specific statute[35] for writers, adaptors, illustrators, photographers, translators and editors, but not for composers and performers. Remuneration is paid for the lending of books only. Lending in general public libraries, but not by research and other libraries, is covered by the scheme.

### (b) Author of Films, Presumptions of Transfer and Unwaivable Remuneration Right

The author of a film is taken to be "the person by whom the arrangements necessary for the making of a film are undertaken" (Section 9(2)(a) of the Act); Section 77 *et seq.* of the Act do not give the director of a film the qualities of an "author," but only confer specific moral rights.

In the case of employed authors, the employer, not the author, is the first owner of copyright, subject to any agreement to the contrary (Section 11(2) of the Act).

In general, no presumption of transfer of performers' rights to the film producer is provided, nor is there an unwaivable remuneration right in accordance with Article 4 of the Directive. However, Section 190 of the Act provides

---

[34] Copyright, Designs and Patents Act 1988 (c. 48).
[35] Public Lending Right Act 1979 (c. 10) with Public Lending Right Scheme 1982, Commencement Order 1982 No. 719 and numerous Amendment Orders.

for a compulsory licence in respect of the performer's reproduction rights under specified circumstances.

## (c) Rights of the type dealt with in Chapter II of the Directive

### *Performers*

Performers are protected not only by criminal law, but also by statutory civil rights of action which amount to exclusive rights to authorise or prohibit certain acts of exploitation. These rights include the fixation of live performances, their direct or indirect reproduction, broadcasting and inclusion in a cable program service. Performers also have exclusive rights of public communication, broadcasting and inclusion in a cable program service of their performances "by means of a recording which was, and which a person knows, or has reason to believe, was made without the performer's consent" (Section 183 of the Act). In addition, performers enjoy exclusive rights in relation to the importation and distribution of illicit recordings under the terms of Section 184(1) of the Act. These rights are not transferable except on the death of the person entitled to performer's rights or upon the assignment of the benefit of a contract or licence (Section 192 of the Act). However, a performer may grant licences in relation to his performances (Section 193(1) of the Act).

### *Producers*

Phonogram producers are protected, in so far as they have an exclusive recording contract with a performer, in the same way as performers (Section 185 *et seq.* of the Act). In addition, they enjoy exclusive rights of reproduction, showing and playing, broadcasting, inclusion in a cable program service and issuing of copies to the public (Sections 17, 19(3), 20(b) and 18 of the Act, respectively). Film producers enjoy the same rights as phonogram producers.

### *Broadcasters*

Broadcasting organisations and cable program services are granted the same rights as phonogram producers, with the exception of the rights set out in Section 185 *et seq.* of the Act. The right of "broadcasting" a broadcast amounts to a rebroadcasting right.

## 2. The Position under the Directive

### (a) Rental and Lending Rights

The exclusive rental right under UK law will have to be extended to all groups of authors and performers as first rightholders; the performers' rental right under Section 184(1)(b) of the Act is restricted to illicit recordings and depends on the infringer's knowledge or "reason to believe," and therefore does not meet the requirements of the Directive.

If the United Kingdom wishes to preserve exclusive lending rights in respect of films and phonograms, it will have to include the authors (for example the composer, director of the film) and performers contributing to the film or phonogram as first rightholders. In accordance with the purpose of Article 4 of the Directive and the discussions which took place among the Member States, it would seem advisable to introduce an unwaivable right to equitable remuneration under Article 4 of the Directive for authors and performers.[36]

Since the rental right must be an exclusive right, it is doubtful whether Section 66 of the Act in its present form can be retained.

Besides these exclusive rights, the UK public lending right scheme can largely continue to subsist under the Directive, since Article 5 of the Directive offers a large degree of flexibility. However, *all* groups of authors, including composers will have to be remunerated, and those lending objects which are not or will not be covered by the exclusive right, such as sheet music, will have to be included as part of a public lending right scheme.

### (b) Author of a Film, Presumptions of Transfer and Unwaivable Remuneration Right

With respect to rental and lending rights, there will have to be provision for the principal director of a film to be its author or one of its authors. In addition, Article 2(2) of the Directive does not permit employed authors of a film to be deprived of their authorship or first ownership of copyright. Accordingly, Section 11(2) of the Act will need to be amended. For consistency, it is recommended that the principal director of a film be considered as the author or one of its authors on a general basis rather than being limited to rental and lending rights only.

There will need to be provision for a presumption of transfer (or licensing) of the performers' exclusive rental right in accordance with Article 2(5) of the Directive. In addition, the UK law will have to incorporate the unwaivable right to equitable remuneration for authors and performers under Article 4 of the Directive. Although the Directive will permit UK law to designate the producer of a film as its co-author, the context of the term "author" in the Directive shows that this term does not include a performer or producer.[37] This is particularly evident from Article 4 of the Directive, the purpose of which is to protect the typically weaker parties to a contract, namely performers and authors, as opposed to producers. Thus, the remuneration right contained in Article 4 of the Directive may not be granted to film producers, even if they are considered to be co-authors under UK law.

Since the performer's reproduction right must be an exclusive right, Section 190 of the Act does not satisfy the provisions of the Directive and cannot be retained.

---

[36] See the comments on Art. 4, p. 65.

[37] See the comments on Art. 2(1) of the Directive, p. 45, referring to similar argument in relation to the term "work." See also notes 15 and 19, above.

### (c) Performers' Rights in the Light of Chapter II of the Directive

With respect to performers' rights, a right of public communication of live performances has to be provided for. The right to use a recorded performance for broadcasting and communication to the public must not be restricted to recordings made without the consent of the performer and will have to include *indirect* use for broadcasting and public communication; under Article 8(2) of the Directive, a right to an equitable remuneration would, however, be sufficient rather than the exclusive right provided for by UK law. Similarly, the distribution right must not be restricted to illicit recordings; this right can *only* be exhausted in accordance with the conditions of Article 9(2) of the Directive in particular not by first sale outside the Community. The requirement of transferability of exclusive rights (see for example Article 7(2) of the Directive) are met since the performer may grant contractual licences.[38] Thus, Section 192 of the Act may continue to apply.

### (d) Producers' and Broadcasters' Rights in the Light of Chapter II of the Directive

The reproduction rights of phonogram and film producers and broadcasting organisations will have to specifically include indirect reproduction. The rights granted to phonogram producers' in relation to communication (showing and playing) and broadcasting will have to include *indirect* use of commercial phonograms for communication to the public and for broadcasting. This must, at the very least, take the form of a right to remuneration under Article 8(2) of the Directive. The rights of phonogram and film producers and broadcasting organisations to issue copies to the public will have to be amended so as to comply with Article 9(2) of the Directive; in particular, exhaustion of the right may only occur if copies are issued to the public within, but not outside, the Community.[39]

---

[38] See the comments on Art. 2(4) of the Directive, p. 53.
[39] See the comments on Art. 9(2) of the Directive, p. 104.

SECTION IV

# THE POSITION IN THE EFTA COUNTRIES

# Introduction[1]

Five members of the European Free Trade Association (EFTA), namely Austria, Finland, Norway, Sweden and Switzerland, have applied for E.C. membership. In order to become Member States of the E.C., these countries will, in principle, have to adapt their national laws so as to embrace Community Law which includes Directives on copyright. Prior to this they will, like the other EFTA countries Iceland and Liechtenstein, but not Switzerland,[2] have to incorporate all the Community's single-market legislation. This is in accordance with the European Economic Area Treaty (EEA Treaty) which was signed by the E.C. and EFTA foreign ministers on May 2, 1992 and will come into force upon ratification of that Treaty and of the protocol signed on March 17, 1993 by all contracting parties.[3] A consequence of the EEA Treaty will be the application of E.C. rules on the free circulation of goods, services, persons and capital within a single market of 370 million consumers. The EFTA countries, except Switzerland, will have to implement those parts of the Community's primary and secondary law (the so-called "*acquis communautaire*,") which relate to the single market, including harmonisation measures in the field of intellectual property.

The EEA Treaty includes Protocol No. 28 on intellectual property. With regard to copyright, the protocol specifies that the contracting parties shall "adjust their legislation on intellectual property so as to make it compatible with the principles of free circulation of goods and services and with the level of protection of intellectual property attained in Community Law, including the level of enforcement of those rights." In addition, the six EFTA countries, except Switzerland undertake to "adjust, upon request and after consultation between the Contracting Parties, their legislation on intellectual property in order to reach at least the level of protection of intellectual property prevailing in the Community upon signature of this Agreement." Accordingly, those EFTA countries (without, for the time being, Switzerland) will have to incorporate the rental right Directive into their national laws.

---

[1] The position in central and eastern European countries will not be dealt with in the framework of this book, not least because at the moment the legislation is in a constant state of flux. Most of these countries have already concluded trade and co-operation agreements or even association agreements which are intended to lead to E.C. membership. These agreements make provision for the adequate protection and enforcement of intellectual property rights; it may be assumed that the countries will model their national copyright legislation on the E.C. standard.

[2] Following the negative result of the Swiss referendum on December 6, 1992, Switzerland decided not to be a party to the EEA Treaty.

[3] The contracting parties are the E.C. Member States, the Community and, after the decision of Switzerland not to take part in the EEA, the six remaining EFTA countries. The adjusting protocol of March 17, 1993 modifies the EEA Treaty to reflect the above-mentioned decision by Switzerland.

# 1. Austria

## 1. THE LAW IN THE LIGHT OF CHAPTER I OF THE DIRECTIVE

The Austrian Copyright Act[4] ("the Act") provides for an exclusive rental right and for a right to obtain equitable remuneration for lending for authors, performers, phonogram and film producers and broadcasting organisations. Since the Directive does not provide a rental right for broadcasters, the Austrian law will have to provide that broadcasters may enjoy the rental and lending rights only if they qualify, at the same time, as phonogram or film producers.[5]

In Austria, the author of a film is, *inter alios*, its principal director. However, by Article 38(1) of the Act, the exploitation rights of commercially produced films, except adaptations or translations, are originally vested in the film producer. The Austrian provision therefore amounts to a non-rebuttable presumption of transfer of the exploitation rights. With respect to the exclusive rental right, this provision will have to be amended in order to comply with Article 2(6) of the Directive. Hence, if it were to be maintained at all, it would have to be changed into a rebuttable presumption which is subject to the payment of remuneration to the author in accordance with Article 4 of the Directive.

Article 69(1) of the Act amounts to a non-rebuttable presumption that the performer has authorised, *inter alia*, the distribution (including rental) of a film in which he/she has performed. If this provision were to be maintained at all, it would have to be made subject to a signed contract and the unwaivable remuneration right set out in Article 4 of the Directive (see Article 2(7) of the Directive). However, it would seem more appropriate to provide, instead of the presumption under Article 2(7) of the Directive, a rebuttable presumption of transfer in accordance with the provisions of Article 2(5) of the Directive.[6]

The new Article 16a(5) of the Act, which was drafted, as were the other relevant provisions of the Amendment Act of 1993, on the basis of the Commission's Amended Proposal of 1992, does not entirely fulfil the requirements of Article 4 of the Directive. The remuneration right, which cannot be waived, will have to be granted to authors and performers only, but not to producers or broadcasters. In addition, the preconditions for the remuneration right in Article 16a(5) of the Act do not correspond to those in Article 4 of the Directive and, thus, will have to be amended to comply with them. For example, not

---

[4] Copyright Act of April 9, 1936, as last amended by the Act of January 29, 1993: Austrian Official Journal No. 93/1993.
[5] See the comments on Art. 2(1) of the Directive, p. 45.
[6] See the comments on Art. 2(5) to 2(7), p. 55.

only the rental or lending of films will have to be covered, but also that of phonograms.

## 2. The Law in the Light of Chapter II of the Directive

With respect to the rights contained in Chapter II of the Directive clarification will be required to the effect that the reproduction rights of performers, phonogram and film producers include indirect reproduction, *i.e.* the fixation of a broadcast which was made on the basis of fixed or already broadcast performances; this is not made sufficiently clear in Article 15(1) of the Act.

There will also need to be clarification that the exhaustion of the distribution right of performers, phonogram and film producers and broadcasters under Article 16(3) of the Act fulfils the requirements of Article 9(2) of the Directive; in particular, the first sale outside the EEA without any specification by the rightholder as to the area of distribution may not result in the exhaustion of the distribution right within the EEA; this is not made sufficiently clear in Article 16(3) of the Act.

It is advisable to state explicitly in the law that the broadcasting right of performers and phonogram producers and the broadcasting right of broadcasters include broadcasting by satellite; this may be assumed, but does not follow necessarily from Article 17 of the Act. With respect to the payments of remuneration for the use of commercial phonograms (Article 76(3) of the Act), *indirect* use for broadcasting and communication to the public will have to be explicitly included. Likewise, the remuneration will have to be extended explicitly to the use of *copies* of commercial phonograms.

With respect to the limitation of performers' rights, it seems doubtful whether the limitation of the public communication right under Article 72(5) of the Act is covered by Article 10 of the Directive.

It will have to be ensured that the rights of organisers of spectacles and other events (Article 66(5) of the Act) may not present any limitation to the performers' rights. Accordingly, it must be made clear that organisers do not have the right to prohibit any exploitation of a performance once the performer has consented to the exploitation.

With respect to the possible presumption of transfer of performers' rights under Chapter II of the Directive, the remarks mentioned above in connection with the rental right in Article 69(1) of the Act will have to be taken into account. With respect to the rights contained in Chapter II, it may even be possible not to provide for any presumption of transfer (or any similar provision, such as Article 69(1) of the Act) at all.

The definition of broadcasting organisations (beginning of Article 76a(1) of the Act) will have to be amended in order to clearly comply with the requirements of the Directive; in particular, it will have to explicitly cover satellite broadcasters and correspond to Article 6(3) of the Directive; it is not sufficiently clear from the law whether these requirements are fulfilled. The broadcasters' exclusive right of public communication can no longer be restricted to illegally fixed or distributed broadcasts (Article 76a(2) of the Act), but will have to be extended in accordance with Article 8(3) of the Directive.

# 2. Finland

## 1. The Law in the Light of Chapter I of the Directive

The Finnish Copyright Act[7] ("the Act") provides an exclusive rental right only for authors of musical works in the form of sheet music. Since the distribution right is not exhausted in the case of films, it may be concluded that authors of films also enjoy an exclusive rental (and lending) right. In order to comply with the Directive, Finnish law will need to provide an exclusive rental right for authors of all kinds of works and in whatever medium except for three-dimensional buildings and works of applied art. This right must also extend to performers, phonogram and film producers. In addition, the unwaivable right to remuneration for authors and performers set out in Article 4 of the Directive, as well as the presumption of transfer of the performers' rental rights to film producers in accordance with Article 2(5) of the Directive will have to be incorporated into Finnish law. Articles 39 and 27(3) of the Act provide for a rebuttable presumption of transfer of certain rights of authors of a literary or artistic work to the film producer. If this presumption is to apply to the rental right, it will have to be made subject to the unwaivable remuneration right (Articles 2(6), 2(5) and 4 of the Directive).

The existing exclusive lending right with respect to films may be preserved if, not only authors, but also performers and film producers are granted the exclusive lending right. The existing public lending right scheme, which is based on particular legislation providing for certain scholarships and other assistance for writers and translators,[8] provides grants only for writers and translators of fiction and non-fiction literature. Consequently, it would have to be amended so as to make provision for a system of remuneration for authors of all kinds of works on all work supports, except three-dimensional buildings and works of applied art. To the extent that exclusive lending rights are intended to be preserved or introduced, authors, performers and producers must all be right-owners.

## 2. The Law in the Light of Chapter II of the Directive

Some clarifications or additions will have to be made in the field of neighbouring rights. In particular, the reproduction rights of performers, phonogram producers and broadcasters must include indirect reproduction.

---

[7] Act No. 404 of July 8, 1961, as last amended by Act No. 34 of January 11, 1991.
[8] Act No. 236 of May 3, 1961.

Performers need to be granted a distribution right in accordance with Article 9 of the Directive. The right to remuneration for the use of phonograms for broadcasting (Article 47 of the Act) will need to be extended to indirect use for broadcasting and to direct and indirect use for communication to the public. In addition, the remuneration must be equitable.

Phonogram producers and broadcasting organisations should be granted a distribution right in accordance with Article 9 of the Directive. To the extent that neighbouring right-owners are granted broadcasting rights of any kind, it must be made clear that these rights cover satellite broadcasts; this does not clearly follow from the law.

Clarification will also be required to the effect that a broadcasting organisation which enjoys protection in accordance with the provisions of the Directive will have to fulfil the requirements of Article 6(2) and (3) of the Directive.

Film producers must be granted rights of reproduction and distribution in their own right.

# 3. Iceland

## 1. THE LAW IN THE LIGHT OF CHAPTER I OF THE DIRECTIVE

An exclusive rental (and lending) right is given only to authors of musical works in the form of sheet-music and, according to prevailing opinion, to authors of films (Articles 2, 24, 25 of the Copyright Act[9] ("the Act")). Therefore, the exclusive rental right will have to be extended to authors of all kinds of works in whatever medium except three-dimensional buildings and works of applied art, and to performers, phonogram and film producers. Likewise, the unwaivable right of remuneration set out in Article 4 of the Directive will have to be introduced for authors and performing artists, and the presumption of transfer contained in Article 2(5) of the Directive will have to be introduced with respect to the performer's exclusive rental right. If Article 41 of the Act, which may be regarded as a presumption of the author's authorisation of certain acts, is extended to the rental right, the presumption will need to be linked to a right to remuneration, as set out in Article 4 of the Directive (see Article 2(6) and (5) of the Directive).

The Icelandic public lending right scheme, which is based on the Library Act[10] and the related Order on the Icelandic Writers' Fund,[11] provides, besides scholarships and similar payments, a remuneration for writers for the lending of their books. Either this remuneration will need to be extended to authors of all kinds of works and in whatever media except three-dimensional buildings and works of applied art, or an exclusive lending right will need to be introduced in respect of all or certain categories of objects which may be lent, for example films on video cassettes, or sheet-music; in this case, not only the authors (as is the case under Finnish law) but also the other groups of right-owners concerned (for example, performers and film producers), would need to be granted the exclusive right. Given the broad flexibility of the Directive provisions on lending rights, it seems that no further fundamental amendment to the existing public lending right scheme would have to be introduced.

## 2. THE LAW IN THE LIGHT OF CHAPTER II OF THE DIRECTIVE

With respect to neighbouring rights, the following amendments will be required. Reproduction rights of performers, phonogram producers and broadcasters must specifically include indirect reproduction; the performers'

---

[9] Act No. 73 of May 29, 1972.
[10] Act No. 50 of May 25, 1976, Art. 11.
[11] Order No. 84 of February 1, 1977.

reproduction right must not be restricted to the reproduction of recorded performances made with the consent of the performer. The right to remuneration for the use of commercial phonograms (Article 47 of the Act) will have to be extended to reproductions of commercial phonograms and to indirect use for broadcasting, that is, rebroadcasting broadcasts that were themselves based on a phonogram. There will need to be a clear statement that the remuneration is to be equitable.

Performers, phonogram producers and broadcasters must be granted a distribution right in accordance with Article 9 of the Directive.

The broadcasters' fixation right (Article 48(1) of the Act second item) must be amended so as not to be restricted to fixation the purpose of a repeat broadcast. Likewise, the broadcasters' right of communication to the public will need to be adapted so as to comply with the requirements of Article 8(3) of the Directive. In particular, the restriction to television broadcasts has to be deleted.

Specific provision must be made to ensure that protected broadcasting organisations fulfil the requirements of Article 6(2) and (3) of the Directive; it is not clear that the Act does so.

The (re-)broadcasting rights of performers, phonogram producers and broadcasters must specifically include broadcasting via satellite.

Neighbouring rights protection must also be granted to film producers in accordance with the provisions of the Directive.

# 4. Liechtenstein

## 1. The Law in the Light of Chapter I of the Directive

Article 12(2) of the Copyright Act of Liechtenstein[12] ("the Act") provides for the exclusive right of an author to sell, offer or otherwise put into circulation copies of his work. Since one may consider rental and lending as forms of putting works into circulation, and since the law does not provide for the exhaustion of such a right one might, but need not necessarily conclude that authors enjoy an exclusive rental and lending right. Because of this legal uncertainty, it seems necessary to clarify that an exclusive rental right exists for authors; with respect to lending, a right to remuneration in place of the exclusive right for authors would be sufficient under Article 5 of the Directive.

In addition, performers, phonogram and film producers will need to be granted an exclusive rental right and, subject to a possible exemption under Article 5 of the Directive, an exclusive lending right.

Furthermore, authors and performers have to be granted an unwaivable right of remuneration for rental according to Article 4 of the Directive, and a rebuttable presumption of transfer of the performer's exclusive rental right to the film producer will have to be introduced according to Article 2(5) of the Directive.

## 2. The Law in the Light of Chapter II of the Directive

Performing artists seem to be protected in Liechtenstein in respect of their performances of literary and musical works in the same way as authors (Article 4(2) of the Act). However, the wording is not sufficiently clear and it may be inferred from practice that the law is not considered to protect performers. Therefore, it will be necessary to clarify the law, so that the rights provided for performers by the Directive are also granted by the law of Liechtenstein.

Since the law does not contain any protection for phonogram and film producers or for broadcasting organisations, such protection will have to be introduced so as to comply with the provisions of the Directive.

---

[12] Act of October 26, 1928, as amended by Act of August 8, 1959.

# 5. Norway

## 1. The Law in the Light of Chapter I of the Directive

The Norwegian Copyright Act[13] ("the Act") grants an exclusive rental right only to authors of musical works. According to the prevailing literature, this is also the case, even as regards lending, for authors of films, because the exhaustion of the distribution right does not extend to films (see Articles 2(1) and (3), 21; 23 of the Act). Under the Directive, this exclusive rental right will have to be extended to authors of all kinds of works, except three-dimensional buildings and works of applied art, as well as to performers, phonogram and film producers. In addition, the unwaivable right to remuneration for authors and performers, under the provisions of Article 4 of the Directive, and a rebuttable presumption of transfer of the performers' exclusive rental rights to film producers, according to Article 2(5) of the Directive, will have to be introduced. If the rebuttable presumption of transfer of authors' rights under Article 39(2) is to be preserved at all (the Directive does not require any presumption of transfer of authors' rights), it will need to be made subject to the remuneration right under Article 4 of the Directive as far as the rental right is concerned.

The Norwegian Public Lending Right Act[14] provides for authors of all kinds of works to be remunerated. Although the public lending right is regulated otherwise than by the Copyright Act and several provisions do not correspond to general principles of copyright (for example the fact that the authors cannot claim, but only apply for a remuneration and that the authors' successors are not entitled to obtain any remuneration for the lending of the authors' books, but may in some cases only apply for subsidies), the Norwegian system may be considered to comply with the provisions of the Directive.[15]

## 2. The Law in the Light of Chapter II of the Directive

With respect to the rights under Chapter II of the Directive, it will have to be made clear that the reproduction right of performers and phonogram producers includes indirect reproduction. The new Article 45b of the Act will

---

[13] Act No. 2 of May 12, 1961, as last amended by Act No. 86 of June 21, 1985.
[14] Act No. 23 of May 29, 1987.
[15] See also the comments on the Danish and Dutch provisions on public lending right, pp. 140, 166, as well as on Art. 5 of the Directive, p. 77.

have to be extended to *indirect* use for broadcasting and public communication. In addition, the remuneration must be equitable (see Article 8(2) of the Directive). Not least, the right will have to be granted to phonogram producers to participate in this remuneration. Article 3 of the Norwegian Act No. 4 of December 14, 1956 on a levy for public performances by performers does not fulfil the requirements of Article 8(2) of the Directive because, *inter alia*, it does not provide rights, but only subsidies.

Performers and phonogram producers must also be granted a distribution right in accordance with Article 9 of the Directive.

A reproduction and distribution right will need to be introduced for film producers.

Clarification will be required to the effect that broadcasting organisations include satellite broadcasters and exclude cable distributors within the meaning of Article 6(3) of the Directive. Likewise, it will have to be stated clearly that the exclusive rights of broadcasters include the right of public communication as set out in Article 8(3) of the Directive and the distribution right in accordance with Article 9 of the Directive; this does not seem to be made clear enough in Article 45a(c) of the Act.

In all cases, where a broadcasting right in any form is granted to performers, phonogram producers and broadcasting organisations, it will have to specifically include satellite broadcasting (or rebroadcasting).

# 6. Sweden

## 1. THE LAW IN THE LIGHT OF CHAPTER I OF THE DIRECTIVE

According to the Swedish Copyright Act,[16] ("the Act") which has a similar structure to the Norwegian and other Scandinavian Copyright Acts, an exclusive rental right is vested only in authors of film works, musical works and computer programs. The rental right will need to be extended to authors of all kinds of works, except three-dimensional buildings and works of applied art, and to performers and producers of phonograms and films.

In addition, the unwaivable right to remuneration contained in Article 4 of the Directive and the presumption of transfer of the performer's exclusive rental right in accordance with Article 2(5) of the Directive will need to be introduced.

Article 39 of the Act provides for a presumption of transfer of rights of authors of a literary or artistic work to the film producer. This presumption is rebuttable, since it applies, as does the whole of Chapter 3 of the Act, only in the absence of agreement to the contrary. However, if it will apply to the rental right, it will have to be made subject to the unwaivable remuneration right (Articles 2(6), 2(5) and 4 of the Directive).

An exclusive lending right is vested in authors of films and, it may be assumed, authors of musical works (see Articles 2(1) and (3), 23 and 25 of the Act). This exclusive lending right may be preserved as part of Swedish law if, in addition to authors, performers and film or phonogram producers are also granted the exclusive lending right as regards videograms and phonograms. Other possibilities for implementation are set out below.

The Swedish public lending right scheme, which is based on the "Decree on the Swedish Authors' Fund" of November 23, 1962[17] provides, besides measures for social assistance, a remuneration right for authors of literary works which are incorporated into books or audio-cassettes. This remuneration right will need to be extended to authors of all kinds of works in whatever media. Alternatively, it will also be possible to extend this right to remuneration beyond authors of all kinds to performers and/or phonogram or film producers. Yet another possibility would be to provide exclusive rights for authors, performers, phonogram and film producers – as the case may be – in respect of all or certain types of media which are lent in public libraries, such as videograms. Given the wide flexibility of Article 5 of the Directive, the Swedish public lending right scheme may be considered as complying with the

---

[16] Act of December 30, 1960, as last amended by the Act of June 1, 1989.
[17] Most recently amended by Decree No. 415 of 1989.

Directive, if authors of all kinds of works (in whatever media) obtain the remuneration.

## 2. The Law in the Light of Chapter II of the Directive

With regard to the rights contained in Chapter II of the Directive, it will need to be made clear that the reproduction rights of performers, phonogram and film producers and broadcasters include indirect reproduction. In addition, the existing rights of broadcasting and rebroadcasting will have to explicitly include (re-)broadcasting by satellite. The law is not sufficiently clear in these two respects.

A distribution right in accordance with Article 9 of the Directive will need to be granted to performers, phonogram and film producers and broadcasting organisations. The remuneration for the use of phonograms according to Article 47 of the Act must be equitable and must extend to indirect use for public communication.

The broadcasters' right of communication to the public (Article 48(1) of the Act, second phase) must apply not only to television broadcasts, but to all kinds of broadcasts. At the same time, the condition mentioned in Article 8(3) of the Directive may be introduced although this is not a requirement since Article 8(3) of the Directive provides minimum protective measures only.

# 7. Switzerland

Chapter (7) has been included on the basis that Switzerland will be obliged, at some stage in the future, to incorporate the Directive into its national law. This has, however, become questionable following the negative result of the Swiss referendum on the European Economic Area and the Swiss decision not to participate therein. In the event that Switzerland is not obliged in the future to incorporate the Directive into its national law, whether on the basis of an amendment to the EEA Treaty or otherwise, this Chapter will have to be disregarded.

## 1. The Law in the Light of Chapter I of the Directive

The new Swiss Copyright Act of October 9, 1992 ("the Act") provides an exclusive rental right only for authors of computer programs (Articles 10(3), 13(4) of the Act); a right to remuneration for rental is vested in authors of all other kinds of works, performers, phonogram producers and broadcasters (Articles 13 and 38 of the Act). In order to comply with the Directive, an exclusive rental right for authors, performers, phonogram and film producers will have to be introduced; however, the right to remuneration contained in Article 13 of the Act may be preserved alongside the exclusive right if it is to be employed for the (obligatory) implementation of Article 4 of the Directive and adapted so as to comply with the requirements of Article 4. In this case, the remuneration right will have to be limited to authors and performers, and it must be made clear that the right cannot be waived. Not only copies, but also originals of works will need to be covered by the remuneration right. It will also need to apply in the situation covered by Article 4(1) of the Directive. The remuneration must be equitable.

With respect to the exceptions to the right (Article 13(2) of the Act), it will have to be made clear that only three-dimensional works of architecture ("buildings") are excluded and that the situation envisaged in Article 13(2)(c) of the Act corresponds to the situation envisaged in Recital (13); this does not clearly follow from the Swiss law. Broadcasting organisations may only be granted a rental right in so far as they qualify, at the same time, as phonogram or film producers.

With respect to the performers' exclusive rental right, a rebuttable presumption of transfer to the film producer, subject to the unwaivable right to remuneration under Article 4, will have to be introduced in accordance with Article 2(5) of the Directive.

The Swiss legislature finally decided not to introduce a lending right. According to Articles 1, 2 and 5 of the Directive, provision must at least be made for the payment of remuneration to authors for the lending of their works.

## 2. The Law in the Light of Chapter II of the Directive

With respect to the rights of Chapter II of the Directive, it will need to be made clear that the reproduction rights of performers, phonogram producers and broadcasters include indirect reproduction, and that the existing broadcasting rights of performers and phonogram producers, as well as the rebroadcasting right of broadcasters, include broadcasting by satellite; this does not clearly follow from the existing law. The provision covering the exhaustion of distribution rights of performers, phonogram producers and broadcasters (Article 12(1); Article 38 of the Act) will have to be explicitly restricted to the situation covered by Article 9(2) of the Directive, in particular to the first sale in the Community (or possibly, under a future agreement, in the EFTA countries). The right to remuneration for the use of commercial phonograms for broadcasting and communication to the public (Article 35 of the Act) will have to be extended to the use of *copies* of such phonograms, and will have to provide for an *equitable* remuneration. Since Article 8(2) of the Directive is a minimum provision, the extension of Article 35 of the Act to sound and visual recordings is in compliance with the terms of the Directive.

There will have to be a grant of neighbouring rights to film producers with respect to reproduction and distribution according to Articles 7 and 9 of the Directive.

It will have to be made clear that broadcasting organisations covered by Article 37 of the Act include satellite broadcasters, but do not include cable distributors as mentioned in Article 6(3) of the Directive.

SECTION V

# THE POSITION AT INTERNATIONAL LEVEL

# 1. The Directive as Compared to International Conventions

## 1. GENERAL

The purpose of a harmonisation Directive like the one on the rental and lending rights is to help create the internal market in the Community by means of harmonising the laws of Member States. The Directive establishes Community law and is by its very nature directed "inwards"; it does not, and indeed cannot, harmonise relations between the Community or its Member States and third countries.

It follows from this purpose that the rental Directive is silent on questions of national treatment: it does not deal with the question of whether and if so to what extent foreign rightholders may enjoy the rights covered by the Directive, such as the rental right or distribution right, in a particular Member State.

With respect to the treatment of rightholders from one Member State in another Member State of the Community, of course the EEC Treaty applies. Not only will the legal position throughout the Community be harmonised as a result of the Directive, but the EEC Treaty also obliges each Member State to accord nationals of another the same treatment as its own nationals; this follows from Article 7, EEC Treaty which explicitly prohibits any discrimination within the Community on the grounds of nationality. There was therefore no need for this principle to be restated in the operational part of the Directive; it is mentioned, however, in Recital (18).

The situation with respect to rightholders from third countries is less clear, however; since the Directive itself does not address this issue, the general rules of national treatment continue to apply. These rules are to be found in the international conventions dealing with copyright and related rights. If a country is not a member of the convention in question, the rules of its national law with respect to the treatment of foreign rightholders apply. The following remarks are intended to outline the application of the rights established by the Directive inside the Community to rightholders from third countries in the light of the relevant international conventions.

## 2. THE BERNE CONVENTION

### (a) Membership

Having more than 90 states as members, the Berne Convention for the Protection of Literary and Artistic Works is the most important international convention on authors' rights. It was established as early as 1886, and has been revised several times since then. All Member States of the Community are members of the Berne Convention. At present, only two of the Member States – Belgium and Ireland – are not bound by the latest revision, the Paris Act of July 24, 1971 ("Paris Act").

With a view to attaining Community-wide acceptance of the Paris Act, and as a consequence, achieving, indirectly, basic harmonisation of authors' rights contained in that Act within the Community, the Commission, in 1991, presented a proposal for a Council Decision,[1] which would have obliged all Member States to adhere to the Paris Act and thus to comply with its provisions. This proposal has, to date, not been successful for purely institutional reasons: a number of Member States have been unwilling to accept the idea that the Community, by means of a Council Decision, would be able to impose on them international obligations in the field of intellectual property. Even constitutional objections have been raised in this context.

When the Commission realised that the proposal for a Council Decision concerning membership of the Berne Convention was being held back, it submitted a proposal for a Council Resolution which had practically the same content. By proposing just a Resolution, having much less, if any, binding force as compared to a Decision, the Commission achieved more success. On May 14, 1992, the Council adopted this Resolution[2] which declares that the Member States "undertake, subject to their constitutional provisions, to become by January 1, 1995 parties to the Paris Act of the Berne Convention ... and to introduce national legislation to ensure effective compliance therewith." A very similar but mandatory rule is included in the Treaty amongst the Community and the EFTA States on the European Economic Area.[3]

As a result, in the very near future all Member States will be bound by the Paris Act. The Community itself, however, as opposed to the individual Member States, is not a member of the Berne Convention and accordingly not bound by its provisions.

### (b) The Rental Directive and the Berne Convention

With regard to authors, the Directive establishes and harmonises only two rights: the rental right and the lending right. The Berne Convention neither includes a rental right nor a lending right, nor does it provide explicitly for a general distribution right, from which a rental or lending right could be derived. In fact, the rental right and the lending right are not related at all to

---

[1] "Proposal for a Council Decision concerning the accession of the Member States to the Berne Convention for the Protection of Literary and Artistic Works, as revised by the Paris Act of July 24, 1971, and the International Convention for the Protection of Performers, Producers of Phonograms and Broadcasting Organisations (Rome Convention) of October 26, 1961," Document COM (90) 582 final; Amended Proposal for a Council Decision, Document COM (92) 10 final.

[2] Council Resolution of May 14, 1992 on increased protection for copyright and neighbouring rights [1992] O.J. C138/1.

[3] Treaty on the European Economic Area between the EEC and its Member States and the EFTA States, signed in Porto on May 2, 1992; published at [1992] 1 C.M.L.R. 921 where it is described as the "Draft Treaty on the European Economic Area," but the text reproduced there is in fact identical with the signed version.

any of the rights explicitly granted by the Berne Convention. As a result, the Berne Convention itself does not establish an international obligation to grant such rental or lending rights amongst its members.

In this situation, however, the wide national treatment obligation set out in Article 5 of the Berne Convention comes into play. According to Article 5, the members of the Berne Convention must grant to each others' nationals (for works originating abroad) not only the rights enshrined in the convention itself, but also all "the rights which their respective laws do now or may hereafter grant to their nationals." This means that states which are members of the Berne Convention must allow authors who are nationals of other Berne Convention Member States, to enjoy those rights which are granted to their own authors in addition to those rights set out in the Berne Convention.

The consequence for the rental and lending right is that, at least in principle,[4] the Member States of the Community, in compliance with Article 5 of the Berne Convention, must grant such rights, as harmonised by the Directive, to authors for works originating in third countries which are members of the Berne Convention.

It must be borne in mind, however, that this national treatment obligation only applies to the rental and lending right in the form it has obtained under the law of the Member State in question, and under the conditions valid there. In other words, Member States are obliged to grant foreign authors who benefit from Article 5 of the Berne Convention, the same, but not better, treatment with respect to these rights as to their own nationals. Accordingly, it is the national law of the Member State where protection is sought which offers protection under its generally applicable law in relation to these rights. This applies to any person who seeks protection within its territory, be it a national, or an individual from a third country who enjoys the same treatment as nationals on the grounds of national treatment obligations in international conventions.

The international conventions which exist do not prevent their members from including in their national law some binding features and some underlying structure and conditions, which a potential rightholder must comply with when seeking protection under that law. Typically, such features are rules on authorship or title, on definitions such as rental or lending, a bar on waiver of certain rights, rules on the assignment of rights, on contractual clauses and on timing.

This also applies to the rights contained in the rental Directive, and to the features which Member States have to attach to these rights. Therefore, all foreign authors who are entitled to national treatment under Article 5 of the Berne Convention have to comply with the rules for the determination of authorship which the Member State in question provides for its own nationals in line with the Directive, as well as with any other condition, if they are to gain protection for their rental and lending rights. One important example of this in the Directive is Article 4, the "unwaivable right to equitable

---

[4] See below.

remuneration." Even if an author of a film script and a film producer from a third country have concluded a contract in that jurisdiction, in which the author has agreed to a single "buy-out" payment for his script and has waived any further claims for remuneration, such a contractual clause would be void in a Member State of the Community where the Directive applies, where the rightholders seek protection for their rental right, and where the script writer is considered to be a genuine author. As a result, he would still, despite the terms of the contract, be entitled to invoke the "right to equitable remuneration" for rental income in that Member State. Take another example: a foreign principal director of a film, under the national treatment obligation and according to Article 2(2) of the Directive, would enjoy in the Member States of the Community his own exclusive rental right with respect to that film, no matter where the film was made, or whether the contract specifically excluded such a right.

The above is but a natural and logical consequence of national treatment; it is not, however, undisputed.[5] But even if the general rules of private international law combined with the rule of "ordre public" were to apply to national treatment, one would still arrive at the same result for the binding features of the rental Directive. In other words, even within the framework of such a legal approach, the foreign script writer in the above-mentioned example would not have been able to waive the right he had in that Member State under Article 4 of the Directive, nor would the foreign principal director of a film lose the status he is accorded in Member States under Article 2(2) of the Directive.

The foregoing remarks are, of course, only valid in cases where the national treatment obligation actually arises under Article 5 Berne Convention. However, a somewhat different situation might occur in the context of the lending right, where Member States are given maximum flexibility with regard to implementation of the right, and are entitled, under Article 5 of the Directive, to derogate from a copyright-based lending right.[6] Should a Member State choose to introduce for authors a remuneration scheme for lending which in its substance is outside of copyright protection[7] – be it part of its social or tax system – the national treatment obligation under Article 5 of the Berne Convention may no longer apply, as the Member State in question would not be providing for *copyright* protection for authors in addition to the Berne Convention rights. To be sure, the question as to if, and to what extent, Article 5 of the Berne Convention may be applied to public lending right schemes is still under discussion in WIPO and not settled yet amongst its Member States.

---

[5] E. Ulmer, *Intellectual Property Rights and the Conflict of Laws* (Kluwer, Deventer, 1978), p. 46; P. Geller [1992] 1 E.I.P.R. 4; *cf.* German Supreme Court (BGH) of June 17, 1992: [1992] GRUR 697; French Supreme Court, Cass.Civ. I, May 28, 1991, ICP 1991. II 21731, with note by Françon.

[6] See above, commentary on Art. 5, p. 77, *et seq.*

[7] S. von Lewinski, "National Treatment, Reciprocity and Retorsion – The Case of Public Lending Right" in Beier/Schricker (eds.), *GATT or WIPO? New Ways in the International Protection of Intellectual Property*, IIC-Studies (Weinheim, 1989), Vol. 11, p. 53 (–62).

## 3. THE ROME CONVENTION

### (a) Membership

The International Convention for the Protection of Performers, Producers of Phonograms and Broadcasting Organisations of 1961 (Rome Convention) establishes several rights for these rightholders, such as rights of fixation, reproduction, broadcasting and communication to the public. The Rome Convention thus deals with rights which are, whilst not being authors' rights themselves, closely allied to authors' copyright; it is for this reason that they are often called neighbouring rights or related rights.[8]

At present, a total of 40 States are members of the Rome Convention. The two Member States of the Community which are presently not Rome Convention members – Belgium and Portugal – are preparing legislation so as to adhere to it in the near future. The Commission, for its part, has taken several initiatives to encourage the Member States to accede to the Rome Convention. The proposals for a Council Decision[9] and the Council Resolution[10] have been described in detail above,[11] and mention has also been made of the agreement with the EFTA States on the European Economic Area. The rental Directive (in its Chapter II) has also gone a long way to harmonise within the Community the rights laid down in the Rome Convention.

It can reasonably be expected, therefore, that all Member States of the Community will be members of the Rome Convention before too long. The Community, as such, is not a member of the Rome Convention. However, on the basis of the rental Directive, the Council has given the Commission the mandate to negotiate on behalf of the Community improvements on the international protection of certain neighbouring rights.[12] In an international context the Rome Convention, for the time being, is the relevant treaty to be considered for the protection of performers, phonogram producers and broadcasting organisations covered by the rental Directive.

### (b) The Rental Directive and the Rome Convention

Some rights which the rental Directive establishes or harmonises for performers, phonogram producers and broadcasting organisations, are identical with those provided in the Rome Convention on an international level. This is particularly true for the reproduction right for phonogram producers, and the rights to broadcast or rebroadcast for broadcasting organisations. With respect to these rights, Member States (if they are members of the Rome Convention) must grant national treatment in any event, according to the general rule of Article 2 of the Rome Convention, to foreign rightholders from other

---

[8] On the title of the proposal, see p. 9, above.
[9] See n. 1, above.
[10] See n. 2, above.
[11] See p. 200, above.
[12] Decision of the Council concerning the participation of the Community in the committee of governmental experts entrusted with the elaboration of a possible new instrument for the protection of performing artists and phonogram producers under the auspices of WIPO (World Intellectual Property Organisation), of June 24, 1993.

States which are members of the Rome Convention. As explained above,[13] all domestic conditions and rules of the Member State where protection is sought apply to this national treatment obligation; the foreign rightholder in question would be accorded the same, but not better treatment than the national rightholders.

Most neighbouring rights established under the Directive, however, go further than the Rome Convention. Performing artists enjoy exclusive rights under the Directive; their reproduction right goes beyond what is stated in the Rome Convention. The Rome Convention does not specifically recognise a distribution right, nor a rental right or lending right, as covered by the Directive. The Directive in part also deals with the protection of cable broadcasters which the Rome Convention does not. The right to remuneration in Article 8(2) of the Directive goes beyond what is stated in Article 12 of the Rome Convention, by additionally covering indirect broadcasting or communication to the public, and by providing for mandatory remuneration for both performers and phonogram producers. Unlike Article 13(d) of the Rome Convention, the rights of broadcasting organisations in Article 8(3) of the Directive are not limited to television broadcasts. Finally, the Directive provides for separate rights of film producers which are not mentioned at all in the Rome Convention.

Article 2(2) of the Rome Convention renders the national treatment obligation more limited, as compared to the parallel provision for authors' rights in Article 5 of the Berne Convention. Rome Convention members, under Article 2(2), are not obliged to extend national treatment to the neighbouring rights which are accorded under their national law over and above the rights enshrined in the Rome Convention itself. Consequently, those rights harmonised under the rental Directive which go further than the Rome Convention are not subject to the national treatment obligation in Article 2 of the Rome Convention. Thus Member States are not obliged to let rightholders from third countries enjoy these rights, even if their respective countries of citizenship are members of the Rome Convention.

---

[13] See pp. 201–202, above.

# 2. The Directive in the Light of International Activities

## 1. GENERAL

The assessment given in Chapter 1 of this Section, above, concerning the implications of the rental Directive at an international level is based on, and reflects, the application of the existing conventions and rules in the framework of international protection for copyright and neighbouring rights. However, the international situation is faced with constant changes. New technological developments and the increase of worldwide piracy must be dealt with on an international level, and there is a steadily growing awareness of the relationship between intellectual property and world trade.

The rental Directive, by going beyond the standards offered by the international conventions in the sector, already tries to cope with these concerns and to indicate new solutions. In fact, the relationship between the Directive and other international activities has been one of mutual advantage. As the proposal for the Directive was drafted and discussed in parallel with some international negotiations, it certainly benefited from them. On the other hand, now that the Directive has been adopted, it may well serve as a pathfinder for some of the forthcoming multilateral activities.

It seems therefore worth looking at these international activities in the light of the direction which the Community has chosen to take in the rental Directive. These activities will be of crucial importance for the future development of international copyright law.

## 2. INITIATIVES IN WIPO

### (a) Negotiations on a Possible Protocol to the Berne Convention

The last revision of the Berne Convention[14] dates back to 1971. It is easy to see that developments in the cultural and technological sector over the past 20 years, such as the exploitation of films on video, satellite broadcasting and the widespread use of computer software and electronic databases, have to be recognised on the international level and accordingly may call for adjustments of the Berne Convention with respect to authors' rights.

The World Intellectual Property Organisation (WIPO) is part of the United

---

14 Berne Convention for the Protection of Literary and Artistic Works of September 9, 1886, as revised at Paris on July 24, 1971.

Nations. It administers the Berne Convention and has, in this capacity, already taken several initiatives with a view to preparing the necessary adjustments to this convention. The first step in this direction has been the preparation of an international model law on the protection of authors' rights. Several new elements, as compared with the Berne Convention, were included in these "model provisions for legislation in the field of copyright."

When the Committee of international experts on the model law concluded its work under the auspices of WIPO in 1990, it was all too obvious that not just national legislation on copyright, but also the most important convention in the field, the Berne Convention, would have to be looked at with a view to possible revision. This confirmed that what had already been envisaged in WIPO's biennial program for the period 1990–91 (the "elaboration of a Possible Protocol to the Berne Convention for the Protection of Literary and Artistic Works")[15] had to progress.

Discussions with regard to this possible Protocol have begun. When they will be concluded is as difficult to predict as the question of whether these negotiations will lead ultimately to a revision of the Berne Convention. However, as far as the substance is concerned, the issues have been identified.

The rental right for authors is one of these issues. There seems to be almost a consensus that, on the international level, authors should be granted a rental right for their works. Likewise, there largely seems to be agreement that this right should be exclusive and thus enable the author to authorise or prohibit any acts of commercial rental, rather than granting him merely a right to remuneration. Moreover, the rental right will probably cover all types of literary and artistic works, without regard to their medium of expression. On the other hand, the introduction of a lending right has not been accepted yet as part of the multilateral framework; a lending right, even as a right to remuneration rather than an exclusive right, has met with objections based on financial considerations and concerns about the public accessibility of culture.

Therefore, the negotiations on the Berne Protocol seem to indicate that the rental Directive is moving in the right, and also internationally acceptable, direction when it provides for a general exclusive rental right for authors with respect to all categories of works and media. Time seems to be less ripe for a lending right, though; and whether other "inventive steps" of the rental Directive, for instance with respect to the definition of rental or to the unwaivable right to participate in the revenues from rental, will be adopted in the framework of the Berne Convention, remains to be seen.

### (b) Negotiations on a New Instrument for Neighbouring Rights

With respect to the rights accorded to rightholders other than authors, the situation on the international scene is more complex. The Rome Convention of 1961[16] which deals with some of these rightholders, namely with performing artists, phonogram producers and broadcasting organisations, is more than 30 years old and has never been revised. Such a revision seems all the

---

[15] WIPO document AB/XX/2 of May 31, 1989.
[16] International Convention for the Protection of Performers, Producers of Phonograms and Broadcasting Organisations of October 26, 1961.

more overdue, since in some of the main fields covered by this convention, such as phonograms or broadcasting, new technology such as digital recordings or satellite broadcasting which was unheard of in 1961, has become part of our everyday life.

One obstacle to a timely revision of the Rome Convention has probably been the fact that this convention is jointly administered by three organisations, WIPO, UNESCO and the ILO (International Labor Office), a fact which tends to make any initiatives more cumbersome. Another reason, however, relates more to the substance of the Rome Convention itself. It would certainly be very difficult to reach a new consensus amongst all the rightholders involved, with their somewhat divergent interests, on improvements to the Rome Convention. Depending on their respective points of view, what could be seen as an improvement for one group of rightholders, might be considered to be an impediment to the rights or interests of others.

Moreover, agreement on a revision appears to be even less likely in the audiovisual sector, where different legal approaches or dogmatic differences are of particular importance. It would certainly not be the easiest task, for instance, to discuss anew the question of which rights a performer should enjoy with respect to a film. It is the same range of reasons which are responsible for the limited international acceptance of the Rome Convention, including the fact that the USA is not numbered among its members, which would stand in the way of a possible revision.

For all these reasons, WIPO has chosen a somewhat different approach for the updating of certain sectors of international neighbouring rights protection. At first, in accordance with the program of WIPO for the 1992–93 biennium, a Committee of experts was convened for the elaboration of a "draft model law for the protection of the intellectual property rights of producers of sound recordings." However, this attempt of WIPO to progress matters by concentrating on the rights of one group of rightholders did not succeed. In the view of the experts, no model law for the protection of sound recordings should be drafted without considering the rights of performers alongside the rights of phonogram producers. As a consequence, in September 1992 the Assembly of the International Union for the Protection of Literary and Artistic Works (Berne Union) took the decision to create a Committee of Experts for the elaboration of a "possible new instrument on the protection of performing artists and phonogram producers."[17]

Therefore the idea of drafting a model law was not immediately pursued, and initiative has now been taken to draft a "new instrument," possibly a new convention, for the protection of certain neighbouring rights under the auspices of WIPO. Negotiations on this new instrument have just begun, and no final decisions have been taken on its exact coverage.

Some predictions concerning the main elements of this instrument can already be made, however. The rights envisaged will probably include rental rights and distribution rights. These rights are likely to be exclusive in nature for all rightholders covered by the instrument. The scope of broadcasting and

---

[17] WIPO document B/A/XIII/2 of September 29, 1992.

communication to the public would be enlarged. All this can be expected to be very similar to the contents of the rental Directive. Whether the new instrument will cover rights of individuals other than performers and phonogram producers, remains to be seen. Furthermore, while the new instrument is likely to cover audiovisual performances, it is possible, but not yet decided, that its scope will be extended beyond sound recordings to other subject matter, such as videograms. A rather delicate question of horizontal character to be dealt with will be the application of national treatment under the new instrument.

On the whole, it may be expected that the rental Directive will serve as a point of reference, if not as a guideline, for the drafting of this new instrument. Many of the elements will overlap.

## 3. GATT/URUGUAY ROUND: THE AGREEMENT ON TRIPS

### (a) The Mandate and the Negotiations

As has been indicated above, it is traditionally WIPO which administers the most important conventions in the field of copyright and neighbouring rights, be it by itself or jointly with other international organisations. WIPO, however, has not been able to fulfil all the expectations and needs relating to international protection in this field. At the same time, the relevance of intellectual property rights in the context of international trade has become increasingly recognised.

This being so, it was only natural to discuss the trade related aspects of intellectual property, including copyright and neighbouring rights, in the forum which represents the international "codex" of world trade, the GATT.[18] Moreover, negotiating these matters in the GATT may have other advantages, due to its more dynamic and goal-orientated process of decision-making, and its well established mechanism for the settlement of international disputes.[19]

The "Trade Related Aspects of Intellectual Property" (in short, TRIPs) were therefore accepted as one of the new trade subjects in the Uruguay Round of the GATT, which started in 1986. Five years later, after lengthy discussions and a first attempt to conclude the Uruguay Round in the Ministerial Conference of Brussels in December 1990, the Director General of the GATT on December 20, 1991 presented a comprehensive proposal entitled "Draft Final Act Embodying the Results of the Uruguay Round of Multilateral Trade Negotiations."[20] The draft agreement on TRIPs forms part of this document and reflects, in substance, the consensus which was found on the subject of TRIPs amongst the negotiating group.

Part II of the TRIPs text contains substantive standards for the protection of intellectual property, including "copyright and related rights," whereas the other parts are dedicated to basic provisions of a horizontal nature, such as

---

[18] General Agreement on Tariffs and Trade of October 30, 1947.
[19] See Reinbothe/Howard, [1991] 5 E.I.P.R. 157.
[20] GATT document MTN.TNC/W/FA of December 20, 1991.

national treatment or application in time, or to the enforcement of rights. At the time of writing, this draft agreement on TRIPs has not yet come into force. Being only a part of the complete "package" of the Uruguay Round issues, the final adoption of the TRIPs text depends on whether agreement can be reached on all the other elements discussed at the Uruguay Round.

### (b) "Copyright and Related Rights" in TRIPs

Many of the elements contained in the copyright section of the TRIPs text have their roots in proposals submitted by the Community in the course of the negotiations. In particular the comprehensive proposal for a draft agreement which the Community presented in March 1990,[21] can be said to have influenced the negotiations to a large extent. It was elaborated in parallel with the proposal for the rental Directive, and both proposals therefore had some considerable impact on each other.

It therefore comes as no surprise that the TRIPs text includes a rental right. It is the first time that such a right has formed part of an international (draft) agreement. According to Article 11 of the TRIPs text, countries are obliged to provide at least authors of computer programs and film works (cinematographic works) with an exclusive rental right. With respect to film works, this obligation is, however, qualified in respect of private copying: there is no such obligation if the rental has not "led to widespread copying of such [film] works which is materially impairing the [author's] exclusive right of reproduction." In addition, Article 14(4) of the TRIPs text provides that phonogram producers and other "rightholders in phonograms," as defined under domestic law, are entitled to an exclusive rental right; in most cases, these would be authors and performing artists.

Furthermore, the TRIPs text provides in Article 14(1) that performers enjoy rights of fixation and reproduction of their unfixed performances, as well as rights of broadcasting and communication to the public with respect to their live performances. To be sure, these rights are not exclusive, as they do not entitle the performer to authorise or prohibit the acts in question; instead, they only give the "possibility of preventing" such acts, which is set out in the same way in Article 7 of the Rome Convention.

Phonogram producers under the TRIPs text enjoy a reproduction right which corresponds to Article 10 of the Rome Convention.

If we compare these substantive rights stated in the TRIPs text with the rental Directive, it is obvious that the TRIPs text falls short of the level of protection provided for in the Community by the Directive. This reflects the character of TRIPs as an international compromise between more than 100 participating countries. Nevertheless, TRIPs would signify an important step forward and would gain its real value from the high degree of international acceptance of the agreement, and from the link to the efficient GATT mechanisms for the settlement of disputes.

As far as the other, more general provisions in the TRIPs text are concerned, a close relationship between the provisions on the "Application in time" in

---

[21] EEC proposal "Draft Agreement on Trade Related Aspects of Intellectual Property Rights," GATT document MTN.GNG/NG 11/W/68 of March 29, 1990.

Article 13 of the Directive, and on the "Protection of Existing Subject Matter" in Article 70 of TRIPs should be noted. Both the Directive and TRIPs intend to make sure that the new rules also apply to already existing works, sound productions, audiovisual productions, and the like. The respective provisions have in fact mutually benefited from each other in the drafting process, to the extent that the formulation in the Directive (Article 13(1): "This Directive shall apply in respect of all ... works ... which ... meet the criteria for protection under the provisions of this Directive ... ") is very similar to the one chosen in the TRIPs text (Article 70(2): " ... this Agreement gives rise to obligations in respect of all subject matter ... which meets ... the criteria for protection under the terms of this Agreement.") In fact, the TRIPs text was agreed before the respective provision was introduced into the proposal for a rental Directive, and served as a model for that formulation.

The provisions on national treatment in the TRIPs text follow along the lines of, and make reference to, Article 5 of the Berne Convention for authors' rights and Article 2 of the Rome Convention for neighbouring rights. Therefore, with respect to the application of rights harmonised under the rental Directive to nationals from third countries, the above observations on the Berne Convention and the Rome Convention[22] apply.

## 4. Initiatives in the Council of Europe

Some brief remarks for the sake of completeness should be made on the Council of Europe. The Council of Europe is a regional multilateral organisation. Among its members are all Member States of the Community. In the field of copyright and neighbouring rights, several agreements have been concluded under the auspices of the Council of Europe. However, these agreements focus on broadcasting and need not be explained here in detail.

Neither the agreements already concluded under the auspices of the Council of Europe, nor the work at present under way in the various committees there, have had substantial impact on the substance of the rental directive. It has rather worked the other way: European developments in the field of copyright, with respect to European countries outside the Community, have been strongly influenced by Community initiatives. In particular, the rental Directive with its important provisions on neighbouring rights and piracy has already been taken into account in the course of the ongoing discussions in the Council of Europe.

Moreover, the international obligations of the Member States towards third countries with respect to the rights established and harmonised by the Directive, which are not explicitly mentioned therein, follow the rules set out in the relevant international conventions.[23] The Council of Europe and the agreements concluded under its auspices do not come into play here.

---

[22] See pp. 199, 203 *et seq.*, above.
[23] See p. 199 *et seq.*, above.

# APPENDICES

# Appendix One: Original and Amended Proposals for the Directive[1]

<table>
<tr><td>ORIGINAL PROPOSAL</td><td>AMENDED PROPOSAL</td></tr>
</table>

| | |
|---|---|
| **PROPOSAL FOR A COUNCIL DIRECTIVE**<br>**On Rental Right, Lending Right and on certain rights related to Copyright**[2] | **PROPOSAL FOR A COUNCIL DIRECTIVE**<br>**On Rental Right and Lending Right and on certain rights related to Copyright in the Field of Intellectual Property**[3] |
| THE COUNCIL OF THE EUROPEAN COMMUNITIES, | THE COUNCIL OF THE EUROPEAN COMMUNITIES, |
| Having regard to the Treaty establishing the European Economic Community and in particular Articles 57(2), 66 and 100A thereof, | unchanged |
| Having regard to the proposal from the Commission, | unchanged |
| In co-operation with the European Parliament, | unchanged |
| Having regard to the opinion of the Economic and Social Committee, | unchanged |
| (1) Whereas[4] differences exist in the legal protection provided by the laws and practices of the Member States for copyright works and subject matter of related rights protection as regards rental and lending, and such differences are sources of barriers to trade and distortions of competition which impede the proper functioning of the internal market; | (1) unchanged |

---

[1] The Explanatory Memoranda are not reproduced here.
[2] COM (90) 586 final – SYN 319; [1991] O.J. C53/35; Brussels, January 24, 1991.
[3] COM (92) 159 final – SYN 319; [1992] O.J. C128/8; Brussels, April 30, 1992: this document set out the Original Proposal and Amended Proposal side by side as here.
[4] Recitals have been numbered editorially for ease of reference. They were not numbered in the Commission documents.

| ORIGINAL PROPOSAL | AMENDED PROPOSAL |
|---|---|
| (2) Whereas such differences in legal protection could well become greater as Member States adopt new and different legislation or as national jurisprudence interpreting such legislation develops differently; | (2) unchanged |
| (3) Whereas such differences should therefore be eliminated by 31 December 1992 in accordance with the objective of introducing an area without internal frontiers as set out in Article 8A of the Treaty; | (3) Whereas such differences should therefore be eliminated by 31 December 1992 in accordance with the objective of introducing an area without internal frontiers as set out in Article 8A of the Treaty so as to establish, pursuant to Article 3(f) of the EEC Treaty, a system ensuring that competition in the common market is not distorted; |
| (4) Whereas rental and lending of copyright works and the subject matter of related rights protection is playing an increasingly important role in particular for creators, artists and a broad range of industries, and piracy is becoming an increasing threat; | (4) unchanged |
| (5) Whereas the adequate protection of copyright works and subject matter of related rights protection by rental and lending rights as well as the protection of the subject matter of related rights protection by the fixation right, reproduction right and distribution right can accordingly be considered as being of fundamental importance for the Community's industrial and cultural development; | (5) Whereas the adequate protection of copyright works and subject matter of related rights protection by rental and lending rights as well as the protection of the subject matter of related rights protection by the fixation right, reproduction right, distribution right, right to broadcast and communication to the public can accordingly be considered as being of fundamental importance for the Community's industrial and cultural development; |
| (6) Whereas copyright and related rights protection must adapt to new economic developments such as new forms of exploitation; | (6) unchanged |
| (7) Whereas the creative and artistic work of authors and performing artists necessitates an adequate income as a basis for further creative and artistic work, and the investments required particularly for the production of phonograms and films are especially high and risky and the possibility for securing that income and recouping that investment can only effectively be guaranteed through adequate legal protection; | (7) Whereas the creative and artistic work of authors and performing artists necessitates an adequate income as a basis for further creative and artistic work, and the investments required particularly for the production of ₁ ₊no-grams and films are especially high and risky and the possibility for securing that income and recouping that investment can only effectively be guaranteed through adequate legal protection of the first rightholders concerned; |

ORIGINAL PROPOSAL | AMENDED PROPOSAL

(8) Whereas without effective and harmonized protection throughout the Member States, such creative and artistic work as well as such investment might decrease or never be made;

(8) unchanged

(9) Whereas these creative, artistic and entrepreneurial activities are, to a large extent, activities of self-employed persons, and the pursuit of such activities must be made easier by providing a uniform legal protection within the Community;

(9) unchanged

(10) Whereas, to the extent that these activities constitute services, their provision must equally be facilitated by the establishment in the Community of a uniform legal framework;

(10) Whereas, to the extent that these activities principally constitute services, their provision must equally be facilitated by the establishment in the Community of a uniform legal framework;

(11) Whereas protection by rental and lending rights and protection in the field of rights related to copyright by existing legislation, administrative practice, and court jurisprudence does not exist at all in some Member States and, where it exists, is not the same or has different characteristics;

(11) unchanged

(12) Whereas the uncoordinated development in the Community of legal protection in these fields in the Member States could result in the creation of new disincentives to trade to the detriment of further industrial and cultural development and of the completion of the internal market;

(12) unchanged

(13) Whereas existing differences having such effects need to be removed and new ones having a negative impact on the functioning of the common market and the development of trade in cultural goods and services need to be prevented from arising;

(13) unchanged

(14) Whereas the legislation of the Member States should be harmonized in such a way so as not to conflict with the existing international conventions on which many Member States' copyright and related rights laws are based;

(14) unchanged

(15) Whereas the Community's legal framework on the rental and lending right and on certain rights related to

(15) Whereas the Community's legal framework on the rental and lending right and on certain rights related to

215

| ORIGINAL PROPOSAL | AMENDED PROPOSAL |
|---|---|
| copyright can be limited to establishing that Member States provide rights with respect to rental and lending for certain groups of right owners and further to establishing the exclusive rights of fixation, reproduction and distribution for certain groups of right owners in the field of related rights protection; | copyright can be limited to establishing that Member States provide rights with respect to rental and lending for certain groups of right owners and further to establishing the exclusive rights of fixation, reproduction, distribution, broadcasting and communication to the public for certain groups of right owners in the field of related rights protection; |
| | (16) Whereas Member States may provide for more far-reaching protection for authors and owners of rights related to copyright than that required by Article 6 bis of this Directive; |
| | (17) Whereas it is necessary for Member States to define clearly the groups of rightholders covered by this Directive; |
| (16) Whereas the harmonized rental and lending rights and the harmonized protection in the field of rights related to copyright should not be exercised in a way which constitutes a disguised restriction on trade between Member States; | (18) unchanged |
| | (19) Whereas the harmonized legal protection resulting from the implementation of the provisions of this Directive may create a new situation in regard to Member States' relations with certain third countries; whereas therefore it will be necessary to step up negotiations and consultations with such third countries, in particular within the relevant international organizations, with a view to securing at least reciprocal legal protection; |
| HAS ADOPTED THIS DIRECTIVE: | HAS ADOPTED THIS DIRECTIVE: |
| CHAPTER I | CHAPTER I |
| **RENTAL AND LENDING RIGHT** | **RENTAL AND LENDING RIGHT** |
| *Article 1* | *Article 1* |
| **Object of Harmonization** | **Object of Harmonization** |
| (1) In accordance with the provisions of this Chapter, Member States shall provide a right to authorize or prohibit the rental and lending of originals and copies of copyright works, and other subject matter as set out in Article 2(1). | (1) unchanged |

ORIGINAL PROPOSAL

AMENDED PROPOSAL

(2) For the purposes of this Directive, "rental" means making available for use, for a limited period of time and for profit-making purposes, without prejudice to paragraph 3.

(2) For the purposes of this Directive, "rental" means making available for use, for a limited period of time and for direct or indirect economic advantage, without prejudice to paragraph 3. "Rental" within the meaning of this paragraph does not cover making available for the purpose of public performance.

(3) For the purposes of this Directive, "lending" means making available for use, for a limited period of time, and not for direct profit-making purposes, if it is made through institutions which are accessible to the public, such as public libraries, research libraries, specialized libraries, school libraries, church libraries, collections of new media or of works of visual art, libraries organized or sponsored by public or private companies, and other collections of subject matter as set out in Article 2(1).

(3) For the purposes of this Directive, "lending" means making available for use, for a limited period of time, and not for profit-making purposes, if it is made through institutions which are accessible to the public, such as public libraries, research libraries, specialized libraries, school libraries, church libraries, collections of new media or of works of visual art and other collections of subject matter as set out in Article 2(1). "Lending" within the meaning of this paragraph does not cover making available for the purpose of public performance.

(4) The rights referred to in paragraph 1 shall not be affected by any sale, or other act of distribution, of originals and copies of works and other subject matter, as set out in Article 2(1).

(4) The rights referred to in paragraph 1 shall not be exhausted by any sale, or other act of distribution, of originals and copies of works and other subject matter, as set out in Article 2(1).

*Article 2*

*Article 2*

**First Owner and Subject Matter of Rental and Lending Right.**

**First Owner and Subject Matter of Rental and Lending Right.**

(1) The right to authorize or prohibit the rental and lending shall belong
  – to the author in respect of the original and copies of his work,
  – to the performing artist in respect of fixations of his performance,
  – to the phonogram producer in respect of his phonograms, and
  – to the producer of the first fixations of cinematographic works and moving images in respect of his visual recordings, and visual and sound recordings.

(1) unchanged

(2) For the purposes of this Directive the prinicipal director of a cinematographic work shall be its author. Member States may provide for others to be its co-authors.

ORIGINAL PROPOSAL

AMENDED PROPOSAL

(2) A rental and lending right does not arise in relation to buildings and to works of applied art.

(3) A rental and lending right does not arise in relation to buildings and to works of applied art.

(3) The provisions of this Directive shall be without prejudice to any provisions of Council Directive (EEC)No. ... of ... on the legal protection of computer programs.[5]

(4) The provisions of this Directive shall be without prejudice to Article 4(c) of Council Directive 91/250/EEC of 14 May 1991 on the legal protection of computer programs.[6]

(5) Any contract concerning film production between a performing artist and a producer of a film, as set out in paragraph 1, 4th indent, must be concluded in writing. When the performing artist signs a contract concerning film production with the film producer as set out in paragraph 1, he shall be presumed, subject to contractual provisions to the contrary, to have assigned his rental and lending right, subject to the provisions of Article 3.

*Article 3*

*Article 3*

**Authorization of Rental and Lending**

**Authorization of Rental and Lending**

If the rightholders authorize to a third party against payment the rental or lending of a sound recording, visual recording or visual and sound recording, then each of the rightholders set out in Article 2(1) shall retain the right to obtain an adequate part of the said payment, notwithstanding any assignment of the rental or lending right or granting of licences. This right to obtain an adequate part of the payment cannot be waived, but its administration may be assigned.

If the rightholders set out in Article 2(1) authorize to a third party against payment the rental or lending of a sound recording, visual recording or visual and sound recording, then each of the said rightholders shall retain the right to obtain an adequate part of the said payment, notwithstanding any assignment of the rental or lending right or granting of licences. This part shall be adequately proportional to the importance of the contribution of the rightholders concerned to the sound recording, visual recording or visual and sound recording. This right to obtain an adequate part of the payment cannot be waived, but its administration may, for authors and performing artists, be entrusted to collecting societies representing the professional categories concerned.

[5] At the time of the Original Proposal, the Software Directive had not yet been adopted.
[6] [1991] O.J. L122/42.

| ORIGINAL PROPOSAL | AMENDED PROPOSAL |
|---|---|

*Article 4*

**Derogation from exclusive lending right**

Member States may, for cultural or other reasons, derogate from the copyright based exclusive lending right referred to in Article 1(1) for one or several categories of objects, provided that
  – at least authors obtain an equitable remuneration through administering bodies for such lending; and
  – such derogation measures comply with Community law, in particular Article 7 of the EEC Treaty.

*Article 4*

**Derogation from exclusive lending right**

unchanged

*Article 4 bis*

**Moral Rights**

No changes, cuts or additions may be made to work by the person making it available for rental, the rentor, the lender or the borrower without specific authorization of the author.

CHAPTER II

**PROTECTION IN THE FIELD OF RIGHTS RELATED TO COPYRIGHT**

CHAPTER II

**PROTECTION IN THE FIELD OF RIGHTS RELATED TO COPYRIGHT**

*Article 5*

**Fixation Right**

Member States shall provide for performing artists the right to authorize or prohibit the fixation of their performances. Likewise, they shall provide for broadcasting organizations the right to authorize or prohibit the fixation of their broadcasts.

*Article 5*

**Fixation Right**

unchanged

*Article 6*

**Reproduction Right**

Member States shall provide the right to authorize or prohibit the direct or indirect reproduction:

*Article 6*

**Reproduction Right**

(1) unchanged

ORIGINAL PROPOSAL

AMENDED PROPOSAL

– for performing artists, of fixations of their performances,
– for phonogram producers, of their phonograms,
– for producers of the first fixations of cinematographic works or moving images, of their visual recordings, and visual and sound recordings,
– for broadcasting organizations, of fixations of their broadcasts.

(2) When the performing artist signs a contract as set out in Article 2 paragraph 5, he shall be presumed, subject to contractual provisions to the contrary, to have assigned his reproduction right, subject to the provisions of Article 3 which apply mutatis mutandis.

*Article 6 bis*

**Broadcasting and Communication to the Public**

(1) Member States shall provide for performing artists the right to authorize or prohibit the wireless broadcasting and the communication to the public of their performance, unless the performance is itself already a broadcast performance or is made from a fixation.

(2) Member States shall provide the right to be paid a single equitable remuneration to both performing artists and phonogram producers by the user, if a phonogram published for commercial purposes, or a reproduction of such phonogram is used for wireless broadcasting, or for any communication to the public. In the absence of agreement between the performing artists and the phonogram producers, Member States may fix the conditions determining how the payment is to be shared between them.

(3) Member States shall provide for broadcasting organisations the right to authorize or prohibit the wireless rebroadcasting of their broadcasts and the communication to the public of their

television broadcasts if such communication is made in places accessible to the public against payment of an entrance fee.

(4) The provisions of this Article shall be without prejudice to those provisions of Council Directive . . ./EEC on the coordination of certain rules on copyright and related rights applicable to satellite broadcasting and retransmission by cable which provide for performing artists and producers of phonograms the right of communication to the public by satellite, and for broadcasting organisations the right of simultaneous retransmission of their broadcasts by satellite.

*Article 7*

*Article 7*

**Distribution Right**

**Distribution Right**

(1) Member States shall provide
– for performing artists in respect of fixations of their performances,
– for phonogram producers in respect of their phonograms,
– for producers of the first fixations of cinematographic works and moving images in respect of their visual recordings, and visual and sound recordings,
– for broadcasting organizations in respect of fixations of their broadcasts,
the exclusive right to make available, for an unlimited period of time, their respective subject matter to the public by sale or otherwise, without prejudice to paragraph 2.

(1) Member States shall provide
– for performing artists in respect of fixations of their performances,
– for phonogram producers in respect of their phonograms,
– for producers of the first fixations of cinematographic works and moving images in respect of their visual recordings, and visual and sound recordings,
– for broadcasting organizations in respect of fixations of their broadcasts,
the exclusive right to make available, for an unlimited period of time, their respective subject matter to the public by sale or otherwise, without prejudice to paragraph 3.

(2) When the performing artist signs a contract as set out in Article 2 paragraph 5, he shall be presumed, subject to contractual provisions to the contrary, to have assigned his distribution right, subject to the provisions of Article 3 which apply mutatis mutandis.

221

| ORIGINAL PROPOSAL | AMENDED PROPOSAL |
|---|---|
| (2) If a subject matter referred to in paragraph 1 has been put into circulation within the Community by the right owner or with his consent, then its import into another Member State may not be prohibited by virtue of the right referred to in paragraph 1. | (3) unchanged |

*Article 8*

**Limitations to Rights**

| | |
|---|---|
| *Article 8* (left) | *Article 8* (right) |

| | |
|---|---|
| (1) Member States may provide limitations to the rights referred to in Chapter II in respect of: | (1) unchanged |

(a) private use;
(b) use of short excerpts in connection with the reporting of current events;
(c) ephemeral fixation by a broadcasting organization by means of its own facilities and for its own broadcasts;
(d) use solely for the purposes of teaching or academic research.

(2) Irrespective of paragraph 1, any Member State may provide the same kinds of limitations with regard to the protection of performers, producers or phonograms, broadcasting organizations and of producers of the first fixations of cinematographic works and moving images, as it provides in connection with the protection of copyright in literary and artistic works. However, compulsory licences may be provided only to the extent that they are compatible with the Rome Convention (International Convention for the Protection of Performers, Producers of Phonograms and Broadcasting Organizations).

(2) unchanged

(3) Paragraph 1(a) shall be without prejudice to any existing or future legislation on remuneration for reproduction for private use.

(3) unchanged

ORIGINAL PROPOSAL                                    AMENDED PROPOSAL

CHAPTER III                                              CHAPTER III

DURATION                                                    DURATION

*Article 9*                                                  *Article 9*

**Duration of Authors' Rights**                    **Duration of Authors' Rights**

Until further harmonization, the authors'          unchanged
rights referred to in this Directive shall
not expire before the end of the term provided by the Berne Convention for the
Protection of Literary and Artistic
Works; this shall be without prejudice to
the particular terms of protection of authors' rights not explicitly dealt with by
that Convention.

*Article 10*                                                *Article 10*

**Duration of Related Rights**                      **Duration of Related Rights**

Until further harmonization, the rights            unchanged
referred to in this Directive of performing
artists, phonogram producers and broadcasting organizations shall not expire
before the end of the respective terms provided by the Rome Convention. This
shall apply mutatis mutandis to the rights
referred to in this Directive, of producers
of the first fixations of cinematographic
works and moving images.

CHAPTER IV                                               CHAPTER IV

**COMMON PROVISIONS**                           **COMMON PROVISIONS**

*Article 11*                                                *Article 11*

**Application in Time**                               **Application in Time**

The provisions of this Directive shall             (1) The provisions of this Directive shall
apply also in respect of all copyright            apply in respect of all copyright works,
works, performances, phonograms,                performances, phonograms, broadcasts
broadcasts and first fixations of cine-          and first fixations of cinematographic
matographic works and moving images             works and moving images referred to in
referred to in this Directive which are, on      this Directive which are, on 1 January
1 January 1993, still protected by the           1993, still protectable by the national
national legislation in the field of au-         legislation or this Directive in the field of
thors' rights and related rights.                authors' rights and related rights.

223

| ORIGINAL PROPOSAL | AMENDED PROPOSAL |
|---|---|

(2) Contractual rights and obligations arising from legislation applying prior to the date laid down in Article 12 shall not be affected by this Directive for a period of three (3) years from its entry into force. All parties concerned shall, however, within a period of three (3) years from the entry into force of this Directive, review the terms of their contracts with a view to bringing them into line with the provisions of this Directive. Member States in which no exclusive right within the meaning of Article 1 paragraph 1 existed before 1 January 1993 shall provide that the rightholders are deemed to have given their authorization to the rental or lending of an object set out in Article 2 Paragraph 1, which is proven to have been made available to third parties for this purpose or to have been acquired before 1 January 1993.

*Article 11 bis*

**Relation between Copyright and Related Rights**

Protection of copyright related rights under this Directive shall leave intact and shall in no way affect the protection of copyright as such.

| *Article 12* | *Article 12* |
|---|---|
| **Final provisions** | **Final provisions** |

Member States shall bring into force the laws, regulations and administrative provisions necessary to comply with this Directive not later than 1 January 1993.

unchanged

Member States shall forthwith inform the Commission thereof and communicate to the Commission the provisions of national law which they adopt in the field covered by this Directive.

When Member States adopt these provisions, these shall contain a reference to

| ORIGINAL PROPOSAL | AMENDED PROPOSAL |
|---|---|

this Directive or shall be accompanied by such reference at the time of their official publication. The procedure for such reference shall be adopted by Member States.

| *Article 13* | *Article 13* |
|---|---|

This Directive is addressed to the Member States.

unchanged

Done at Brussels,

*For the Council*
*The President*

# Appendix Two: The Directive as Adopted

COUNCIL DIRECTIVE 92/100/EEC

of November 19, 1992

**on rental right and lending right and on certain rights related to copyright in the field of intellectual property**

THE COUNCIL OF THE EUROPEAN COMMUNITIES,

Having regard to the Treaty establishing the European Economic Community, and in particular Articles 57(2), 66 and 100a thereof,

Having regard to the proposal from the Commission,[1]

In cooperation with the European Parliament,[2]

Having regard to the opinion of the Economic and Social Committee,[3]

(1) Whereas[4] differences exist in the legal protection provided by the laws and practices of the Member States for copyright works and subject matter of related rights protection as regards rental and lending; whereas such differences are sources of barriers to trade and distortions of competition which impede the achievement and proper functioning of the internal market;

(2) Whereas such differences in legal protection could well become greater as Member States adopt new and different legislation or as national case-law interpreting such legislation develops differently;

(3) Whereas such differences should therefore be eliminated in accordance with the objective of introducing an area without internal frontiers as set out in Article 8a of the Treaty so as to institute, pursuant to Article 3(f) of the Treaty, a system ensuring that competition in the common market is not distorted;

(4) Whereas rental and lending of copyright works and the subject matter of related rights protection is playing an increasingly important role in particular for authors, performers and producers of phonograms and films; whereas piracy is becoming an increasing threat;

---

[1] [1991] O.J. C53/35 and [1992] O.J. C128/8.
[2] [1992] O.J. C67/92 and Decision of 28 October 1992; [1992] O.J. C305/73.
[3] [1991] O.J. C269/54.
[4] Recitals have been numbered editorially for ease of reference. They are not numbered in the official text.

(5) Whereas the adequate protection of copyright works and subject matter of related rights protection by rental and lending rights as well as the protection of the subject matter of related rights protection by the fixation right, reproduction right, distribution right, right to broadcast and communication to the public can accordingly be considered as being of fundamental importance for the Community's economic and cultural development;

(6) Whereas copyright and related rights protection must adapt to new economic developments such as new forms of exploitation;

(7) Whereas the creative and artistic work of authors and performers necessitates an adequate income as a basis for further creative and artistic work, and the investments required particularly for the production of phonograms and films are especially high and risky; whereas the possibility for securing that income and recouping that investment can only effectively be guaranteed through adequate legal protection of the rightholders concerned;

(8) Whereas these creative, artistic and entrepreneurial activities are, to a large extent, activities of self-employed persons; whereas the pursuit of such activities must be made easier by providing a harmonized legal protection within the Community;

(9) Whereas, to the extent that these activities principally constitute services, their provision must equally be facilitated by the establishment in the Community of a harmonized legal framework;

(10) Whereas the legislation of the Member States should be approximated in such a way so as not to conflict with the international conventions on which many Member States' copyright and related rights laws are based;

(11) Whereas the Community's legal framework on the rental right and lending right and on certain rights related to copyright can be limited to establishing that Member States provide rights with respect to rental and lending for certain groups of rightholders and further to establishing the rights of fixation, reproduction, distribution, broadcasting and communication to the public for certain groups of rightholders in the field of related rights protection;

(12) Whereas it is necessary to define the concepts of rental and lending for the purposes of this Directive;

(13) Whereas it is desirable, with a view to clarity, to exclude from rental and lending within the meaning of this Directive certain forms of making available, as for instance making available phonograms or films (cinematographic or audiovisual works or moving images, whether or not accompanied by sound) for the purpose of public performance or broadcasting, making available for the purpose of exhibition, or making available for on-the-spot reference use; whereas lending within the meaning of this Directive does not include making available between establishments which are accessible to the public;

(14) Whereas, where lending by an establishment accessible to the public gives rise to a payment the amount of which does not go beyond what is necessary to cover the operating costs of the establishment, there is no direct or indirect economic or commercial advantage within the meaning of this Directive;

(15) Whereas it is necessary to introduce arrangements ensuring that an unwaivable equitable remuneration is obtained by authors and performers who must retain the possibility to entrust the administration of this right to collecting societies representing them;

(16) Whereas the equitable remuneration may be paid on the basis of one or several payments at any time on or after the conclusion of the contract;

(17) Whereas the equitable remuneration must take account of the importance of

the contribution of the authors and performers concerned to the phonogram or film;

(18) Whereas it is also necessary to protect the rights at least of authors as regards public lending by providing for specific arrangements; whereas, however, any measures based on Article 5 of this Directive have to comply with Community law, in particular with Article 7 of the Treaty;

(19) Whereas the provisions of Chapter II do not prevent Member States from extending the presumption set out in Article 2(5) to the exclusive rights included in that chapter; whereas furthermore the provisions of Chapter II do not prevent Member States from providing for a rebuttable presumption of the authorization of exploitation in respect of the exclusive rights of performers provided for in those articles, in so far as such presumption is compatible with the International Convention for the Protection of Performers, Producers of Phonograms and Broadcasting Organizations (hereinafter referred to as the Rome Convention);

(20) Whereas Member States may provide for more far-reaching protection for owners of rights related to copyright than that required by Article 8 of this Directive;

(21) Whereas the harmonized rental and lending rights and the harmonized protection in the field of rights related to copyright should not be exercised in a way which constitutes a disguised restriction on trade between Member States or in a way which is contrary to the rule of media exploitation chronology, as recognised in the Judgment handed down in Société Cinéthèque v. FNCF,[5]

HAS ADOPTED THIS DIRECTIVE:

## CHAPTER I

### RENTAL AND LENDING RIGHT

*Article 1*

#### Object of harmonization

1. In accordance with the provisions of this Chapter, Member States shall provide, subject to Article 5, a right to authorize or prohibit the rental and lending of originals and copies of copyright works, and other subject matter as set out in Article 2(1).

2. For the purposes of this Directive, 'rental' means making available for use, for a limited period of time and for direct or indirect economic or commercial advantage.

3. For the purposes of this Directive, 'lending' means making available for use, for a limited period of time and not for direct or indirect economic or commercial advantage, when it is made through establishments which are accessible to the public.

4. The rights referred to in paragraph 1 shall not be exhausted by any sale or other act of distribution of originals and copies of copyright works and other subject matter as set out in Article 2(1).

*Article 2*

#### Rightholders and subject matter of rental and lending right

1. The exclusive right to authorize or prohibit rental and lending shall belong:

- to the author in respect of the original and copies of his work,
- to the performer in respect of fixations of his performance,
- to the phonogram producer in respect of his phonograms, and

---

[5] Cases 60/84 and 61/84, *Société Cinéthèque* v. *Federation Nationale des Cinemas Français*: [1985] E.C.R. 2605, [1986] 1 C.M.L.R. 365.

– to the producer of the first fixation of a film in respect of the original and copies of his film. For the purposes of this Directive, the term 'film' shall designate a cinematographic or audiovisual work or moving images, whether or not accompanied by sound.

2. For the purposes of this Directive the principal director of a cinematographic or audiovisual work shall be considered as its author or one of its authors. Member States may provide for others to be considered as its co-authors.

3. This Directive does not cover rental and lending rights in relation to buildings and to works of applied art.

4. The rights referred to in paragraph 1 may be transferred, assigned or subject to the granting of contractual licences.

5. Without prejudice to paragraph 7, when a contract concerning film production is concluded, individually or collectively, by performers with a film producer, the performer covered by this contract shall be presumed, subject to contractual clauses to the contrary, to have transferred his rental right, subject to Article 4.

6. Member States may provide for a similar presumption as set out in paragraph 5 with respect to authors.

7. Member States may provide that the signing of a contract concluded between a performer and a film producer concerning the production of a film has the effect of authorizing rental, provided that such contract provides for an equitable remuneration within the meaning of Article 4. Member States may also provide that this paragraph shall apply *mutatis mutandis* to the rights included in Chapter II.

*Article 3*

### Rental of computer programs

This Directive shall be without prejudice to Article 4(c) of Council Directive 91/250/EEC of 14 May 1991 on the legal protection of computer programs.[6]

*Article 4*

### Unwaivable right to equitable remuneration

1. Where an author or performer has transferred or assigned his rental right concerning a phonogram or an original or copy of a film to a phonogram or film producer, that author or performer shall retain the right to obtain an equitable remuneration for the rental.

2. The right to obtain an equitable remuneration for rental cannot be waived by authors or performers.

3. The administration of this right to obtain an equitable remuneration may be entrusted to collecting societies representing authors or performers.

4. Member States may regulate whether and to what extent administration by collecting societies of the right to obtain an equitable remuneration may be imposed, as well as the question from whom this remuneration may be claimed or collected.

*Article 5*

### Derogation from the exclusive public lending right

1. Member States may derogate from the exclusive right provided for in Article 1 in respect of public lending, provided that at least authors obtain a remuneration for

---

[6] [1991] O.J. L122/42.

such lending. Member States shall be free to determine this remuneration taking account of their cultural promotion objectives.

2. When Member States do not apply the exclusive lending right provided for in Article 1 as regards phonograms, films and computer programs, they shall introduce, at least for authors, a remuneration.

3. Member States may exempt certain categories of establishments from the payment of the remuneration referred to in paragraphs 1 and 2.

4. The Commission, in cooperation with the Member States, shall draw up before 1 July 1997 a report on public lending in the Community. It shall forward this report to the European Parliament and to the Council.

## CHAPTER II

## RIGHTS RELATED TO COPYRIGHT

### Article 6

### Fixation right

1. Member States shall provide for performers the exclusive right to authorize or prohibit the fixation of their performances.

2. Member States shall provide for broadcasting organizations the exclusive right to authorize or prohibit the fixation of their broadcasts, whether these broadcasts are transmitted by wire or over the air, including by cable or satellite.

3. A cable distributor shall not have the right provided for in paragraph 2 where it merely retransmits by cable the broadcasts of broadcasting organizations.

### Article 7

### Reproduction right

1. Member States shall provide the exclusive right to authorize or prohibit the direct or indirect reproduction:

- for performers, of fixations of their performances,
- for phonogram producers, of their phonograms,
- for producers of the first fixations of films, in respect of the original and copies of their films, and
- for broadcasting organizations, of fixations of their broadcasts, as set out in Article 6(2).

2. The reproduction right referred to in paragraph 1 may be transferred, assigned or subject to the granting of contractual licences.

### Article 8

### Broadcasting and communication to the public

1. Member States shall provide for performers the exclusive right to authorize or prohibit the broadcasting by wireless means and the communication to the public of their performances, except where the performance is itself already a broadcast performance or is made from a fixation.

2. Member States shall provide a right in order to ensure that a single equitable remuneration is paid by the user, if a phonogram published for commercial purposes, or a reproduction of such phonogram, is used for broadcasting by wireless means or for any communication to the public, and to ensure that this remuneration is shared between the relevant performers and phonogram producers. Member States may, in the absence of agreement between the performers and phonogram producers, lay down the conditions as to the sharing of this remuneration between them.

3. Member States shall provide for broadcasting organizations the exclusive right to authorize or prohibit the rebroadcasting of their broadcasts by wireless means, as well as the communication to the public of their broadcasts if such communication is made in places accessible to the public against payment of an entrance fee.

*Article 9*

### Distribution right

1. Member States shall provide

- for performers, in respect of fixations of their performances,
- for phonogram producers, in respect of their phonograms,
- for producers of their first fixations of films, in respect of the original and copies of their films,
- for broadcasting organizations, in respect of fixations of their broadcast as set out in Article 6(2),

the exclusive right to make available these objects, including copies thereof, to the public by sale or otherwise, hereafter referred to as the 'distribution right'.

2. The distribution right shall not be exhausted within the Community in respect of an object as referred to in paragraph 1, except where the first sale in the Community of that object is made by the rightholder or with his consent.

3. The distribution right shall be without prejudice to the specific provisions of Chapter I, in particular Article 1(4).

4. The distribution right may be transferred, assigned or subject to the granting of contractual licences.

*Article 10*

### Limitations to rights

1. Member States may provide for limitations to the rights referred to in Chapter II in respect of:

(a) private use;

(b) use of short excerpts in connection with the reporting of current events;

(c) ephemeral fixation by a broadcasting organization by means of its own facilities and for its own broadcasts;

(d) use solely for the purposes of teaching or scientific research.

2. Irrespective of paragraph 1, any Member State may provide for the same kinds of limitations with regard to the protection of performers, producers of phonograms, broadcasting organizations and of producers of the first fixations of films, as it provides for in connection with the protection of copyright in literary and artistic works. However, compulsory licences may be provided for only to the extent to which they are compatible with the Rome Convention.

3. Paragraph 1(a) shall be without prejudice to any existing or future legislation on remuneration for reproduction for private use.

CHAPTER III

### DURATION

*Article 11*

### Duration of authors' rights

Without prejudice to further harmonization, the authors' rights referred to in this Directive shall not expire before the end of the term provided by the Berne Convention for the Protection of Literary and Artistic Works.

*Article 12*

### Duration of related rights

Without prejudice to further harmonization, the rights referred to in this Directive of performers, phonogram producers and broadcasting organizations shall not expire before the end of the respective terms provided by the Rome Convention.

The rights referred to in this Directive for producers of the first fixations of films shall not expire before the end of a period of 20 years computed from the end of the year in which the fixation was made.

## CHAPTER IV

## COMMON PROVISIONS

*Article 13*

### Application in time

1. This Directive shall apply in respect of all copyright works, performances, phonograms, broadcasts and first fixations of films referred to in this Directive which are, on 1 July 1994, still protected by the legislation of the Member States in the field of copyright and related rights or meet the criteria for protection under the provisions of this Directive on that date.

2. This Directive shall apply without prejudice to any acts of exploitation performed before 1 July 1994.

3. Member States may provide that the rightholders are deemed to have given their authorization to the rental or lending of an object referred to in Article 2(1) which is proven to have been made available to third parties for this purpose or to have been acquired before 1 July 1994. However, in particular where such an object is a digital recording, Member States may provide that rightholders shall have a right to obtain an adequate remuneration for the rental or lending of that object.

4. Member States need not apply the provisions of Article 2(2) to cinematographic or audiovisual works created before 1 July 1994.

5. Member States may determine the date as from which the Article 2(2) shall apply, provided that that date is not later than 1 July 1997.

6. This Directive shall, without prejudice to paragraph 3 and subject to paragraphs 8 and 9, not affect any contracts concluded before the date of its adoption.

7. Member States may provide, subject to the provisions of paragraphs 8 and 9, that when rightholders who acquire new rights under the national provisions adopted in implementation of this Directive have, before 1 July 1994, given their consent for exploitation, they shall be presumed to have transferred the new exclusive rights.

8. Member States may determine the date as from which the unwaivable right to an equitable remuneration referred to in Article 4 exists, provided that that date is no later than 1 July 1997.

9. For contracts concluded before 1 July 1994, the unwaivable right to an equitable remuneration provided for in Article 4 shall apply only where authors or performers or those representing them have submitted a request to that effect before 1 January 1997. In the absence of agreement between rightholders concerning the level of remuneration, Member States may fix the level of equitable remuneration.

*Article 14*

### Relation between copyright and related rights

Protection of copyright-related rights under this Directive shall leave intact and shall in no way affect the protection of copyright.

*Article 15*

### Final provisions

1. Member States shall bring into force the laws, regulations and administrative provisions necessary to comply with this Directive not later than 1 July 1994. They shall forthwith inform the Commission thereof.

When Member States adopt these measures, they shall contain a reference to this Directive or shall be accompanied by such reference at the time of their official publication. The methods of making such a reference shall be laid down by the Member States.

2. Member States shall communicate to the Commission the main provisions of domestic law which they adopt in the field covered by this Directive.

*Article 16*

This Directive is addressed to the Member States.

Done at Brussels, 19 November 1992.

*For the Council*
*The President*
E. LEIGH

# Index

QMW LIBRARY
(MILE END)

WITHDRAWN
FROM STOCK
QMUL LIBRARY